CW00971805

Advance praise for *Jealousy and Envy*

"This book's quite extraordinary accomplishment derives from two factors. The authors' editing and careful explication provide a coherent overview on the topics of envy and jealousy by defining these strong feelings thoroughly, and also differentiating them from other feelings like shame and admiration. In addition, this book helps clinicians to widen the perspective on the dynamics of envy and jealousy. Understanding both feelings in the context of oedipal and/or preoedipal conflicts enriches psychoanalytic theory and practice. This valuable book shows a great breadth of theoretical and clinical issues around envy and jealousy."

— Manfred Cierpka, M.D., Director of the Institute for Family Therapy, University of Heidelberg

"It is not easy to comment on this rich and profound work, which deepens and enriches our understanding of two central motives and affects almost ever-present in our daily analytic and psychotherapeutic work, but there are three points which, above many other in this book, exert a lasting impression on me and will surely influence my understanding of these motivations and my clinical work profoundly: the understanding of envy and jealousy not as entities and last causes not to be further explored in their origin, but as processes; the fundamental role of shame in these processes; and the fundamental role of traumatic experiences in the development of both jealousy and envy. Especially in the contributions of the editors and main authors of this monograph, the profound psychoanalytic, developmental, and historical investigations are enlarged and explained by transparently described case-material without any obscuring overload of conceptual interpretations, which are too often found in other contemporary psychoanalytic or psychodynamic accounts. A particular merit of this book is the broad inclusion of a sociocultural and gender perspective by literature (Othello), examination of sacrifice rituals, womb envy, and especially the scrutiny on the "Evil Eye." It is not difficult to predict that this book will inspire many readers in their clinical work as well as more research on the many facets of the discussed phenomena."

— Günter Reich, Ph.D., Department for Psychosomatic Medicine and Psychotherapy, University of Göttingen

"Envy and jealousy, demons that inhabit the human breast and ingredients in numerous plots in film, literature, and the theater, are frequent problems in people who seek therapy. In this timely and very readable book, editors Wurmser and Jarass and contributors offer a wealth of experience, information and wisdom which should be of interest to both the professional and general reading public."

— Zvi Lothane, M.D., Author, In *Defense of Schreber: Soul Murder and Psychiatry* (Analytic Press, 1992)

"Léon Wurmser has once more taken psychoanalysts into areas of pain and madness usually avoided. In previous work he confronted us with issues of shame, of sadomasochism, of tyrannical superego functioning, and now, with his colleague Heidrun Jarass, he challenges us to face the devastating experiences of jealousy and envy. With the participation of an impressive group of international experts, the editors help us reclaim the crucial importance of jealousy and envy in our theory and clinical work. This book is essential reading for all thoughtful students of human behavior."

— Jack Novick, Ph.D., Co-author, *Fearful Symmetry and Good Goodbyes*

Vol. 1: *Reflections on Self Psychology*—Joseph D. Lichtenberg & Samuel Kaplan (eds.)

Vol. 2: *Psychoanalysis and Infant Research*—Joseph D. Lichtenberg

Vol. 4: *Structures of Subjectivity: Explorations in Psychoanalytic Phenomenology*—George E. Atwood & Robert D. Stolorow

Vol. 7: *The Borderline Patient: Emerging Concepts in Diagnosis, Psychodynamics, and Treatment, Vol. 2*—James S. Grotstein, Marion F. Solomon & Joan A. Lang (eds.)

Vol. 8: *Psychoanalytic Treatment: An Intersubjective Approach*—Robert D. Stolorow, Bernard Brandchaft & George E. Atwood

Vol. 9: *Female Homosexuality: Choice without Volition*—Elaine V. Siegel

Vol. 10: *Psychoanalysis and Motivation*—Joseph D. Lichtenberg

Vol. 11: *Cancer Stories: Creativity and Self-Repair*—Esther Dreifuss Kattan

Vol. 12: *Contexts of Being: The Intersubjective Foundations of Psychological Life*—Robert D. Stolorow & George E. Atwood

Vol. 13: *Self and Motivational Systems: Toward a Theory of Psychoanalytic Technique*—Joseph D. Lichtenberg, Frank M. Lachmann & James L. Fosshage

Vol. 14: *Affects as Process: An Inquiry into the Centrality of Affect in Psychological Life*—Joseph M. Jones

Vol. 15: *Understanding Therapeutic Action: Psychodynamic Concepts of Cure*—Lawrence E. Lifson (ed.)

Vol. 16: *The Clinical Exchange: Techniques Derived from Self and Motivational Systems*—Joseph D. Lichtenberg, Frank M. Lachmann & James L. Fosshage

Vol. 17: *Working Intersubjectively: Contextualism in Psychoanalytic Practice*—Donna M. Orange, George E. Atwood & Robert D. Stolorow

Vol. 18: *Kohut, Loewald, and the Postmoderns: A Comparative Study of Self and Relationship*—Judith Guss Teicholz

Vol. 19: *A Spirit of Inquiry: Communication in Psychoanalysis*—Joseph D. Lichtenberg, Frank M. Lachmann & James L. Fosshage

Vol. 20: *Craft and Spirit: A Guide to the Exploratory Psychotherapies*—Joseph D. Lichtenberg

Vol. 21: *Attachment and Sexuality*—Diana Diamond, Sidney J. Blatt & Joseph D. Lichtenberg

Vol. 22: *Psychotherapy and Medication: The Challenge of Integration*—Fredric N. Busch and Larry S. Sandberg

Vol. 23: *Trauma and Human Existence: Autobiographical, Psychoanalytic, and Philosophical Reflections*—Robert D. Stolorow

Vol. 24: *Jealousy and Envy: New Views about Two Powerful Emotions*—Léon Wurmser & Heidrun Jarass

Vol. 25: *Sensuality and Sexuality Across the Divide of Shame*—Joseph D. Lichtenberg

Jealousy and Envy

Psychoanalytic Inquiry Book Series

Volume 24

Jealousy and Envy

New Views about Two Powerful Feelings

Edited by
Léon Wurmser and Heidrun Jarass

The Analytic Press
Taylor & Francis Group
New York London

The Analytic Press
Taylor & Francis Group
270 Madison Avenue
New York, NY 10016

The Analytic Press
Taylor & Francis Group
27 Church Road
Hove, East Sussex BN3 2FA

Printed in the United States of America on acid-free paper
10 9 8 7 6 5 4 3 2 1

International Standard Book Number-13: 978-0-88163-470-9 (Hardcover)

Library of Congress Cataloging-in-Publication Data

Jealousy and envy : new views about two powerful emotions / edited by Leon Wurmser and Heidrun Jarass.
p. cm. -- (Psychoanalytic inquiry book series ; no. 24)
Includes bibliographical references and index.
ISBN-13: 978-0-88163-470-9 (alk. paper)
1. Jealousy. 2. Envy. I. Wurmser, Leon. II. Jarass, Heidrun.

BF575.J4J43 2007
152.4'8--dc22 2007015025

Visit the Taylor & Francis Web site at
http://www.taylorandfrancis.com

and The Analytic Press Web site at
http://www.analyticpress.com

Contents

Foreword

ANNE-MARIE SANDLER

When the two main authors of this monograph invited me to add a few lines to this publication, I was especially pleased, as I felt that a serious study of the topic of jealousy and envy was greatly overdue. This neglect seemed surprising in view of the very central role that jealousy and envy play in mental life.

It is interesting to notice that in the work of Freud, jealousy is referred to quite often and generally in connection with the oedipal situation and with conflicts around siblings. Envy, on the other hand, is more sparingly mentioned in the writings of Freud and if so, mostly linked with the idea of penis envy. This has greatly changed since Melanie Klein brought in her concept of primary envy of the good breast. This has awakened a general interest in the role of envy in our inner life, whether we believe in primary envy or not.

It is important and fruitful to clearly delineate the differences between envy and jealousy. The *Oxford English Dictionary*'s definition of jealousy implies a resentfulness toward another on account of known or suspected rivalry; troubled by the belief, suspicion, or fear that the good that one desires to gain or keep for oneself had been or may be diverted to another; resentfulness toward another on account of known or suspected rivalry, for example in love and affection, especially in sexual love. It is interesting that jealousy is also defined as intolerant of unfaithfulness, solicitous for preservation of rights, vehement in wrath, desire, or devotion. This last meaning seems to involve passion and a certain belief in and reliance on justice and loyalty.

The meaning of envy is rather different. The definition speaks of grudging contemplation of more fortunate persons, of people with advantages; envy is related to *invidere*, to look upon in a bad sense; malice, enmity; mortification, and ill will occasioned by the contemplation of another's superior advantages. Also in a more neutral sense, to wish oneself on a level with another in some respect, or possessed of something that another has.

These definitions help us to reflect on the rather different place these two strong feelings occupy in our mental apparatus. Envy refers to grudging, malice, and enmity in the face of someone else's advantages and appears to be linked with strong personal feelings of offense and hurt.

The perceived exalted state of the other produces a narcissistic wound in the subject, which evokes in that person hatred and ill will toward the other. The conflict is a two-person conflict and is strongly linked with fantasies of being exploited, belittled, and forced into a submissive position. The individual feels attacked in his or her omnipotence and sense of superiority by the object of this envy, which forces the individual to face in an unbearable way his or her dependency on the object.

Jealousy requires the capacity of relating on a three-person relationship level, on an oedipal level. Jealousy is linked with rivalry for the love, attention, and possible privileges from a third. It arises from a belief or fear that the love object may divert some or all of his or her love or attention to another. A profound feeling of unfairness and betrayal is often present in the fantasies of the jealous person and can often be the basis for the hatred and wish of revenge the individual experiences. We have all had to struggle in the course of development with our feelings of ambivalence toward our love objects, and jealousy is usually linked with suspiciousness toward the desired object or the rival. The feeling of jealousy can call for violent hatred and a strong wish for revenge. It is often accompanied by powerful feelings and fantasies of being tricked and deceived, both by the object of devotion and by the rival. The difference between jealousy and feelings of envy has mainly to do with the fact that the victim of jealousy feels less completely at the mercy of the other as he or she has already achieved more complex, somewhat more mature and multiple object relationships.

It is with great expectations and pleasure that I look forward to the opportunity of reading what the authors of the essays in this book will bring to us.

Introduction

LÉON WURMSER AND HEIDRUN JARASS

Jealousy and envy belong to the basics of psychoanalytic and psychotherapeutic work, form much of the daily warp and woof of sessions and interpretive work, and go back to the very inception of psychoanalytic reflection on feelings at play in development and conflict. Yet, some new observations, some new thinking, and some new relevance of old, but neglected ideas about these two feeling states and their origins warrant special attention, both as to theory and practice.

Often it is not easy to determine to what extent something is an issue of jealousy and how much envy, resentment, and vengefulness play into it. Often, the words are used interchangeably and seem to flow into each other. Behind these aggressive affects and impulses, giant forces (Nietzsche [1948] talked of "*Urkatzen*", primal cats) are lurking, forces of humiliation, shame, and of outer and, still more, inner condemnation, hence of guilt.

In order to clarify more those affects most closely involved, I offer my own words: In *jealousy* I feel: "I am the one who has been excluded from love. I am standing outside of an intimate relationship that is particularly precious to me."[1] Behind jealousy, there is always a sense of loss, and with that, acute pain and sadness, but also a feeling of humiliation and shame. Either it means: "I am the excluded third and want to be the excluding first instead," or it implies: "I am excluded from belonging to a larger community, and my pain and shame are so strong that I want to hurl myself against this exclusion, but feel helpless to do anything about it." Very easily this leads to the desire for revenge. Yet another, very frequent way to deal with these forms of jealousy is its radical turn-around: "Instead of that I *am* jealous, I *make* jealous." Or: "In order to avoid feeling jealous I try to pit one against the other." Yet another prominent way is reaction formation against jealousy in the form of altruistic surrender: "I generously cede my love to someone else." All this largely goes on unconsciously, and the consequences of this hidden repetition assault us with dreadful force. "*Eifersucht ist eine Leidenschaft, die mit Eifer sucht, was Leiden schafft*" ("Jealousy is a passion that assiduously searches for what creates suffering"), a wonderful play on words in German attributed to the philosopher Schleiermacher (Büchmann, 1965).

In *envy* the individual says: "The other has more, is better and more respected than I am, and I feel inferior and therefore humiliated. I want to take away and destroy the good he has and is."[2] Also shame always lies behind envy, even much more so than is the case in jealousy (Lansky & Morrison, 1997; de Paola panel report, 2001). The impulse is to wipe out the perceived difference by taking, by hook or by crook, that wherein one feels shortchanged and diminished, even if this entails the humiliation and destruction of the other person or his or her worth.

It should be mentioned, however, that there may be an inner differentiation within envy. In Switzerland one speaks of "green envy" versus "yellow envy," and similarly in Russia about "white envy" and "black envy": the former entails the pain of a felt lack (e.g., of youth and strength), and a wish and yearning to have or regain what the other enjoys without wanting to destroy it or him or her.

Another interesting differentiation is one that goes back to Nietzsche and was introduced into the analytic debate by the Swiss analyst Brigit Barth (1990)—the one between common envy and existential envy: common envy is conscious, loud, and vehement. It wants to take what the other has and demands a simple reversal of inequality, not the establishment of justice. Existential envy is secret, veiled, and quiet. This envy knows it cannot have what it admires. This hopelessness causes despair, rage, rebellion, and hatred, together with the conviction not to be able to survive without the desired value. It wants the humiliation, disempowerment, and destruction of the envied one.

In *resentment,* the wounded sense of justice stands in the foreground: "Injustice has happened to me; I have been robbed of what was most valuable to me." Behind resentment, we therefore commonly encounter envy and jealousy, but what is typically allied with those affects is the marked sense of helplessness and impotence about being able to redress the balance of justice.

Finally, *revenge* is the impulse and attitude to remove the causes of shame, guilt, envy, jealousy, and resentment, and to seemingly undo the suffered pain and shame by its reversal: "If I inflict upon the other at least as much suffering, or, still better, a multiple of what had been done to me, then I am freed from it"—the talion principle, derived from the Latin word *"talis,"* "the same." Mostly, this reckoning does not tally, already internally for reasons of one's own sense of guilt and remorse, and even less so externally because it leads to the well-known cycles of retaliation where every act of revenge only conjures up a much greater vendetta.

The unbearability of shame––remembered, continually feared, or reexperienced in fantasy––drives vindictiveness on and blocks the possibility of *forgiveness.* In order to allow forgiveness in therapeutic work, Lansky (2001) urges "the exploration of shame fantasies" because it

> provides necessary details about their unbearableness. … If attention to this shame is bypassed in analysis in favor of attention to more visible rage or resentment at the transgression of the betrayer and the guilt that attends that rage, this many-faceted model of forgiveness is oversimplified. Inexact interpretation … is the likely result, and with it an overfocus on rage, control, and guilt at the expense of the dynamics of shame. (pp. 1030–1031)

The vicious circle of shame, resentment, and revenge is replaced in therapy by a process that gradually leads to forgiveness. This process, however, requires a very detailed working through of the dynamics of hidden shame.

Now to an outline of this Psychoanalytic Inquiry monograph devoted to this broad spectrum of feeling states.

In the work with cases of pathological jealousy, it became obvious to several of us how limited our literature is about its dynamics (see also Coen, 1987). It is mostly restricted to sexual jealousy and to the dialectic between oedipal and preoedipal conflicts. As essential as these are, there is more to this: the deep correlation between early and chronic traumatization and the sense of being excluded and humiliated is clinically very relevant, but has barely been commented upon. Moreover, recent systematic infant studies (Hart, Carrington, Tronick, & Carroll, 2004) as well as anecdotal evidence give clear indication for the appearance of jealousy reactions at the age of 6 months and earlier.

On the other side, a great deal has been expatiated upon about envy, mostly by Melanie Klein and Kleinian authors (most impressively stated by Spillius, 1993). More recently, some neo-Kleinian authors have moved away from Klein's original emphasis on the infantile relationship with the breast to focus on envy more generally as an affective force shaping the clinical process. Several contributions, both by non-Kleinians and neo-Kleinians, have appeared that deal specifically with the envy of the female body and of woman's procreativity, summarized under the heading of "womb envy" or "birth envy" (Balsam, 2003; Barth, 1990; Benz, 1984; Eschbach, 2004; Seelig, 2002; and Eschbach in this volume). The concept, in its application to both genders and to cultural history, goes far back in analytic writings (Freud, Horney, Jones, Rank, Bettelheim, Jacobson), but it has been undervalued, even omitted, in favor of "penis envy." The concept of womb envy helps to understand some important aspects both in male and female patients that hitherto have been overlooked, for example, in regard to ritual sacrifice (Janowitz, in this volume). Especially its precipitation in the ego ideal is crucially important in many forms of individual and social pathology, as the detailed case description presented in this volume by Jarass (with Wurmser) will show.

We have arranged the contributions of these connected issues so that we start off with a plea for greater attention to the affect of jealousy, its very early antecedents, and its later intimate relationship to guilt (Wurmser and Jarass) and shame (also spelled out in more detail by Morrison and Lansky) and a study of the dramatic dialectic between two personalities whose characters are organized around jealousy (in Othello's case) and envy (in Iago's case) respectively (Lansky). Then the focus shifts to a detailed study of womb envy (Eschbach; Shabad), its pernicious role when it is transmitted in the form of hostility against anything feminine from one generation to the other in the form of superego introjects and ego ideal. Its deep cultural and social effects can be seen in the rituals of sacrifice throughout history and in most cultures (Janowitz) and in the underground of the most dangerous of all prejudices, anti-Semitism (Wurmser and Jarass). Envy more generally is one ingredient in the ubiquitous fear of the "Evil Eye," but very important superego and shame aspects have hitherto been overlooked in its studies (Kilborne; Wurmser and Jarass). Whereas Morrison and Lansky emphasize the sequence of shame → envy → guilt and deepened shame, the concluding essay by Balsam reverses the view and describes admiration → shame → envy.

Now a little more about the individual essays.

Léon Wurmser (collaborating with Heidrun Jarass) observes how the psychoanalytic literature about pathological jealousy has largely been confined to sexual jealousy and its dialectic between oedipal and preoedipal conflicts. It neglected the deep correlations between early traumatization, especially in cases of manifestly nonsexual jealousy (e.g., siblings, mother–daughter), with the core sense of being excluded and humiliated and the wish: "I am the excluded third, but want to be the excluding first." Typically, pathological jealousy defends against guilt of complex origin (not just about infidelity) and hides behind sadness and "symbiotic" demands. Recent systematic infant studies indicate the early and nonderived appearance of jealousy.

Another aspect deserves emphasis: To what extent has there been a facile connection of jealousy with oedipal conflicts, and of triangularity with the oedipal stage? These need to be resolutely uncoupled from each other. A special case of these disclaimers is the high valence and relevance of the conflicts around sibling rivalry. In much analytic work, this theme has been eclipsed by the classical positive and negative Oedipus constellations. This one-sidedness has recently been eloquently questioned by the German analyst Franz Wellendorf (1995) and tracked back to some prejudice on Freud's side against his own siblings.

Melvin Lansky focuses on the intimate and complex relationships of jealousy and envy with underlying and subsequent shame conflicts. In his view, Freud sometimes conflated jealousy per se with simple rivalry among approximate equals for the love of the opposite sex parent. This ignores the dimension of oedipal shame, shame at the sense of diminishment in realizing the physical, sexual, material, and psychological weakness compared both to the rival and to the love object. Klein conceives of envy in terms of the original relationship of the infant to the breast. She ignores the shame on comparison with the admired or needed other with whom one is also rivalrous. Lansky exemplifies the complexity of these feeling states of envy and jealousy, which cannot be reduced to simple affects, by a thorough analysis of the main personalities in Shakespeare's *Othello.*

Cheryl Eschbach seeks to show the clinical relevance of a part-object–based theory, anchored not strictly in the breast but in the concrete and abstract idea of the womb. She defines it as envy of woman as sexual object *and* mother, envy both of the sexuality of the inner space and of the consequent life-giving and life-denying powers that accrue to the mother. Penis envy usually remains closer to consciousness than womb envy. In men, exaggerated phallic assertiveness and aggression, especially against women, harbors a deep horror of the female body, conjoined with envy of its procreative power.

Peter Shabad deepens this aspect of womb envy by postulating that the existential fact of being born of a woman has a profound psychological and cultural impact on the male quest for significance in the eyes of the cosmos: his need to undo the shame of being an inferior creature born of woman and thus to attain some sense of dignity as a creative human being in his own right, by destroying the power of women. Shabad applies these insights into the "causa-sui fantasy of self-creation" to a new interpretation of the Oedipus myth, especially to the interaction of Oedipus with the Sphinx, but also to the background of Dostoyevsky's Raskolnikov and Nietzsche's *Übermensch* fantasy, and to modern German history (post–World War I male fantasies with their fascistic idealization of hardness and their development into Nazi ideology).

Heidrun Jarass (in cooperation with Léon Wurmser) reports on the case of an extremely traumatized patient, with enlarged suicide of her mother at age 1 and similar suicide by her stepmother at age 18, where one crucial element in the transformative work of analysis has been the understanding of her father's intense hatred of women and femininity, hypothetically rooted in his womb envy, and how this envy and hatred have become leading factors in the girl's inner life. Generally, the incorporation of this hatred against women into the superego, especially the ego ideal of girls and boys, is clinically very frequent and socially of great relevance. The case lends itself to some reflections about the consequences of very early, very severe, and ongoing traumatization and the figure of the "vampire" symbolizing both severe trauma and the disastrous superego introjects.

But it also raises important questions about how to deal with so severely traumatized patients. One of the many relevant elements in this long lasting and complex treatment deserves some special consideration: the complementarity and possible opposition of psychoanalytic technique and psychoanalytic relationship. The profound analytic insights are only truly mutative if they occur in the matrix of an emotionally intimate relationship, a deep trustful togetherness that far transcends intellectual insight. Here Buber's philosophy of dialogue appears particularly helpful. In no way should it supplant the understanding by conflict; it should only complement it. The intrapsychic and the interpersonal or relational way of understanding are dialectically bound to each other. One without the other does not do justice to the complexity of our work.

Naomi Janowitz sees animal and originally human sacrifice as the structural opposite of birth and as an expression of the basic problem of envy of women and of their procreativity. Sacrifice undoes the natural birth experience via culturally enacted death. Strikingly, this power of rebirthing is almost exclusively given over to men: Sacrifice gives birth by killing and redirects natural productivity to men, as is borne out by traditions of sacrifice in Judaism, Christianity (the Eucharist!), Islam, Brahmanism, and Buddhism. Something similar is at work in initiation rites (see also Janowitz, 2005).

Benjamin Kilborne tracks the great importance of beliefs in the Evil Eye, reviews some of the rituals around it, and studies an example from Moroccan field work. He sees a whole cultural belief system organized around this concept of the Evil Eye and implies that the psychology of envy is the cornerstone of motivation. He contrasts the two systems of understanding human motivation: the psychoanalytic theory and the belief system revolving around the Evil Eye. Psychoanalytic understanding is a universalist kind of theory that has none of the specificity of the Evil Eye explanations, which inevitably designate a particular person in the patient's world as the source of the misfortune, evil, or sickness. Evil Eye explanations are two-person explanations and are oriented to the here and now. The Evil Eye belief system privileges one set of dynamics, those of envy, over a more global view and understanding of psychodynamics.

The study by Heidrun Jarass and Léon Wurmser on the "magic eye" is a parallel study of the phenomena of Evil Eye, magically penetrating, destructive looks, and the shining, divinely inspired face. This essay brings examples from the Bible and Talmud and from two literary works, one situated in Sicily, written by the Swedish author Selma Lagerlöf, describing the Jettatore, and the other Edgar Allan Poe's story "The Telltale Heart." Freud's view that this widespread sociocultural phenomenon can be understood as projected envy is expanded also to prominently recognize in it the important roles of jealousy and of the punishment aspect, especially the role of shame and guilt, and the archaic experience of merger, of magical power, penetrating force, and destructive violence ascribed to looking and showing. The core of the Evil Eye is the pernicious power of internalized object relations, in which the sequence of shame, jealousy, envy, and revenge is replicated in the conscience, above all in its unconscious parts. Admiration and idealization or humiliation of others may hide the sequence outlined, but this inner Evil Eye keeps breaking through with its own kind of penetrating gaze, its own kind of magical force and searing force. Such regression of the cognitive and perceptual processes is due to trauma with its many forms of overstimulation and overexcitement, or of self-annihilation by fragmentation and devastating shame. Thus, behind the projection of envy, jealousy, revenge, and the superego sanctions lies as the nucleus traumatogenic shame. The shining face is viewed as part of a "trauma compensatory scheme" (Fischer & Riedesser, 2003). This is illustrated by two cases, studied in depth.

Andrew Morrison and Melvin Lansky emphasize the complexity of such seemingly simple affects like jealousy and envy by studying the shame conflicts specifically underlying envy. The paranoid-schizoid position, one of the pillars of Kleinian theory, is understood as a state of persecutory shame anxiety. Envy is one of the consequences of such deep shame, not of a primary aggressive drive. Similarly to Rosemary Balsam, the authors see envy as reflecting a destructive idealization of the other in comparison with whom the self appears as lesser. Envy can be seen as one type of defense against unbearable shame. In the light of this shift of accents, some of the work of Spillius is reinterpreted. Envy is a comparative and self-conscious emotion lying "downstream" from shame.

Rosemary Balsam's essay starts out with a rejection of Freud's distorted view of the woman as primarily a being without a penis suffering from castration shame that leads inexorably to penis envy. A deeper understanding of female psychology turns to general female body anxieties (e.g., those concerning loss of virginity, penile penetration anxiety, or rape anxiety), the female counterpart to castration anxiety, or anxieties arising from loss of control of flow in menstruation and of the expansion of the body in pregnancy. Envy and admiration form a tight relation with each other whereby Balsam sees admiration as preexisting envy. Such gender specific amazements are: (a) pregnancy and childbirth and (b) penile erection. If the growth potential seems blocked and the admired body enlargement not achievable, admiration itself may become dangerous and feared to be toxic. Rapid repression occurs, and intense admiration can turn into bitter, hopeless envy, a very painful emotion. The other has to be diminished so that the balance of self-esteem can be righted—where Morrison and Lansky would speak of shame that needs to be countered by envy and its aggression. A magic transformation is sought by which weak turns into powerful, ordinary into amazing, and so forth. Righting the bitterness of imbalance becomes the cornerstone of character development.

We would like to conclude with some linguistic reflections: "Envy" is derived from *invidia* in Latin. The verb *invidére* originally means "to throw an evil look," to harm by the evil, envious eye. Literally, it signifies "looking into the other," "throwing the magically powerful, destructive gaze through the eye's window into the soul." The eye is most of all a window of the conscience: looking into the conscience and looking out from the conscience; this look may indeed be the lightning bolt of the conscience's power. Closely related to the Evil Eye as carrier of projected envy and power of conscience is fascination. *Fascinare* means "to bewitch, to cast a spell, to exert magical power." It is derived from *fascinum*, a Latin word for the male member. Eye and penis, looking and showing oneself, exploring curiosity and sexual exhibition have a deep connection and, in primary process, are often interchangeable. At the same time, *fascinare* is related to the Greek *baskainein*, which means not only "to bewitch, to bring about a magic transformation," but significantly also to envy and to libel (derived from *bazein*, "to gossip"). The exhibitionist wants above all to fascinate with his member, as a defense against his deep shame and castration anxiety. The hypnotizing look of the leader (*Führer*) and seducer (*Verführer*) exerts not only power and terror, but also a strongly erotic, specifically sadomasochistic fascination. In treatments, we hear how such a gaze is that of the "Devil" (i.e., that of the repressed sexuality). Yet, in a curious reversal, the Kabbala calls the "Power of Evil" Samael, the god of blindness or the blind god.

"Jealousy" is indirectly derived from the Greek *zelos*, meaning "ardor, intense desire, eagerness, fieriness." The same is true for its German, Slavic, and Hebrew equivalents: Heat and fire inhere in this very profound affect.

In these two emotions, we are dealing with very deep and culturally enormously powerful emotions, whether they are primary affects or not. Certainly they evolve into complex feeling states that shape to a considerable, often decisive, extent character and object relations in most human beings. Yet, they are woven into the rich texture of human emotions and connected with them in untold variations. To tease out some of these threads has been the purpose of bringing together the essays in this volume.

NOTES

1. Spillius quotes Melanie Klein: "Jealousy she describes as a three person situation in which the love that the subject feels is his due ... has been taken away, or is in danger of being taken away, from him by his rival" (1993, p. 1199).
2. Melanie Klein's definition in 1957: "Envy is the angry feeling that another person possesses and enjoys something desirable—the envious impulse being to take it away or spoil it" (quoted by Walter Joffe, 1969, p. 538).

REFERENCES

Balsam, R. H. (2003). The vanished pregnant body in psychoanalytic female developmental theory. *Journal of the American Psychoanalytical Association, 51*, 1153–1179.

Barth, B. (1990). Die Darstellung der weiblichen Sexualität als Ausdruck männlichen Uterusneides und dessen Abwehr. *Jahrbuch der Psychoanalyse, 26*, 64–101.

Benz, A. E. (1984). Der Gebärneid der Männer. *Psyche, 38*, 307–328.

Büchmann, G. (1965). *Geflügelte Worte und Zitatenschatz*. Zürich: Classen.

Coen, S. J. (1987). Pathological jealousy. *International Journal of Psycho-Analysis, 68*, 99–108.

de Paola, H. (2001). Panel Report: Envy, Jealousy and Shame. *International Journal of Psycho-Analysis, 82*, 381–384.

Eschbach, C. (2004). *Womb envy in character development.* Presented at American Psycho-Analytic Association meeting in San Francisco.

Fischer, G., & Riedesser, P, (2003). *Lehrbuch der Psychotraumatologie* (3rd revised ed.). München: Reinhardt.

Hart, S. L., Carrington, H. A., Tronick, E. Z., & Carroll, S. R. (2004). When infants lose exclusive maternal attention: Is it jealousy? *Infancy, 6*(1), 57–78.

Janowitz, N. (2005, January). *Lusting for death: Some unconscious meanings of martyrdom traditions.* Presented at American Psychoanalytical Association meeting, New York.

Joffe, W. G. (1969). A critical review of the status of the envy concept. *International Journal of Psycho-Analysis, 50,* 533–546.

Lansky, M. R. & Morrison, A. P. (1997). *The Widening Scope of Shame.* Hillsdale, NJ: The Analytic Press.

Lansky, M. R. (2001). Hidden shame, working through, and the problem of forgiveness in *The Tempest. Journal of the American Psychoanalytical Association, 49,* 1005–1033.

Nietzsche, F. (1948). *Gedichte. Parnass-Bücherei.* Bern: Alfred Scherz.

Seelig, B. (2002). The rape of Medusa in the temple of Athena. *International Journal of Psycho-Analysis, 83,* 895–911.

Spillius, E. B. (1993). Varieties of envious experiences. *International Journal of Psycho-Analysis, 74,* 1199–1212.

Wellendorf, F. (1995). Zur Psychoanalyse der Geschwisterbeziehung. *Forum der Psychoanalyse, 11*(4), 295–310.

Editors

Léon Wurmser, M.D., Ph.D., Humboldt University, Berlin, is the author of *The Hidden Dimension,* Jason Aronson, Lanham, MD 1978; *The Mask of Shame,* Jason Aronson Lanham, MD, 1981; *The Power of the Inner Judge,* Jason Aronson Lanham, MD, 2000; *Flight from Conscience,* Springer, New York, 1980; *The Riddle of Masochism,* Springer, New York 1993; *Magic Transformation and Tragic Transformation,* Vandenhoeck and Ruprecht, Göttingen, Germany 1999; *Values and Ideas of Judaism in Psychoanalytic View,* Vandenhoeck, and Ruprecht, Göttingen, Germany 2001; recipient of Egnér and *Journal of the American Psychoanalytic Association* prizes. Dr. Wurmser is a supervising and training analyst with the New York Freudian Society, and a clinical professor of psychiatry with the University of West Virginia, and he teaches extensively in Europe. His book *"Torment me, but don't abandon me!" The Psychoanalysis of the Severe Neuroses in a New Key* will be published by Rowman & Littlefield, Lanham, MD, in 2007.

Heidrun Jarass, M.D., is a general practitioner working as a psychoanalyst in private practice. She teaches and is a training and supervising analyst at the Institute for Psychoanalysis of the German Psychoanalytic Society (DPG) in Nuremberg. Dr. Jarass is vice president of the board of directors of the Nuremberg-Regensburg Psychoanalytic Society, and since 2004 has been a member of the International Psychoanalytic Association, and served on the larger board of the German Society for Psychotherapy (DGPT). Since 2005 she has been active in psychoanalytic research focusing on the psychodynamic processes in supervision and has presented her work with severely ill patients at international meetings.

Contributors

Rosemary H. Balsam, M.D., is Associate Clinical Professor of Psychiatry, Yale Medical School, Staff Psychiatrist, Department of Student Health, Yale University, and Training and Supervising Analyst, Western New England Institute for Psychoanalysis. She is Editor of the Book Review Section of *JAPA*, and was the National Woman Psychoanalytic Scholar of the American Psychoanalytic Association, 2004-05.

Cheryl L. Eschbach, M.D., is Assistant Clinical Professor of Psychiatry and Behavioral Sciences at the Emory University School of Medicine. She is a psychoanalyst in private practice in Atlanta, Georgia.

Naomi Janowitz, Ph.D., is Director of the Religious Studies Program at University of California – Davis, and is the author of numerous articles on Judaism, Christianity and Graeco-Roman religions in late antiquity as well as three books: *The Poetics of Ascent: Rabbinic Theories of Language in a Late Antique Ascent Text* (SUNY Press, 1989), *Magic in the Roman World: Pagans Jews and Christians* (Routledge, 2001), and *Icons of Power: Rituals Strategies in Late Antiquity* (Penn State Press, 2002), which was chosen as a *Choice* Journal Outstanding Academic book for 2003. She is currently an Advanced Candidate at the San Francisco Psychoanalytic Institute and has a private practice in Berkeley, California.

Benjamin Kilborne, Ph.D., was educated in the US and in France, and has published extensively in fields as various as history, anthropology, literature, and psychoanalysis. Professor at UCLA and the Sorbonne, Visiting Professor at the University of Moscow, and Training and Supervising Analyst in Istanbul, he is currently in private practice in clinical psychoanalysis and psychotherapy in West Stockbridge, Massachusetts. He is the author of scores of papers and, most recently, of *Disappearing Persons: Shame and Appearance* (SUNY Press, 2002). He is also a Julliard-trained pianist.

Melvin R. Lansky, M.D., is a Training and Supervising Analyst at the New Center for Psychoanalysis in Los Angeles, a Clinical Professor of Psychiatry at the UCLA Medical School, and the author or editor of seven books and over a hundred articles and book chapters, mostly on psychoanalysis or applied psychoanalysis. His books include *Fathers Who Fail: Shame and Psychopathology in the Family System* (Analytic Press, 1992);

Posttraumatic Nightmares: Psychodynamic Explorations (Analytic Press, 1995) and (as Co-Editor with Andrew P. Morrison) *The Widening Scope of Shame* (Analytic Press, 1997). He was the recipient of the *JAPA* prize for 2005.

Andrew P. Morrison, M.D., is Associate Clinical Professor of Psychiatry, Harvard Medical School, Supervising Analyst, Massachusetts Institute for Psychoanalysis, and faculty, Boston Psychoanalytic Society and Institute. A member of the Editorial Board of *Psychoanalytic Dialogues,* he is the author of *Shame: The Underside of Narcissism* (Analytic Press, 1989) and *The Culture of Shame* (Ballantine, 1996), and editor of *Essential Papers on Narcissism* (New York University Press, 1986) and (with Melvin R. Lansky) *The Widening Scope of Shame* (Analytic Press, 1997). He has written many papers on shame and other psychoanalytic matters as well, and is in private practice of psychotherapy and psychoanalysis in Cambridge, Massachusetts.

Peter Shabad, Ph.D., is Clinical Associate Professor of Psychology in the Department of Psychiatry at Northwestern University Medical School, and Adjunct Professor at the Chicago School of Professional Psychology. He is the author of *Despair and the Return of Hope: Echoes of Mourning in Psychotherapy* (Jason Aronson, 2001), and co-editor of *The Problem of Loss and Mourning: Psychoanalytic Perspectives* (International Universities Press, 2000), and is the author of numerous book chapters and journal articles in psychoanalysis. He also has a full-time private practice in Chicago, Illinois.

1

Pathological Jealousy
The Perversion of Love

LÉON WURMSER AND HEIDRUN JARASS

A PLEA FOR TAKING JEALOUSY MORE SERIOUSLY

A number of experiences in the past few years have caused us to pay more attention to the affect of jealousy and the outer and inner conflicts connected with it.

First, it was the observation in supervision that nowadays, particularly in Germany, much more weight is being given to the dyadic and, therefore, to envy than to triangular relations and to issues of jealousy. Yet, in clinical work it becomes quite evident that this turning away from the dynamics that are in the widest sense oedipal (i.e., triadic) is problematic and one-sided. In supervised analyses it strikes us how often conflicts of closeness and distance, understood as being of symbiotic origin, really hide unconscious jealousy, and that in these instances the dyadic defends against what really is triadic. Often the reverse is true as well: that the triadic conflict hides a deeper dyadic conflict (and this doubleness has also been noted by Coen [1987]). But this state of affairs tends to be more easily acknowledged and is less particularly repressed than its obverse (i.e., when jealousy and the disavowed shame going with it are hidden by fears of separation or closeness and are clinically overlooked).

Second, there were personal experiences and observations with relatives and friends, which have, from childhood on and into our old age, ever again caused us to be deeply concerned about what devastating power the unreflected living out of jealousy has on all intimate and close relationships, how the most precious parts of our lives—love, respect, and creativity—may be poisoned and destroyed by its force, and how often such jealousy is looked upon as "normal" and not questioned any further.[1]

Third, it was and is our own self-analytic and self-critical reflection that keeps making it painfully conscious to us how the ghosts of that distant personal past (i.e., our own feelings of jealousy, envy, and resentment) are never completely banished and continue to sneak into our own feelings and behaviors without us being aware of it.

It is, therefore, all the more surprising that we hardly find any articles on this topic in the psychoanalytic literature, a fact also regretted in the last major work on the topic of pathological jealousy written by Stanley Coen (1987). This is really quite curious. It impresses us somewhat like the way it occurred 40 years ago when shame was an affect hardly anyone paid attention to: Nobody in psychoanalysis talked about it (exceptions were Gerhard Piers, Helen Lynd, Erik Erikson, Sidney Levin, and Helen Block Lewis), and yet Shakespeare and the Greek tragedians were replete with it! Exactly the same could be stated now about jealousy. Moreover, these two affects, shame and jealousy, are very intimately linked (just as it is true for envy and shame).

As mentioned in the prologue of this book, new insights demand an uncoupling of issues of jealousy from the Oedipus conflicts as well as a separate study of triangularity and the oedipal phase. A third issue to be considered is the great relevance of jealousy in sibling rivalry as clearly distinguished from oedipal rivalry. Franz Wellendorf (1995), who devoted a valuable study to this neglected topic, summarizes this by saying: "Looking at the history of psychoanalysis one is struck by the discrepancy between frequent and intense sibling conflicts among psychoanalysts and the neglect of this issue in the psychoanalytic literature. One can find this discrepancy already in Freud" (p. 309).

Yet, we start out with a case study of the intense jealousy problems between mother and daughter and their dynamics.

PATHOLOGICAL JEALOUSY: THE SENSE OF INJUSTICE AND THE "GAPING FLAW"

And when I love thee not, / Chaos is come again.

Othello, A. III, sec. 3, v. 91/92

Jane, a woman in her 50s in a European academic institution seen by a colleague, a woman analyst, many years ago, was married for the fourth time with two grown-up daughters. She came to treatment because of severe depressive episodes, with at times suicidal despair. From the beginning of therapy, an obtrusive problem in her work was her vehement jealousy in regard to her younger, by far preferred daughter, the only one from her third marriage. This had been a bond to a man whom she loved very much, but whom she also divorced because of financial disagreements and who soon afterward died. If that daughter did not call her every day and spend every weekend with her, if she cultivated her own friendships and especially when she thought of marrying, Jane went into towering rages and accused her for hours in telephone harangues that she (the daughter) was not loving her really, otherwise her own mother would come above everybody else. When the daughter did not give in to her tantrums, Jane took it to mean that she did not care at all about her mother. If she did really love her, she would yield to her. No other relationship should ever replace this most intense of all bonds—that by blood. Either there existed this absolute irreplaceability and closeness, or Jane saw herself as completely alone. Something of this showed also in her then current fourth marriage to a very troubled, severely narcissistic, and exploitative man. It was also in regard to this almost delusional jealousy that the analytic process momentarily collapsed: All ability to step out of the immediate experience, to reflect about it with the help of the inner eye, and all rationality transiently vanished. The part became the whole. When the analyst questioned this, she too became, for the moment, the enemy.

A contributing fact about Jane's history is that when she was 4 months old, her mother killed herself by shooting herself in the head. The two older siblings stayed with the alcoholic father, whereas Jane was given to a relative of his. This adoptive mother was quite possessive, phobically intrusive, and clinging toward Jane. Until she was 12, Jane did not know anything about her real life story, although she always had a vague sense that something was not right, that "nothing was real." With tragic irony and envious cruelty her adoptive mother used to say: "You think you are so smart, but you do not know everything!" The decisive truth had been hidden from her. Only at 12 she learned from her intoxicated "uncle" that he really was her biological father, and the reason why she had been raised apart from her brother and sister was because of her mother's suicide. This threw her into such deep despair that for weeks she was not able to return to school and was hiding in her bedroom. Most galling, and even more extremely shaming was the fact that everybody in her wider family knew all along the truth and assiduously kept the secret from her, and her alone.

When the girl was praised for her intelligence, her adoptive mother would sarcastically object: "She is so smart that she does all these stupid things." The same happened when her prettiness was admired: "Everything positive had to be undone. Everything that made me myself was wrong." This invidious devaluation continued incessantly in her own mind: a voice of envy and resentment that could not permit her anything good, no pleasure, pride, or joy. As seen in the case of Nora described by one of us (HJ, in the Jarass and Wurmser essay in this volume), parental envy became very much part of the introject and was now vehemently effective against the self-as-agent.

In her childhood, everything seemed unreal, false, and in one sense this was accurate because it was built on the veiling of the truth, and in another sense, because nothing could ever replace the lost primal reality, yet, she was herself a stranger and did not fit in. Now she postulated again and again that only blood relationship counted, not her adoptive family. Her jealousy manifested itself in this longing for something real. Orality, the images of eating and smoking, and most of all an indissoluble bond and exclusivity stood in her experience for a *core reality* and an original *meaningfulness,* in contrast to her basic experience of strangeness and meaninglessness, of total unlovability (i.e., of the feeling in her inmost being of not being worthy of love and appreciation)—therefore, something much like *primal shame.* She spoke of a *gaping flaw* in herself: "How can anybody with a flaw create somebody without a flaw?"—referring to her suicidal mother and her alcoholic father. It is indeed that concept of the *hamartía* (flaw) postulated by Aristotle as the character flaw present in every tragic hero. It is at once an image of shame and an image of pain, the feeling of a *mortal wound.* Both belong to the basic trauma. As she stated herself: "I am not being punished for something that I do, but I am rejected for what I am"—*shame, not guilt.* Behind the absoluteness of the fantasy, the too-much is hidden in the repetition of the trauma: "I am rejected for who I am."

We also have an indication that there was, parallel to this, a kind of *existential guilt*: that it had been her own existence that had caused the death of her mother (cf. Hirsch, 2002). She constantly felt she should apologize for who she was and that she existed.

Besides the basic feeling of unreality and estrangement, there was a second element—the demand for distributive *justice*—and for her the basic experience that she had been wronged, that she had suffered grievous injustice. This sense of injustice dwelled in the very core of her being, of her self, of her identity. So severely traumatized patients like Jane testify to the fact that chronic, early, and enduring traumatization, as indicated here by loss and soul blindness, causes not only an all-encompassing feeling of shame, a kind of shame mood, but also a smoldering resentment. Both lead not only to a fundamental attitude of "all or nothing," but also to that of entitlement: "I have the *right for reparation,*" an attitude accompanied by anger, but painstakingly hidden and suppressed. This burning resentment joined with a deep sense of being defective.

But we deal here not simply with a lack of object and a defect, but with a conflict. The intolerability of her shame, her helplessness, the feeling of having been betrayed and of being a stranger, and the panic about this, all were being hidden by the resentment, and this made it impossible to go beyond it. She feared the unbearable shame that if she trusted, she again would be betrayed: "not to be again the trusting victim." All questioning by her analyst led to a furious transference protest: "Do you think I am stupid!?" Its vehemence might trigger in the countertransference feelings of helpless rage.

The judgment "Who leaves me and who is not constantly immediately reachable, does not love me and is therefore a traitor" becomes her *idée fixe* and her leading myth.

SEPARATION IS EQUATED WITH SOUL MURDER

In her jealousy, all three—the shame, the resentment, and the claim for reparation—lived on in a most powerful way. Clearly, on the face of it, the structure of jealousy seems to be triadic. But at its core, there is sheltered, as it were, the fantasy of an all-powerful *twosome unity* from which everybody else, even the entire world, should be banished. Pathological jealousy is, therefore, in no way limited to sexual jealousy (although the psychoanalytic literature deals, as far as we can see, only with this form). In fact, the latter is a special case of a more general search for, and addiction to, the exclusivity of the intimate relationship—the fantasy of total possession of, and power over, the intimate other. *The essence of jealousy lies in this absoluteness and exclusivity of the demanded relationship.*

This can be deepened: Whoever did not maintain this principle of absolute exclusivity in the intimate relationship was deemed totally guilty. Thus, separation guilt became the foundation stone for her entire ethics. "I made myself my own child in order to have this place in life," Jane confessed, "and when my daughter leaves I lose my place." She did not want anyone else to be close to her children: "They were mine." And: "I made her so I would *have* someone." She did not want anyone to doubt that she was the mother who did everything for her children; nobody could take away her affection, in the sense of contesting it. There could not be any separation. She also took her husband's visit with his family of origin as betrayal. Everything that was not exclusive was considered betrayal and a fundamental breach of trust. Love was possession and meant: "Either I own you or I kill you. You have no right of having your own life." She often dreams of tigers and other "feral beasts." These devouring animals represent more than her deep neediness ("the devouring need for love") and desperate and deeply aggressive demands for love and jealous rages; they also express the consuming nature of the affects themselves. In turn, it is so as the *Othello* quote at the beginning of this section says: "If I do not have you I am faced with the nothingness of a total lack of relationship and with that a complete loss of self." Early traumatization leads to this structural emptiness, to this abyss of not-being (Green, 1993; Küchenhoff, 1990).

This claim for exclusivity was the defense against her deep knowledge of having in fact been an excluded one, that indeed there was a hidden reality that she was sensing, but was not allowed to know. Her judgmentalism defended her against exploring these connections and working through these conflicts. Clinging to the absoluteness and exclusivity endowed her with structure and constancy; without them she would have felt completely lost. It was a defense that she had "zero empathy" for her daughter: It would have been too dangerous to put herself into the other; she would then lose the hold that her absolute judgment gave her.

This had another important consequence: her superego, her conscience, too showed this implacability and rigid exclusivity, or, more precisely, it had one such aspect of absoluteness.

Suddenly, a wider and deeper meaning of her pathological jealousy opened up—of this expression of the principle of *power instead of love*—and this with a small, yet typical event. Her daughter, who had defied Jane's massive reproaches, had married and then, 1 year later, moved to a far away university town and spent a 1-week vacation with Jane. Once after she and her husband had left the house, Jane went into their bedroom and "discovered" the list of things to do, including buying a present for the first wife of her late father, Jane's third husband. But Jane's jealousy always threw itself with particularly biting ferocity upon the daughter's relationship with her half-sister, the child from the first marriage of her father. And now the daughter wants to give a gift to the mother of that hated rival! Jane was beside herself with indignation and called it an act of utmost disloyalty; her rage was now also directed at her analyst who tried to explore this further. She cried: "I do not mean anything to anybody. I am an awful person!" Thus she puts into words the shame aspect hidden in the core of jealousy, namely, the sense of being the excluded third.

Jane spoke about how that stepdaughter of hers had refused to accept her and made her life hard with her reproaches because Jane had, after all, helped to break up the husband's first marriage and family. Furthermore, the mother of that girl had tried to have the illegitimacy of Jane's daughter legally certified. The analyst asked herself whether Jane had not been feeling guilty because she had taken her husband away from his wife and his two children and that she now expected to be punished by them. Instead of feeling this "real guilt" (*Realschuld*), she externalized it and accused in turn both women of taking her own daughter away from her. In other words, the pathological jealousy was, at least partly, a *defense against her guilt feelings* for having robbed them of their husband and father and given them so much cause for severe jealousy and aggrievement. However, Jane never acknowledged this guilt. What she obsessively, almost delusionally fastened on now manifested itself as *reversal of the guilt and of the reason for jealousy*: now it is *she* who felt herself chronically to be the excluded third and the victim of betrayal and accused the other two, especially her stepdaughter, while she herself seemed to be innocent. The moment the analyst, if ever so tactfully, tried to question this, Jane became furious, and for that moment the main transference became that of feeling blamed. It was a *superego transference* because the guilt feeling within had to be so vehemently defended against by the jealousy.[2] Ultimately, it was not merely the guilt for having broken up that family but for the *soul murder* that she inflicted on her child, actively doing now what she had suffered passively.

Her inability to accept a transitional object and the emphasis on the concreteness of her relationship to her daughter should, therefore, not be simply understood as a developmental deficit, but they stood, among other things, in the service of the defense against guilt feelings and prevented their emergence.[3] It also illustrates what one of us (HJ) in her case study describes as a defense: the concreteness of guilt and submission to an archaic, sadistic superego as a way of dealing with the "hole," the objectless, nameless emptiness left by severest, early trauma, in both cases, Jane's and Nora's (as discussed in the essay by Jarass and Wurmser, chapter 5), by the suicide of the patient's mother during the child's first year of life and the surrounding circumstances, and the jealousy and envy used as strategies defending against this archaic superego as manifest in global feelings of guilt and shame.

In the continued work with the patient, her massive masochism became ever clearer, especially vis-à-vis her husband: Although unemployed, he asked her, who was working in a demanding academic profession, to do everything for him: shopping, taxes, paying all the bills, all the driving, cooking, all negotiations about car leases, and so forth. He was very overweight and spent his days lying in front of the television or playing computer games. At night, he did not let her sleep with his accusations, harangues, and fears. When she underwent a surgical procedure with the suspicion for malignancy, her husband traveled far away; it was a girlfriend who helped her through those difficult days. Yet, she did accept everything: "Suffering is the price I have to pay in order not to be alone." In the treatment she recognized how lonely she was in this misalliance and how much self-punishment there was in this, for the many layers of guiltiness. Her husband embodied her own archaic, resentful, devaluing inner judgment. The main transference gradually turned out to be a reversal of the jealousy scenario: She now had a powerful ally in her analyst against this ogre of man and conscience. It was a type of triangle, where she now became the excluding first. Separating from her husband, she moved out of the miserable situation to a house given to her by some friends. Only now could she see that the categories of blood relationship and matrimony were tottering: Her friends were the ones who truly stood by her.

Her towering superego demands, manifest in the equally dominant moral masochism, could be better understood during the sessions with the help of the sequence visible within the analytic process and also in the transference: yearning for love → omnipotence of responsibility and submitting to all demands → disappointed love and deeper loneliness → rage → turning all the anger against the self → the absoluteness of the inner judge and his condemnation. In the wake of these insights and changes, her pathological jealousy disappeared apparently completely.

These observations can now give us occasion for a deeper exploration of jealousy, and, more broadly, of the conflicted nature of love.

THE DYNAMICS OF PATHOLOGICAL JEALOUSY

Dimitry Karamazov (1979/1980, 1990) states: "But to fall in love does not mean to love. One can fall in love and still hate" (p. 104). This idea contains a very deep truth: Infatuation can harbor and veil very much aggression. It does not have to be that way, but the danger always lurks there. This can be extended to much of what is called love.

Socrates starts his own inquiry into the nature of love in Plato's "Symposium" with the observation that one desires what one does not have, what one feels "in need of" and "deprived of"—*endeés.* As psychoanalysts we would say that there is in the core of love a yearning for something one profoundly feels lacking, a core feeling that we also detect both in envy and in jealousy.

A very important aspect to be considered in much of love is the often quite unabashedly expressed wish for exclusive possession of the partner. In its midst, there crouches, often devouring, even murderous jealousy. It seems that this wish for exclusivity can be observed already in very small children. Newest experimental studies show clear reactions of jealousy in 6-month-old infants in episodes "where the mothers directed positive attention toward a lifelike doll" (as compared with face-to-face play and still-face perturbation):

> Cross-context comparisons of affects and behaviors revealed that jealousy evocation responses were distinguished by diminished joy and heightened anger and intensity of negative emotionality, comparable to levels displayed during the still-face episode; heightened sadness, with durations exceeding those displayed during still-face exposure; and an approach response consisting of interest, looks at mother, and diminished distancing, which was more pronounced than that demonstrated during play. (Hart, Carrington, Tronick, & Carroll, 2004, p. 57)

Fascinatingly, this works in experiments when a lifelike baby doll is used, but not when "the mothers focused positive attention toward a book" (p. 58). Hart et al. therefore conclude: "Because infants were being ignored in both conditions, the results suggest that infants find maternal inattention even more perturbing if the object of maternal attention is another child" (p. 58. Moreover, "5-month-olds were found more upset when maternal attention was directed toward another infant than toward an adult" (p. 58) (Draghi-Lorenz, 1998; Masciuch & Kienapple, 1993). It is also very fascinating to notice that the crucial element is *exclusiveness,* just as we observed in the clinical example (and in introspective inquiry as well). The authors mention that in several previous studies (Fivaz-Depeursinge & Corboz-Warnery, 1999; McHale & Fivaz-Depeursinge, 1999, Murray & Travarthen, 1985)

> infants as young as 3 months old recognize when their mothers are focusing on social objects other than themselves, and operate in triangular

> situations by distributing their affect signals and attention between their conversing parents. These studies suggest that young infants are sensitive to even brief and unintentional instances of social exclusion, and utilize various approach responses toward establishing social exclusion. (Hart et al., p. 59)

Brazelton is quoted as describing an 11-month-old's "'frantic' efforts to reinstate exclusiveness by pushing the rival infant" off the mother's lap (p. 59). As crucial as dyadic relationships are, the similarly critical relevance of triadic constellations from quite early infancy on is shown in these intense efforts by very young children to reestablish "dyadic relationships with attachment figures" after they had been replaced by a triad (p. 60).

In contrast to the still-face situation, there is the combination of sadness and "heightened interest and looks at mother and diminished distancing, suggesting an approach response ... the approach response associated with jealousy evocation was even more pronounced than that demonstrated during play" (Hart et al., 2004, p. 68). *"Overall, these results indicate that expressions of sadness and looks at mother were specific to the jealous evocation situation"* (p. 70, our emphasis).

There are also striking connections between the overall attitudes of mothers and the jealousy responses in their children: "mothers' greater disengagement in play predicted infants' lesser joy during jealousy evocation ... [while] mothers' greater intrusiveness in play predicted infants' lesser interest during jealousy evocation" (p. 70). Another interesting correlation is their reverse: "heightened negativity in infants exposed to jealous evocation was associated with more optimal characteristics of mothers" (p. 61): "infants' anger and sadness during jealousy evocation relate to maternal sensitivity and dyadic vocal turn-taking during play" (p. 70). In other words: *The better the relationship with mother is, the more pronounced the jealousy response is!*

Certainly, this wish to take possession of the other person and establish exclusivity in dyadic attachment turns out to be an innate disposition that shows up extremely early in infancy. What has struck us clinically (and introspectively as well) was a prevalence of sadness and desperate searching that might be the only conscious aspect that veiled an underlying, but repressed, jealousy. Accordingly, the authors state that "infant jealousy is distinguished by the affect expression of sadness" (Hart et al., 2004, p. 71). This relation makes much sense:

> Jealousy's presentation through sadness may be understood in light of this affect's potential effect on caregivers ... loss of exclusiveness represents disrupted attachment, and the infant's expression of jealousy through sadness functions to solicit exclusive caregiving, and thus repair the attachment relationship ... jealousy protest signifies the meaningfulness of the attachment relationship. (p. 72)

The jealousy responses in infants of intrusive and depressed mothers tend to be flattened (p. 73). All these findings also show that it is wrong to view jealousy as a "secondary, or nonbasic emotion" and confirm what, in our own experience, observant mothers long claimed, that they could observe clear signals of jealousy in infants as young as 4 months old.

If we turn now to the psychoanalytic investigation of jealousy, Freud (1922, 1955/1968) differentiates between three forms and layers of jealousy: (a) competitive or normal, (b) projected, and (c) delusional jealousy. Normal jealousy is "compounded of grief, the pain caused by the thought of losing the loved object, and of the narcissistic wound … further of feelings of enmity against the successful rival, and of a greater or lesser amount of self-criticism which tries to hold the subject's own ego accountable for his loss" (p. 223). Freud derived this from the "Oedipus or siblings complex" and saw it as rooted very deeply in the unconscious. Evidently now, with the new findings, we can reach much farther back.

Besides this "normal" jealousy (about which we will have to say more later), there is the projected jealousy: The one who is or wants to be unfaithful accuses the partner of such infidelity in order to assuage his or her own guilt. This is clearly a defensive strategy at the behest of the superego, as both Ernest Jones (1929) and J. Riviere (1932) further emphasized and also borne out by our case study. The third type, the delusional forms of pathological jealousy, is ascribed by Freud to hidden homosexuality: "*I* do not love him, *she* loves him!" (Freud, 1922, p. 225). Freud importantly adds: "In a delusional case one will be prepared to find jealousy belonging to all three layers, never to the third alone" (p. 225).

In his eloquent, elegant, and erudite lecture "Jealousy" at the Sorbonne in Paris, Ernest Jones (1929) summarizes his ideas neatly:

> It is my experience that jealousy is a much less normal phenomenon than is commonly supposed, that for the greater part it rests on an abnormal and neurotic basis. It betokens a failure in the development of the capacity to love, a lack of self-confidence due ultimately to unconscious guiltiness that has not been overcome from childhood days, and an undue dependence on the love object that indicates a tendency in the direction of sex inversion.[4]. This last feature becomes plain enough in insane jealousy, but I consider it is present in a milder degree in the other forms also. In short, jealousy is a sign of weakness in love, not of strength; it takes its source in fear, guilt and hate rather than in love. (p. 340)

As Lansky (1997) did recently in regard to envy (i.e., understand it not simply as an affect but as an entire process), Jones enumerates the psychological stages in jealousy:

> first of the fear of loss, secondly of shame and wounded self-esteem that is derived from the unconscious guiltiness, and thirdly of anger which protects him against both by justifying his hatred, putting him in the right and thus once more restoring his self-esteem. (p. 339)

The impulse of infidelity that is now projected onto the partner originates in the man's fear of a threatening bondage to the woman (p. 338): "There is often a fear of being loved too greatly, a fear of having his personality 'possessed' by the love object" (pp. 336–337)—akin to the fear and envy of femininity that are outlined in other parts of this volume. Quoting La Rochefoucauld, Jones points to the secondary shame caused by jealousy: "*On a honte d'avouer que l'on ait de la jalousie*"[5] (p. 336). Jones would reduce all sense of inferiority and shame to unconscious guilt, "a sentiment of *moral* inferiority" (p. 334) (which we would demur at) and generalizes in a sentence that holds a very great truth, far beyond the topic at hand, albeit again by underplaying the crucial role of shame, besides guilt in this, especially with the sense of having been betrayed (Lansky, 2001):

> Mental health and freedom, with the capacity for happiness that this brings, is essentially dependent on freedom from unconscious guiltiness. With this goes a compensatory self-love. It is the self-love, self-esteem and self-respect that is wounded and damaged by the unconscious guilt, hence the person's sensitiveness to criticism and his constant demand for approval or recognition in various forms. Hence also the unsparing nature of the hatred aroused when one is betrayed; if love is pitiful, self-love is certainly pitiless. La Rochefoucauld justly observed that "*la jalousie est le plus grand de tous les maux, et celui qui fait le moins de pitié aux personnes qui le causent.*"[6] (pp. 334–335)

The single key Jones promises that could unlock all the main secrets of jealousy (p. 327) appears then to be what he calls "unconscious guiltiness" and which we would today enlarge by the factor of unconscious shame.

Joan Riviere (1932) (and later enlarged to encompass a rebuttal of Fenichel's critique; I quote from the German edition of the latter version) correctly points out that both pathological forms of jealousy described by Freud serve the defense against the superego by projecting the guilt feelings for infidelity onto the partner. In her own case description, however, she deepens this concept of jealousy; it has to serve as a protection against guilt feelings for a much more archaic form of fantasy: to steal something from another person on an oral-erotic and oral-sadistic basis. In other words, she postulates the origin of jealousy in the earliest forms of envy. She sees in this also a kind of triadic constellation: the subject, the object that is being deprived, and the thing or person that is being taken away, over, and beyond her acceptance of the very early oedipal conflict postulated by Klein. The guilt feelings for this "ruling passion of her life" (referring to her patient) were then rationalized and "genitalized' by being displaced onto the much less repressed guilt for her projected sexual unfaithfulness. All pleasure was experienced as being stolen from another person. The wish to be preferred to somebody else was the prevalent tone of her psyche. Yet, manifestly the guilt was being reversed, exactly as we have observed with Jane: the others were the guilty ones, they had robbed, deprived, harmed, and destroyed her—instead of her doing this. In her case also, it is *a grand reversal of a guilt situation and turning the blaming from passive to active,* "the liberation of the ego from the burden of responsibility." The "narcissistic injury," the gaping wound experienced by our's and Riviere's patients, is traced by her to the condemnation by the superego and viewed as expiation of the ego for the unconscious robbing and aggressive impulses, ultimately by very early "heterosexual oral-genital envy." In our case we would add the severe real traumatizations as prototype for such woundedness replicated then by the introjects, especially in the form of superego accusations and condemnations. Riviere continues by saying that the jealous person consciously experiences the unfaithfulness of the partner as a retaliation for her (his) own aggressions that she places in the earliest aggressive fantasies, while we would consider these aggressions, above all the wishes to steal, as derived from the severe traumatizations and their perpetuation on the intrapsychic and interpersonal planes. Yet, she sees the true reason for the anxiety not in any fear of outer retaliation but in the ego's fear of its own sadism, the anxiety caused by threatened internal retribution. Riviere rightly adds Othello to her argument: He had won his love object in the first place by taking her away from her father. His central "psychic guilt" cannot be overlooked and yet not recognized as what it is: his "blackness."

Without wanting to enter into a careful study of the debate between Fenichel (1935) and Riviere, we would like to give some of the former's points that may still be salient for us. Like Jones, Fenichel sees pathological jealousy as arising in people incapable of deeper love, a point that we will take up later on in our own thoughts about jealousy as a perversion of love. For him too it is the narcissistic injury:

> The fear of loss of love is strongest precisely in those people to whom loss of love really is the worst that can befall them—to whom it means not only a sexual frustration, but also a severe impairment of their self-regard and under certain circumstances a dissolution of the ego. (Fenichel, 1935, p. 350)

Very importantly, he adds a sociocultural aspect: "a society whose ideology makes one marriage partner appear as the property of the other, for this reason increases the psychoeconomic usefulness of jealousy" (p. 351). He asserts that a longing for other ties is biologically normal, but thwarted by this ideology of possessiveness (p. 353), a point taken up by us later on as well. Like Riviere, he also puts the fantasy of "robbing of what is not given freely" in the center of a dynamic understanding of jealousy, but one mostly on the oedipal and sexual levels: "robbing (or, turned against the ego, being robbed at the same time) became for her a condition of love," ultimately also for him directed, on an oral-sadistic level, against her mother (p. 358). Her sexual excitement was tied to the fantasy: "I am being robbed, and I rob" (p. 358).

La Rochefoucauld (Jones, 1929, p. 328) most succinctly states: *"Il y a dans la jalousie plus d'amour-propre que d'amour"* ("In jealousy, there is more self-love than love"), and Jones (1929) repeats it: "it is not love at all, but a craving to be loved" (p 334). Ping-Nie Pao (1969) takes up this (and Fenichel's) observation of inability for deeper love as a major predisposing dynamic factor in pathological jealousy: "'Let her prove to me' was merely a projection of his own feeling of incapacity for loving. He seemed to be saying: It is not I who cannot love; it is you who does not love" (p. 625). It is replaced by the "belief that to love is to possess" (p. 630). He rightly questions an automatic correlation of pathological jealousy with homosexuality, but joins it in his case rather with "concern over narcissistic self-engrossment" (p. 635) and "concern over narcissistic unrelatedness" (p. 637). He concludes "that jealousy is an ego state that can be reinstated by various conflicts, like those over homosexual impulses, oral-sadistic impulses, etc.," and, as he adds later on, "by conflicts over aggressivity and narcissism" (p. 635). Very important, "jealousy is a complex ego state, involving all components of the psychic structure—id, ego, and superego" (pp. 635–636). Divergent explanations become complementary (p. 637), which is also Joffe's (1969) and Coen's (1987) view.

Finally, we reach the last important contribution to our topic, as already mentioned at the beginning, from Stanley Coen (1987) who stresses, among other things, the dialectic between dyadic and triadic aspects in pathological jealousy: "the jealous triadic scene in pathological jealousy serves simultaneously to defend against as well as to express both dyadic and triadic conflicts" (p. 100).

> [T]he primal scene triadic construction of Mr. A's pathological jealousy protected against dangerous intimacy with one person. ... But not only does the woman protect against homosexuality, the man protects against heterosexuality, against intimacy in a one-to-one relationship. ... Simultaneously, this intense dyadic conflict screens a dangerously aggressive triadic oedipal struggle. (p. 106)

Similarly to Jones, Fenichel, and Pao, Coen observes: "inability to love in pathological jealousy ... is here given central attention. ... The behavioral enactment in pathological jealousy is a substitute for and defense against full, loving and sexual, intimacy with a single, live person" (pp. 106–107). But he significantly adds: "It is a masturbatory equivalent, sometimes a masturbatory prelude, a perverse form of sexual relatedness" (p. 107). Like virtually every author writing about this subject, Coen also emphasizes the superego aspect, that is, "the need for defense against guilt" (p. 105) and in fact its actualization, just as Jane enacted and enacts scenes where she incurs massive real guilt. As generally, sexual masochism is an important defense against moral masochism (Berliner, 1940, 1947; Wurmser, 1993). The essence of jealousy being the sense of exclusion, as we noticed with Jane, is also met by Coen (1987) in his case: "From this perspective,

Mr. A's pathological jealousy was a masochistically elaborated fantasy of exclusion from the primal scene" (p. 106). Like Jones, the third person, the "rival," is needed as a protector against the dangerous intimacy with the woman:

> Relations with an object regarded as similar and equal to oneself (homosexual; narcissistic) are safer than intense needs of an unequal, different object (heterosexual; adult love). From this perspective, the object choice in pathological jealousy is homosexual, narcissistic, even with regard to the heterosexual component. That is, the heterosexual object is regarded as phallic and masculine in her own right and is further pulled into the homosexual narcissistic orbit by her fantasied connexion with another man. Control, equality, and sameness in one's object relations defend against a variety of fantasied dangers in freely needing and loving another. (p. 106)

Jealousy is thus also for Coen a highly complex affective process and, as it has been noted for envy by Joffe (1969), against the Kleinian notion of "primary envy" (see especially Etchegoyen, Lopez, Rabih, 1987; Spillius, 1993), complexly derived from all developmental levels. The various explanations given are seen by Coen as complementary. "The narcissistic deficiency is a complex issue not reducible only to defensive regression from oedipal conflicts nor to presumed developmental arrest or fixation" (again as seen in our patient); "the *conflict* is understood as involving both oedipal and pre-oedipal derivatives" (1987, pp. 106–107). As an organizing focus he suggests "intense fearfulness of allowing oneself to love another single person. The jealous triadic construction serves ... to deal with this danger and need."

The dialectic of dyadic and triadic aspects in jealousy, in my view, does not entail that these are distinctly two types of jealousy. But we can see a spectrum of intensity: the more "pathological" (i.e., compulsive) jealousy is, the stronger the preoedipal over the oedipal components (i.e., the more regressive) the dyadic, "symbiotic" qualities.

This central fear of "intimacy" or "bondage" to the "woman," however, draws a large portion of strength from what we find in the studies on "womb envy" in its larger sense, as studied in detail by one of us (HJ) in the dynamic background to a single case and, on a much larger canvas, by the works of Benz (1984), Barth (1990), Seelig (2002), Balsam (2003), and Eschbach (2004).

We conclude this psychodynamic section with a remark again by La Rochefoucauld: "*La jalousie est, en quelque manière, juste et raisonnable, puisqu'elle ne tend qu' à conserver un bien qui nous appartient ou que nous croyons nous appartenir; au lieu que l'envie est une fureur qui ne peut souffrir le bien des autres*" (p.): "Jealousy is in some ways just and reasonable because it tends to preserve a good that belongs to us or of which we believe that it belongs to us whereas envy is a rage that cannot tolerate the good of others." (personal communication, Dr. E. Natorp-Husmann, 2006)

JEALOUSY AND THE PROBLEM OF THE EXCLUSIVE POSSESSION OF THE OTHER

It has become abundantly clear that jealousy in its pathological expansions has much to do with "self-love" (i.e., narcissism) and hatred, but preciously little to do with love itself. Yet, surely there must be something like "normal" jealousy that is an expression of love and passion, as the history of great literature claims and as is reflected in the justifying legislation that treats *"crimes passionels"* (crimes of jealousy) with much more leniency than, say, murders for robbery. This strange juxtaposition may indeed manifest the primacy of the value of property, of possession: the one who takes away a possessed thing is the primary criminal, and the one who avenges such supposed "robbing" is more or less justified, his violence condoned.

One might even extend this, by some analogy, to the widespread "honor killings" in Muslim lands where it is seen as incumbent upon the males in a family to take revenge for the "honor" taken away by some form of sexual intimacy from the woman and hence from the family as a whole—a form of "robbery" the dishonor and shame of which can only be expunged if the woman herself is annihilated. Here too both the woman as a whole and her sexual "intactness" are concretistically seen as things that the man possesses, and the deprivation of which is looked upon and treated as a cardinal crime. Holding possession, however, as supreme value is utterly dehumanizing.

This raises deeper questions about "normal" jealousy and the largely uncontested equation of "faithfulness" with exclusivity, that is, exclusive possession (Fenichel raises the same question in a footnote challenging Jones's view that "much more marital infidelity is of neurotic origin than is generally supposed" [1935, p. 353]; see also above on his view of the marriage partner being made the property of the other by leading societal ideology).

The question is justified: Doesn't this concept of its "normality" rest on a concept of infatuation or even of love that is founded on total possession and disregards the individuality of the other? There may be complex compromise formations between the claim for exclusivity and respect. Still, the double question remains: On the one side, how is trust, the core of love, possible if the claim for possession is dominant? On the other side, how is trust possible if because of such possessiveness the attractions and ties to other people have to be hidden, if it has to come to lies and secrecy?

If we put aside for the moment this form of love that is founded upon possession and power (the one we encountered in Jane), we still have to admit that in every close and emotionally intimate relationship there are areas of exclusivity from which any third person is barred. Put differently, love has its own private zone. If it is violated by a third person, it generates shame, and if this happens in a particularly forceful way, the offense leads to strong indignation or impotent rage and despair. Similarly, it is true that even in love one guards a reserve of privacy and devotion to oneself and to others besides the beloved. It is a main task of love to discover the right measure, the right balance between several intimate bonds. Thus one may gently and tenderly try in every relationship to find the right equilibrium between the opposing tendencies of total bestowal of love and the equally intense need for other deep relationships. Therefore, the basic question becomes: How do we find the *individually specific balance between exclusivity and sharing?*

One of the great insights seems to be that *love is divisible and that it grows in the very sharing and does not get reduced.* We are reminded of the beautiful parable of the Kabbalist Rabbi David ibn Abi Zimra (1479–1573):

> Just as a woman becomes pregnant and gives birth without lacking anything [of her own being], so too the souls of the righteous and the pious become pregnant and give birth and emanate sparks into this world, to protect the generation or for some other reasons, like one who lights one candle from another, where the first candle is not diminished. (Scholem, 1991, p. 223)

This observation that we have more by giving, and certainly not less, is true not only for love (and having children is the most beautiful example for it) and for goodness, but also for wisdom and justice. They all become more by being shared. The good German phrase "Shared grief is half the grief; shared joy is double the joy"[7] can be extended to love, as unusual as it may sound.

Another very important conclusion is that fidelity and exclusivity are not identical and have to be uncoupled from each other, as much as this may contradict conventional morality. There exists a deep and lasting fidelity to the other, beloved person without which this faithfulness and loyalty would have to entail exclusivity.[8] Quite to the contrary! The more broadly, strongly, and deeply our love and need for being loved are being fulfilled, the more understanding and patient we are toward the other; and the more loving and giving we are toward others, the less we blame them and are intolerant toward them. It was, after all, one of the main insights of psychoanalysis that chronic or constantly repeated frustration of the desire for love (i.e., of libido) is centrally pathogenic. The voice of jealousy does not want to accept this as true.

No one of us is acquitted from this conflict, and if the reconciliation of these two sides fails, as we witnessed with Jane, the most painful wound of being totally unloved opens up—of not being worthy of being loved. Unlovability is the core experience of shame. It comes together with desolate loneliness and sadness, and with that almost inevitably a wish to gain power over what seems to have been lost. In the tragic character, life is ruled by this dilemma: either total affection or total pain and total shame; either exclusivity of love and possession or total abandonment and unworthiness (Wurmser, 1989/2001, 2005). This state leads, however, to traumatization, of both the self and the other. Very deep traumata hide behind it.

In regard to exclusivity in love, we can add that the core feeling of jealousy, that of being excluded from the intimate two-someness of the others, the conviction that "I am the excluded third," and with that the intense sense of loss: "I have lost what would give my life any meaning," are inevitably connected with humiliation (i.e., shame lurks behind jealousy). In turn, the exertion of power and possession toward the other, which becomes so much part of jealousy, is a rape of the other person's individuality and marks with this a guilt that is being really incurred: the possessive lover or spouse should in fact feel guilty because he deprives the other of her (or his) essential humanness. In reverse, the "betrayal" of such exclusivity, the breaking of such love imposed as possessiveness incurs its own guilt because the victim of such a possessive love also feels guilty when he or she tries to break that bond and escape from that prison of dehumanization.

Once these psychodynamic processes are internalized, we are faced with a great superego polarity: the shame for being excluded against the guilt for the taking-over and hence the dehumanization of the other person, or for the rebellion against such an absolute claim.

The operas of the nineteenth century (I think in particular of the works of Verdi and Tchaikovsky) circle, to a large part, around this issue. The tragic character breaks apart in this conflict between love and domination and the ensuing derivative conflicts. In our terms: ultimately, he experiences every intimate relationship in sadomasochistic categories.

Thus it appears that this one conflict is a kind of leitmotiv for pathological jealousy (and more generally, for the tragic character): it is the *conflict between love and power.* It is manifested, for example, in the tipping over of the yearning for the beloved into the compulsion to control this other person completely and thus to functionalize and dehumanize the beloved—as we witnessed in the case of Jane.

DISCUSSION: REFLECTIONS ON THE NATURE OF LOVE

Besides this very large-scale conflict between love and power that dominates, much of human existence encounters yet another conflict. We can go out from Aristotle's beautiful definition of love: "Love means: I want you to be." It goes back to his "Nicomachean Ethics" (1926/1968, Ch. 9.4, 1166a):

> The feelings of love (*philiká, philíai*) are thus defined: the loving (*philón,* also: the friend) is one who wishes, and promotes by action, the real or apparent good of another (more precisely: the next one, *tou pélas*) for that other's sake; or it could also be said that [the loving] one is somebody who wants the

> beloved (*ton phílon*) to be and to live for his own sake—what mothers feel towards their children.

We can now expand on this idea and differentiate it in this way: Love means: (1) It is a main wish and need of mine for you to be, and my happiness crucially depends on your existence.[9] (2) I want to be near you, and if you are far away I miss you very much.[10] (3) I want you not to suffer any damage, and your well-being is as important to me as my own (the meaning of caring, corresponding to Aristotle's alternative definition). (4) Your own will (your autonomy), your identity, your being so as you are, is as essential for me as my own. (5) I want to share with you what I have, what is within, just as what is without. However, a sixth part is added to this that is both important and yet becomes highly problematic: (6) I want to merge with you on all levels, not only on the plane of the mind and the values and on that of the emotions, but also physically, because at that point, immediately a big contradiction opens up: Not only does that not apply for every form of love e.g., that between child and parent, or rather, we know since Freud, that it is very much the case that it exists, but should not and has to be defended against, or it is not so between friends where the sexual aspects have to remain completely sublimated, but it is true especially for many deep love relationships where the sexual wishes are very much present and stormy, cannot be defended against, and are not unconscious at all, but where they are at the same time forbidden and have to be suppressed, precisely in order not to harm the beloved other. In such a case then the conflict may become intolerable, irreconcilable: it becomes tragic. With that, there exists in love a gaping, often utterly painful, inner contradiction that may lead to a dialectic reversal: where the genuine love is overpowered by the frustrated desire and switches over into anxiety and angry rebuff, or into jealousy and furious hatred[11]—murderous jealous rage.

This means that within the just described full essence of love, in all its six constituents, there arises its own adversary; and this foe stands up against love in the guise of a great biological and deep emotional force: sexual desire. Love stands then in conflict with such an important and ultimately undeniable part of itself: the impetuosity of sexual wishes, the "drive" *par excellence.*

This is then one of the fundamental tragic conflicts: the dialectical reversal of love into sexual desire with its inherent aggression, its possessive jealousy, and its shame.[12] Understood in this way, this second conflict, the enmity between love and sexuality, may be only a veiled form of that first conflict, the struggle between love and power.

To put the contradiction very pointedly: Love celebrates individuality, sexuality destroys it. Love wants the singular being, sexuality wants to undo the boundaries and destroy what is singular. The tragic character is incapable of transforming this conflict into complementarity. This, however, is the goal of genuine maturation: to bring these two powers to reconciliation, to harmony, to mutual fulfillment—something very rare, but always alluring as the shining summit of being.

We have all heard the saying that love is never fair. Is this really true? We hold that this is very much true for the power greedy, acquisitive form of love. This is never just and cannot be. Authentic love, however, seeks justice and respects boundaries, or more accurately: aspires for a dialectic between the lifting of boundaries and the respect for them.

A relationship that is supposedly built upon trust, yet insists upon the rights of power, of possession of the other, and hence of the right to jealousy, is in our view deeply flawed, if not false and hypocritical. This entails, therefore, also a different view of sexual fidelity and loyalty. We know from our clinical work and our knowledge about friends that there are situations where a very deep mutual love may coexist with other bonds (e.g., marital ties), and where the limit-setting against physical contact may be artificial, representing a submission to the conventional values of possession and power. And yet this statement itself may be fraught with ethical conflict: Such a deep, but rivaling love relationship may run counter to a deep sense of loyalty and mutual trust to the first tie that cannot be violated without incurring guilt. And to that may come the lies necessary to protect such a doubleness, the violation of the high value of truth. These are paradigms for great tragic conflicts in everyday life. Then the question is: How authentic and genuine can the first attachment still be? To what extent has it been already affected by issues of functionalization, by manipulation and power, by lies?

CONCLUSION

The affects discussed at the beginning of this essay have a particular affinity to narcissism (i.e., to the primacy of power and self-love), and hence partake in the odium with which self-esteem and self-respect—normal as well as pathological—have been historically treated. Ovid (pp. 106–107) describes *invidia,* the monster of envy that devours snakes and is bursting with poison: "*Carpitque et carpitur una*". ("It devours and is at the same time being devoured") ("Metamorphoses," 2:781); "her teeth are red with rust, her breast is green with gall, her tongue suffused with poison, and she never laughs except when watching pain."[13] In Dante's *Inferno* (Canto 6, 74–75), one of the condemned, Ciacco, predicts the calamity of Florence with the words: "*Superbia, invidia e avarizia sone le tre faville c'hanno i cuori accesi*" ("Arrogant self-willedness, envy and avarice are the three sparks that have inflamed their hearts"). Spiteful arrogance, envy, and greed are indeed social evils of the first magnitude, and yet, once we find access to the inner life of someone beset by them, as hard and rare as such access may be, we find the same depth of anxiety and other unmanageable feelings of unpleasure, particularly of shame. Whoever sees himself shortchanged feels not only shame, but envy: "I want to be better, more likeable, etc." The more shame, the more envy; the more envy, the more cause for shame. Another deep motive for shame is: "I ought to hide all my feelings. To show them makes me utterly vulnerable. When I tried to trust, my opening myself up was squashed, either by brutal rebuff or by cold disregard and an icy stare, or simply nobody was willing to listen. I have to cover all my feelings, all my facial expressions behind an iron mask." This is also the shame hidden in jealousy, and the vicious circle can be extended: The more shame, the more jealousy; the more jealousy, the more shame.

The more there is disregard of needs and capabilities, the more intense is the rage about such violation of identity. And, of course, rage, hatred, and spite need to be covered as well—in a steadily deepening vicious spiral. The more shame, the more spite; the more spite, the more cause for shame. Spite (or defiance) can be seen as a last ditch defense of the integrity of the self (Wurmser, 1981, p. 198); elsewhere we spoke of the value of defiance (Wurmser, 1987/2000, chapter. 3).

Because of the moralizing tradition toward these affects and the underlying needs to be respected and treated as somebody special, the therapist has to be particularly cautious: to intervene without condemning and to treat these affects as necessary consequences of deeper conflicts and traumatizations, and especially deal with them from the side of defense: the *fear* of having them possibly arise.

There is a Chassidic interpretation what is said in the "Sayings of the Fathers" (*Pirqé avót*, a part of the Talmud) (4.28): "Jealousy, desire, and [craving for] honor bring the human being out of the world." To this, Rabbi Bunam, one of the Chassidic masters said: "The one who deals with his jealousy, his desire and his [craving for] honor, they lift above this world" (M. Weiss, personal communication, 2006).

We then conclude that everything that happens out of the primacy of power and possession as highest value is dehumanizing and destructive to all human bonds. And here, envy and jealousy assume their "pride of place" indeed. In turn, everything that happens out of love, the way we have described it with our six criteria, appears to us to be good; in fact, it does belong to the highest there is. Goethe wrote these beautiful lines (in "*Rastlose Liebe*", a poem put to music by Schubert): "*Krone des Lebens, Glück ohne Ruh, Liebe bist du*" ("The crown of life, happiness without rest, love, that is what you are!"); and similarly, Dostoyevsky writes in "The Demons": "Love is higher than Being, love is the crown of Being." In another Goetheword (from "Egmont," Act III): "*Glücklich allein ist die Seele, die liebt.*" ("Alone that soul is happy that loves.") Add to this Heine's words: "To love and be loved, this on earth is the highest bliss" (*Lieben und geliebt zu werden, ist das größte Glück auf Erden*) ("*Italien,*" Chap. 16. Ges. W. Bd. 6, S. 30). Adam Smith observed that the "chief part of human happiness arises from the consciousness of being beloved" (quoted by D. Brooks, *New York Times*, July 2, 2006, WK p. 11). All these quotes say one thing, that, in sharp opposition to jealousy, envy, and the search for power, love, in its deepest and broadest understanding, ultimately gives life its meaning.

ACKNOWLEDGMENTS

We express our gratitude for the help received in the preparation of this essay by Dres Natorp-Husmann, C. Mendelson, I. Roski, and F. W. Eickhoff.

NOTES

1. My (LW) 4-year-old granddaughter Serena addressed her infant sister (a few weeks old): "My sweet little piece of garbage!" But a few days later she was stroking the baby's head and singing: "We're making friends, not just sisters."
2. We are reminded of Freud's analysis of Ibsen's "Rosmer of Rosmersholm."
3. One of the participants in a discussion of parts of this paper (Robert Evans, Yale University) mentioned in this context a poem by John Keats: "I had a dove and the sweet dove died. / And I have thought she died of grieving. / But lo, I looked and her feet were tied / By a single strand of my own hands weaving."
4. This is homosexuality.
5. "One is ashamed of admitting that one is jealous."
6. "Jealousy is the greatest of evils and one that creates least pity in the people that cause it." I am not certain whether the latter part refers to the people who are jealous or against whom jealousy is directed. I am inclined to think that it means: that it creates the least pity *toward* the people who cause it (i.e., that give rise to it).
7. *"Geteiltes Leid ist halbes Leid; geteilte Freud ist doppelte Freud."*
8. Again La Rochefoucauld:*"Il y a une certaine sorte d'amour don't l'excès empèche la jalousie"*: "There is a certain form of love the strength of which blocks jealousy."
9. This is what Martha Nussbaum (2005, pp. 379–380) describes as the "eudaimonistic" essence of love: "I love people whom I invest with importance vis-à-vis my own projects of living a rich and complete life," *eudaimonía* being "a rich and flourishing and complete life."
10. What Nussbaum would call "eudaimonistic vulnerability."
11. Cf. William Congreve's famous words: "Heaven has no rage like love to hatred turned, / Nor hell a fury like a woman scorned" ("The Mourning Bride," 1697, III, 8).
12. Whereby I am convinced that also love itself in its full and broad meaning is biologically anchored, just as is sexuality, albeit in a very complex way.
13. *"Livent rubigine dentes, / pectora felle virent, lingua est suffusa veneno, / risus abest, nisi quem visi movere dolores"* (vs. 776–778).

REFERENCES

Aristotle. (1926/1968). *Nicomachean Ethics*. Loeb edition. Trans. H. Rackham. Cambridge, MA: Harvard University Press.

Balsam, R. H. (2003). The vanished pregnant body in psychoanalytic female developmental theory. *Journal of the American Psychoanalytical Association, 51*, 1153–1179.

Barth, B. (1990). Die Darstellung der weiblichen Sexualität als Ausdruck männlichen Uterusneides und dessen Abwehr. *Jahrbuch der Psychoanalyse, 26*, 64–101).

Benz, A. E. (1984). Der Gebärneid der Männer. *Psyche*, 38, 307–328.

Berliner, B. (1940). Libido and reality in masochism. *Psychoanalytical Quarterly, 9*, 322–333.

Berliner, B. (1947). On some psychodynamics of masochism. *Psychoanalytical Quarterly, 16*, 459–471.

Coen, S. J. (1987). Pathological jealousy. *International Journal of Psycho-Analysis, 68*, 99–108.

Dostoyevsky, F. M. (1872/1994). *Demons*. Russian edition. St. Petersburg: Gumanitarnoye Asgenstvo "Akademičesky Projekt," 1994. eng. Trans. R. Pevear and L. Volokhonsky. New York: Vintage Classics, Random House, 1994.

Dostoyevsky, F. M. (1879–1880/1988/1990). *The Brothers Karamozov*. Russian edition, Moscow: "Chudozhestvennaja literature," 1988. Engl. Trans. R. Pevear and L. Volokhonsky. San Francisco: North Point Press, 1990.

Draghi-Lorenz, R. (1998). Jealousy in the first year. Evidence of early interpersonal awareness. Presented at the biennial International Conference on Infant Studies, Atlanta, Georgia.

Eschbach, Ch. (2004). Womb envy in character development. Presented at the American Psychoanalysis Association meeting. San Francisco.

Etchegoyen, H. R., Lopez, B. M., & Rabih, M. (1987). On envy and how to interpret it. Ibid.: 49–62.

Fenichel, O. (1935). A contribution to the psychology of jealouse. In: *The Collected Papers of Otto Fenichel, First Series*. Ed. Hanna Fenichel and David Rapaport, pp. 349–362. New York: Norton, 1953.

Fivaz-Depeursinge, E. & Corboz-Warnery, A. (1999). *The primary triangle: A developmental systems view of mothers, fathers, and infants*. New York: Basic.

Freud, S. (1922/1955/1968). *Some neurotic mechanisms in jealousy, paranoia and homosexuality*. In: Standard Edition 18, pp. 221–232. London: Hogarth Press.

Green, A. (1993). *Le travail du négative*. Paris: Minuit.

Hart, S. L., Carrington, H. A., Tronick, E. Z., & Carroll, S. R. (2004). "When infants lose exclusive maternal attention: Is it jealousy? *Infancy, 6*(1), 57–78.

Hirsch, M. (2002). *Schuld und Schuldgefühl*. Göttingen: Vandenhoeck & Ruprecht.

Joffe, Walter G. (1969). A critical review of the status of the envy concept. *International Journal of Psycho-Analysis, 50*, 533–546.

Jones, E. (1929/1967). Jealousy. In *Papers on psychoanalysis* (pp.). Boston: Beacon Press.

Küchenhoff, J. (1990). Die Repräsentation früher Traumata in der Übertragung. *Forum der Psychoanalyse, 6*(1), 15–31.

Lansky, M. R. (1997). Envy as process. In M. R. Lansky & A. P. Morrison (Eds.), *The widening scope of shame* (pp.). Hillsdale, NJ: Analytic Press.

Lansky, M. R. (2001). Hidden shame, working through, and the problem of forgiveness in *The Tempest*. *Journal of the American Psychoanalytical Association, 49,* 1005–1033.
Masciuk, S., & Kienapple, K. (1993). The emergence of jealousy in children 4 months to 7 years of age. *Journal of Social and Personal Relationships, 10,* 421–435.
McHale, J. P. & Fivaz-Depeursinge, E. (1999). Understanding triadic and family grop interactions during infancy and toddlerhood. *Clinical Child and Family Psychology Review* 2, 107–127.
Morrison, A. P., & Lansky, M. R. (1999). Shame and envy.
Murray, L. & Travarthen, C. (1985). Emotional regulation of interactions between two-month olds and their mothers. In: T. Fields and N. fox (eds.) *Social perceptions in infants,* pp. 177–197. Norwood, NJ: Ablex.
Nietzsche, F. (1948). *Gedichte. Parnass-Bücherei.* Bern: Alfred Scherz.
Nussbaum, M. C. (2005). Analytic love and human vulnerability: A comment on Lawrence Friedman's "Is there a special psychoanalytic love?" *Journal of American Psychoanalytical Association, 53*: 377–384.
Ovide. *Les Métamorphoses.* Ed. J. Chamonard. Paris: Librarie Garnier.
Pao, P.-N. (1969). Pathological jealousy. *Psychoanalytic Quarterly, 38,* 616–638.
Riviere, J. (1932). Eifersucht als Abwehrmechanismus. In *Ausgewählte Schriften* (pp. 114–137). Tübingen: L. Gast, ed.
Scholem, G. (1991). *On the mystical shape of the godhead. Basic concepts in the Kabbalah.* Übers. J. Neugroschel, New York: Schocken.
Seelig, B. (2002). The rape of Medusa in the temple of Athena. *International Journal of Psycho-Analysis,* 83, 895–911.
Spillius, E. B. (1993). Varieties of envious experiences. *International Journal of Psycho-Analysis, 74,* 1199–1212.
Wellendorf, F. (1995). Zur Psychoanalyse der Geschwisterbeziehung. *Forum der Psychoanalyse, 11*(4), 295–310.
Wurmser, L. (1981). *The mask of shame.* Johns Hopkins University Press. *Die Maske der Scham.* New York: Springer, 1990, 1993, 1998.
Wurmser, L. (1987/2000). *Flucht vor dem Gewissen.* Göttingen: Vandenhoeck & Ruprecht.
Wurmser, L. (1989/2001). *Die Zerbrochene Wirklichkeit.* Göttingen: Vandenhoeck & Ruprecht.
Wurmser, L. (1993). *Das Rätsel des Masochismus.* Heidelberg: Springer.
Wurmser, L. (2000). *The Power of the Inner Judge.* Northvale, NJ: Aronson.
Wurmser, L. (2005). *Tragic Character and the Devastating Power of Absoluteness.* Presentation at the Meeting of the American Psychoanalytical Association, January, New York.

2

Jealousy and Envy in Othello

Psychoanalytic Reflections on the Rivalrous Emotions

MELVIN R. LANSKY

> The concept of perspicuous representation is of fundamental significance to us. It earmarks the form of account we give, the way we look at things
>
> *(Wittgenstein, 1953).*

This paper considers envy and jealousy in light of the powerful shame dynamics evidenced in Shakespeare's portrayal of these rivalrous emotions in *Othello* and compares them with the received views of Freud on jealousy and Klein on envy. These dimensions of (usually unconscious) shame conflict, often overlooked or ignored in psychoanalytic theorizing, are important. Shame dynamics play a central role in the instigation of envy and of jealousy and in the transformation of envious and jealous states of mind into vengeful destructive action. The theoretical understanding and, consequently, the clinical handling of jealousy and envy can be seriously impeded, therefore, by the failure to distinguish jealous and envious states of mind per se from predispositions to those states, from the dynamics of instigation of those states and, in turn, from the dynamics of instigation by which those states of mind, with the deployment of splitting, result in destructive and vengeful action that appears coexisting with those jealous and envious states of mind.

Instigatory dynamics of jealous and envious states of mind usually involve unconscious shame dynamics. Unconscious shame fantasies are evoked in response to circumstances in the jealous or envious person's current life. Appreciation of the details of these instigatory dynamics can become obscured within a psychoanalytic perspective if one is held captive by an inadequate conceptualization of conscience—of self-evaluation and a sense of evaluation by others—in respect to which shame and guilt dynamics are played out. To illustrate these points in relation to jealousy and envy, I have drawn upon Shakespeare's masterpiece, not as definitive evidence, but because it reveals with exquisite sensitivity both conscious and unconscious dynamics that I wish to emphasize in this exposition.

RECEIVED PSYCHOANALYTIC NOTIONS OF JEALOUSY AND ENVY

I begin by considering our major psychoanalytic legacy of jealousy and envy: Freud's formulations on jealousy and Klein's on envy. It has been widely accepted as a psychoanalytic truism that jealousy concerns the disruptive, possessive, angry state following the loss of the love object, or the anticipation of that loss to a rival or rivals, a predicament involving at least three parties; and that envy—not to be confused with its sometime colloquial usage of covetousness toward possessions that the other has—is a type of hatred of another who, upon conscious or unconscious comparison with oneself, seems better, not bad, persecutory, or frustrating. Melanie Klein, in *Envy and Gratitude* (1957) distinguishes between envy and jealousy, seeing the former as basically preoedipal and the latter as oedipal. She considers envy to be the earlier of the two, and points to envy as a widespread and usually malignant emotional disposition inferable in a very wide range of clinical situations. Hanna Segal (1973), discussing Klein's contrast of envy and jealousy, writes:

> Jealousy is based on love and aims at the possession of the loved object and the removal of the rival. It pertains to a triangular relationship and therefore to a time of life when objects are clearly recognized and differentiated from one another. Envy, on the other hand, is a two-part relation in which the subject envies the object for some possession or quality; no other live object need enter into it. Jealousy is necessarily a whole-object relationship, whilst envy is essentially experienced in terms of part-objects, though it persists into whole-object relationships. (p. 40)

In the history of psychoanalytic thinking, jealousy was elaborated first. From the beginnings of psychoanalytic thinking, the oedipal rivalry has been seen in terms of jealousy and the child's competition with one or the other parent for the other parent in presumed rivalry with the first and in an erotized interpersonal situation that involves jealousy. Freud (1897/1966, p. 265), in a letter to Fliess, makes oedipal erotism and jealousy the cornerstone of his psychoanalytic thinking.

> One single thought of great value has been revealed to me. I have found, in my own case too, falling in love with the mother and jealousy of the father, and I now regard it as a universal event of early childhood. ... If that is so, we can understand the riveting power of *Oedipus Rex,* in spite of all the objections raised by reason against its presupposition of destiny. (Letter 71, October 15, 1897)

Jealousy finds its first psychoanalytic context in the analytic search for explanations of clinical data—constellations of associations suggesting forbidden sexual desire and hostile competition with, in the positive oedipal situation, the same sex parent for the parent of the opposite sex. Jealousy may be said, therefore, to motor and drive into being the struggles of the oedipal period and, by inference, to confer a unity on the complex of associations called the Oedipus complex in the analytic situation. Let me note here that "oedipal" may have an ambiguous usage, referring both to the complexity of whole object, multiple party relationships in the postoedipal part of life, and to the specific maturational level and states of mind in the oedipal period per se. I will use the term here in the latter sense, referring to properties of the oedipal period including sexual possessiveness felt by one who has both a mind and a body inadequate to actually accomplish the desire to sexually and materially possess the (forbidden) object of sexual desire. I am highlighting, therefore, the regression specifically to oedipal level fixations. In so doing, I am by no means assuming that regressions to preoedipal levels of fixation do not also occur. It is important to realize that, in addition to the dynamics of rivalry specifically, oedipal level conflict includes the dynamics of inadequacy and the sense of oneself as less than and diminished in comparison to the loved one and the rival.

Freud initially deployed an ambiguous usage of the word envy, in the context of penis envy, not distinguishing between envy as covetousness—the little girl's wish for a penis—and envy considered more generally, the hatred of the (admired) possessor of the penis for being presumably more powerful, complete, and lovable than the little girl who does not have one.

Melanie Klein (1957) made valuable contributions to the understanding of envy, first by distinguishing envy generally from penis envy in particular and then from covetousness generally, by accenting the centrality of actual, fantasied, or wishful destructive attack on the admired and envied object—the breast, the mother, later, perhaps, the penis—on whom one depended, but also hated. Envy is uniquely malignant from a social point of view because the envied person is hated for what is admirable about that person, not for what is frustrating or bad. Klein and her early followers theorized that envy is a direct manifestation of the destructive instinct, or *thanatos.* The envious attack on the breast or the mother is ambivalent, since it is a malignant destructiveness aimed at a whole or part object who is also loved and depended on.

The envious one hates the attributes of the object that are good, giving, complete, or lovable about the object, not the shortcomings of the object. It is for that reason that exposure of oneself as envious—as wishing to tear down a person because of what is admirable about that person—gives rise to so much distress, often shame to the point of mortification, so that the prospect of exposure of oneself to self or others as envious brings forth defensive operations and poses technical difficulties for analytic treatment (Etchegoyen, Benito, & Rabih, 1987; Lansky, 1997).

Jealousy, in contrast to envy, involves love for the object. It centers on the actual or anticipated loss of the love object already felt to be one's possession or the fear of that loss to a rival. Jealousy is a problem that seems, at least in the ideation of the jealous person, solvable (i.e., by defeat of the rival and securing of the love object's love). Envy, when it is directed toward the other in an intimate and desperately needed other in a dyadic situation, is more complicated. Klein pointed out that the overpowering ambivalence toward the hated and needed love object necessitates splitting of the ego and severe regression such that the states of mind of love and need are kept apart from the states of mind partaking of shame and destructive rage. Klein (1957) referred to this regression as that from the *depressive to the paranoid schizoid position,* made necessary by the weakened or immature ego's inability to bear the burdens of intense love in the presence of intense hatred toward the same object.

Both of these fruitful legacies partake of serious oversights and theoretical flaws. Both Freud's and Klein's theoretical oversights are, in my opinion, related to the fact that each deployed notions of conscience inadequate to the task of understanding the shame dynamics that are an intimate part of oedipal shame in jealousy and the shame accompanying diminishment of the self in the envy of a "good" object. Both Freud and Klein overemphasize hostile action and fear of retaliation at the expense of considering diminishment in respect to aspirations and ideals, that is to say, overemphasize guilt dynamics (originating from tension with the superego proper) at the expense of shame dynamics (originating from the ego ideal) (Lansky, 2005a).

WHAT ARE JEALOUSY AND ENVY?

One can be held captive by notions of envy as the persistence into later, even adult life of a two-party, basically preoedipal state of mind, and of jealousy as a state of mind that involves three parties and is basically postoedipal. Such captivation by theoretical simplification comes at the cost of attaining a nuanced appreciation of clinical phenomenology to the detriment of both theory and practice. Both envy and jealousy do indeed involve rivalry and hatred, but significant complexities remain in conceptualizing envy and jealousy. One can understand the Freudian and Kleinian formulations and deploy them clinically without facing the essential question: To what do the words jealousy and envy refer? Although jealousy and envy are states of mind recognizable by all, it is far from clear in what sense envy and jealousy are distinct entities, whether they are mutually exclusive states of mind, and, in fact, what entities are referred to by the terms jealousy and envy. Spinoza (1951, Book III), considering jealousy in his definitions and classifications of the emotions, does not consider it a separate emotion, but rather an amalgam or a compounding of more basic emotions. Spinoza sees envy as a kind of hatred, "hatred insofar as it induces a man to be pained by another's good fortune and to rejoice in another's evil fortune" (Book III\XXIII, p. 178). The same contention (i.e., that these rivalrous emotions are amalgams of emotionally laden mental states rather than simple, fundamental emotions) has been eloquently argued by Konstan (2003) from a philological point of view.

What, then, are these rivalrous emotions? Common psychoanalytic usage often equivocates as to what is being referred to when these rivalrous emotions are discussed. Are they affects? They certainly partake of strong hostile and destructive affects, although not necessarily conscious affects, nor are they purely affective states of mind. The words envy and jealousy do not refer to simple basic affects in the sense that shame, guilt, anxiety, and depression are affects. Are they inextricably embedded in specific constellations of object relations? They, of course, do involve relationships, envy, at least two individuals; and jealousy, at least three.

Attempts to explain envy or jealousy completely in terms reducible to aggressive drive or destructive instinct confine the theoretical focus in such a way that obscures the complexities that would accompany a full appreciation of the clinical phenomenology in which envy and jealousy are embedded. That is to say, envy and jealousy as states of mind are always attended by a narrative, a dramatic arc. Although psychoanalysis alludes to such a narrative by evoking the notion of unconscious fantasy in relation to internal objects, Shakespeare's dramatic art has the advantage of directly using narratives of envy and jealousy. Strictly psychoanalytic formulations capture wishes, derived, we may presume, from drives in ascendancy in the developmental period in question, but are not seen in the original form as developmental levels evolve. These formulations, more often than not, partake of an oversimplified view of instigation (Lansky, 2004, 2005a, 2005b) and, especially of the instigating role of hidden shame and shame fantasies. Formulations on presumed wishes fixated at the developmental level to which one has regressed cannot be presumed equivalent to the original states of mind at that developmental level. Furthermore, there is also the risk—both of conflating the actual emotional state, jealousy or envy itself, with the triggering effect of that state of mind, jealous or envious, on fantasied or actual vengeful destructive action—wishes or actions that generate guilt—and of overlooking instigating shame dynamics in favor of the guilt dynamics that result from destructive wishes or actions. In this discussion, I will use the words envy and jealousy such that they refer to states of mind—complex and not necessarily distinct mental states that do include affects and contexts of object relations but cannot be reduced to these or to other simple categories.

In considering both jealousy and envy, it is important not to collapse the distinction between persistence of an unmodified constellation of object relations from early life and a regression to states of mind fixated at the level in question, but including the influences of subsequent developmental levels. The Kleinian Oedipus complex, in fact, is a three-party psychological complex that includes a component of envy of the same sex parent for possessing the parent of the opposite sex and exists in addition to the jealousy of the child that is based primarily on the love for the parent of the opposite sex. The little girl's envy of the mother for possessing the father and his penis coexists with her jealousy that the loved father is lost in competition to the mother. Even within Klein's system, therefore, envy can be seen as involving more than two parties: the dyad of the envier/envied, but also another love object who vies for the envied person's love or a world outside the dyad, which, in the mind of the envious one, values the envied person more than the self.

To assume that envy throughout life is ever an unmodified persistence of the envy presumably felt in the earliest infantile situation is unjustifiable; and it is an unverifiable inference to conclude that actual envy as we use the word can take place prior to self and object differentiation (Joffe, 1969; Neubauer, 1982; Spielman, 1971). Klein and her early followers tended to bypass these conceptual problems with a peculiarly unscientific and unverifiable Platonism that postulated preexisting innate ideas (fully formed fantasy at, or even prior to, birth) involving well-differentiated self and object and by simply defining envy as a direct manifestation of the destructive drive. One is hard pressed to imagine—even in principle—verifiable evidence that sustains either of these assumptions. In adult life, one may envy another who is not loved, needed, and not in a way partaking of the same ambivalence as that postulated by Klein in the early preoedipal period, especially the part/object relationship between the infant and the breast.

It is likewise an error to presume that jealousy that represents a fixation at a strictly oedipal level is the same as the reaction to the loss or the prospect of the loss of the loved object in postoedipal rivalry. We may refer loosely to both as types of jealousy, but the dynamics involved, especially the dynamics of shame, are not the same.

THE ROLE OF SHAME IN ENVY AND JEALOUSY

In both Freud and Klein, we find an abundance of brilliant clinical observation—verifiable and of enduring value in appreciating clinical phenomenology. These lasting contributions to our appreciation of clinical phenomenology are, however, constricted by inadequate conceptualizations of motivation for jealousy and for envy, conceptualizations that are overly reliant on instinct in a reductionistic fashion or on incomplete understanding of conflict in relation to the conscience. In particular, shame arising from conflict with the ego ideal—one's goals or standards for self-respect—is sidestepped in favor of a dynamic involving transgression—destructive actions or wishes—and consequent guilt. Freud (1897/1966) deploys the concept of drive as a fundamental explanatory concept, instead of a (necessary) element in a more complex picture and at times seems to regard jealousy as though it were simple competition among equals for a love object—that is to say, postoedipal rather than truly oedipal in nature—and accounted for entirely by sexual and aggressive wishes, yet ignores or minimizes the element of diminishment by comparison with both the object of desire and with the rival (shame) in the dynamics of the jealous oedipal age child. This sense of diminishment on comparison with a love object or a rival carries with it the anticipation of overwhelming shame. These hidden shame dynamics are essential to a balanced conceptualization of both of these rivalrous emotions.

Klein and her early followers, by conceptualizing envy as a primary manifestation of a more basic instinctual aggressivity that she privileged, did not specifically explore the sense of diminishment that is inevitably found as the trigger of envy, that is to say, the shameful awareness of self in comparison with the desperately needed or admired other with whom one is also rivalrous. This sense of diminishment—shame, conscious or unconscious—that instigates envy is to be found in many of the clinical case reports of Klein and her early followers, but not in their theorizing, which uses a notion of conscience inadequate to account for shame (for details, see Lansky, 2005a). That notion of conscience involves aggressive actions or wishes and consequent persecutory anxiety (in the paranoid-schizoid position) or guilt (in the depressive position). There is no clear relation of the sense of diminishment or shame to the conscience in the *theoretical* work of Klein or her early followers (Lansky, 2005a). As a result, the instigating influence of shame, although evident in Kleinian clinical writings (Joseph, 1986; Mitrani, 1993), does not come to theoretical attention at all. Envy, I have argued elsewhere (Lansky, 1997; Morrison & Lansky, this volume), centers around the diminishment of the self in comparison with a presumably rivalrous other, often, but by no means always, a loved and desperately needed other.

My own investigations of envy (Lansky, 1997; Morrison & Lansky, this volume) and that of others (Hutson, 1996; Wurmser, 1981) emphasize the centrality of (often unconscious) shame conflict (signaling the danger of unlovability or of rejection) as triggering envy. Shame also arises when one is exposed to self and others as envious (i.e., as adjusting one's narcissistic equilibrium by tearing down the other). That is to say, being exposed as envious poses, in and of itself, the danger of mortifying shame, often the shame accompanying exposure of the self as envious, is unbearable. Envy thus presents technical problems in interpretation (Etchegoyen, et al., 1987), more so than jealousy, exposure of which tends to be significantly less humiliating.

Jealousy, insofar as it is distinct from simple competitive rivalry, has a distinct sense of diminishment as well, to the extent that it involves a regression to the earliest oedipal states of mind. By oedipal I am referring to the specifically oedipal period in development; I am not regarding the developmental traversing from preoedipal to oedipal as a simple passage from one type of relatedness (dyadic) to another (multiple party). Jealousy, especially the pathologically delusional type under consideration here, is not simply rivalry for an object of erotic desire. It involves a regression to strictly oedipal states of mind such that the object of desire and the rival are felt to be more intact, powerful, and sexually flourishing than is the jealous self, which is experienced as weak, inadequate, and desperately dependent on the love of the desired object and often that of the rival as well. (See, in this regard, Proust's brilliant portrayal of jealousy in *The Remembrance of Things Past* [1989] especially in "Swann's Way" [pp. 3–52].) The sense of diminishment is prominent, and, hence, tension arises in regard to the judgment of the ego ideal, accompanying either defeat and relegation to asexual status or apparent victory and exposure to inadequacy to provide for the loved one sexually, socially, or materially.

The role of shame dynamics in the oedipal situation has been cursorily acknowledged in theoretical papers but usually neglected and subordinated to the supposedly central dynamic of rivalrous transgression and feared retaliation (castration anxiety). Our literature, by overlooking the powerful role of shame in oedipal rivalry more often than is commonly acknowledged, tends to reduce the Oedipus complex (which involves very complex shame and guilt dynamics) to the castration complex (involving forbidden desire, hostile competition, and retaliation—a guilt dynamic) and to conflate those two complexes. Arlow (1980) has pointed to the sense of humiliation and vengefulness in regard to one's felt rejection from the activities of the primal scene. Kilborne (2002, 2003) has emphasized the notion of oedipal shame, counteracting tendencies among psychoanalytic theorists to view shame as exclusively preoedipal and to see the oedipal situation as exclusively concerned with transgression and retaliation (guilt dynamics). In pathological jealousy, I argue below, shame dynamics are especially powerful.

LITERATURE AS A SOURCE OF DATA

In drawing from *Othello* to explore some points about envy and jealousy, I am not presuming that the play provides evidence that is of the same scientific status as clinical evidence. The marshalling of clinical evidence would require an unwieldy amount of material for a short contribution. I draw upon the play to illustrate, not to demonstrate, some selected points about the rivalrous emotions, points that derive separately and stand independently of the play, yet which develop in very concentrated form within a character who is not only envious, but characterologically organized around envy, Iago, in relation to one who is not only jealous, but becomes organized around overwhelming pathological jealousy, Othello. I rely upon the text not only because it perspicuously highlights the inner and interpersonal worlds of one character riddled with envy with those of another ensnared by jealousy with no implication that the problems posed by the tragedy are equivalent to the use of clinical evidence, but also because the play provides a unique dimension to our understanding of those states of mind.

The use of the play allows me to stress features of each state of mind and character structure in the company of easily inferable fantasies that accompany the moral emotions of shame and guilt. These, in turn, enable me to explore certain dimensions of the rivalrous emotions with greater clarity. I presume, following Edmund Wilson (1929), that the playwright is not only an artist, but also a naturalist, insofar as this great play affects us as it does. The citation of a great literary work cannot be dismissed as the use of mere fiction in contrast, say, to the presumed truth of purely clinical data. As a naturalist, the literary artist serves as coinvestigator in the exploration of the phenomenon under consideration. Aristotle, writing in the fourth century B.C.E., sees poetic art as closer to universal truth than to history (C. Hanly, personal communication, June 16, 2006):

> Poetry, therefore, is a more philosophical and a higher thing than history: for poetry tends to express the universal, history, the particular. By the universal, I mean how a person of a certain type will on occasion speak or act, according to the law of probability or necessity; and it is this universality at which poetry aims. (Aristotle, 1992, IX, pp. 3–4)

Parenthetically, I may note that the clinical vignettes used in strictly clinical contributions are by no means immune from partaking of a faulty epistemology from which erroneous overgeneralizations can be drawn. The brief clinical vignette, considered in isolation, often the principal building block of argumentation in psychoanalytic articles, is, depending on the material chosen, not necessarily more data based, scientific, and fundamentally factual than the work of dramatic or poetic art.

The play allows us to consider a case of simple rivalry as it is manifested in the character of Roderigo. I understand the word rivalry, in this context, to be a more superficial, more general term than are jealousy and envy. Roderigo, whose character structure and motivation are viewed in much less depth than are those of Iago and Othello, is an exemplar of postoedipal rivalry. Envy and jealousy are among the subtypes of rivalry, envy often with a needed other, whose laudable and lovable attributes or accomplishments confer a sense of diminishment on the self, and jealousy, with a presumed rival for the loved other's affections.

Not all erotic rivalry involves jealousy or envy. Roderigo's rivalry involves neither, insofar as we know his character from the text. Rivalry does not refer to a discrete emotional state or to a specific constellation of object relations. It is a term superordinate to jealousy and envy and not necessarily dynamically the same as either. Rivalry has a more shallow explanatory connotation than does either envy or jealousy. For example, athletic, scholastic, or economic rivalry are not necessarily jealous or envious in any simple, reductionistic way, although such rivalry may include or derive elements of jealousy or envy from earlier stages of development. In Roderigo's rivalry, for example, there is revealed to us no convincing evidence for regression to preoedipal or to strictly oedipal states of mind as there is with Othello's jealousy or Iago's envy. Roderigo's character is represented completely at a postoedipal level. Seeing competition for an object of erotic desire as simple rivalry is an acknowledgment of our distance from the character and his motivations. We simply are not made aware of Roderigo's inner workings to the same extent that we are of those of Othello or Iago. We do not know the depths of his personality as we come to know those of Iago and Othello.

In deploying a literary work as the basis of my argument, I am, of course, vulnerable to the criticism that Iago may not be an exemplar of envy per se, but of a constellation of malignant personality traits that cannot be presumed to be captured by the term envy. Othello, likewise, although obviously jealous, manifests a pathological jealousy that may not be, strictly speaking, pathological jealousy as it is referred to psychoanalytically as a clinical entity. Furthermore, Othello's jealousy and Iago's envy are not as dramaturgically striking as states of mind per se as they are as instigators of diabolically destructive vengeful actions. It is the diabolical murder of loved ones, not simply jealous or envious states of mind, that accounts for the tragic impact of the play.

I will persist in seeing Iago as fundamentally an exemplar of characterologically global envy because of the centrality of the sense of personal diminishment (shame, conscious or unconscious) that he feels at the flourishing—the success or completeness—of those at whom his envy is directed, and Othello an exemplar of jealousy because of his enduring love for Desdemona, despite his conviction of her infidelity.

With the presumption that the reader is familiar with the play, I shall proceed to highlight some observations about the rivalrous emotions in the context of the play and some of the points that it illustrates about a character structure dominated by pervasive, destructive envy and another dominated by pathological jealousy.

THE IMMEDIATE CONTEXT OF THE OPENING OF THE PLAY

Othello opens in Venice on an evening in which two momentous events take place concerning the protagonist. First, Othello has eloped with

Desdemona, the daughter of Brabantio, a Venetian senator. Othello and Brabantio, it is made clear, are very closely united in mutual admiration and respect. We may presume that the elopement was felt to be necessary because of vast differences in status that would make a request by Othello for Desdemona's hand unlikely or impossible. Brabantio is a Venetian noble, wealthy, and very much in the center of the city-state's aristocratic power elite. Desdemona is young, beautiful, well born, and very likely to be sought after by the most choice insiders in Venice.

Othello's comments about himself point us to his sense of himself as unlike and less than others, Desdemona in particular. Othello is an outsider: foreign, black, a military man rather than a polished courtier, and he is elderly (all quotes in text are from Shakespeare [1604/1999]:

> for I am black
> And have not those soft parts of conversation
> That chamberers have, or for I am declined
> Into the vale of years.
>
> *Othello*, III, 3, 304–307

Perhaps he is impotent as well:

> Desdemona: Let me go with him
> Othello: Vouch with me, heaven.
> I therefore beg it not
> To please the palate of my appetite,
> Nor to comply with heat (the young affects
> in me defunct).
>
> (I, 1, 294–299)

These matters of status and potency, together with the fact that he took his bride by stealth rather than with the blessing of her father, will enter into the intensity of his reaction to her presumed infidelity.

Second, on the very same evening, we find that the Duke of Venice has ordered an emergency nighttime assemblage of Venetian aristocracy and councilors to face the imminent problem of a Turkish invasion of Cyprus. An expedition must be deployed immediately and, by consensus, the Venetians agree on the choice of their most distinguished general, Othello, as the commander of that expedition. Othello is, at the end of act I, placed in an exalted position vis-à-vis the Venetian Society from which he has, heretofore, been cast an outsider. The circumstances of the Turkish threat confer upon him power and status that, especially when the action of the play switches to Cyprus in the ensuing four acts, are magnified to a position of virtual omnipotence.

ENVY

Iago: If Cassio do remain,
He hath a daily beauty in his life
That makes me ugly.

(V, 1, 19–21)

The play opens on that night in front of Brabantio's house, and we are immediately faced with a dialogue between Iago, Othello's "ancient" or standard bearer, and Roderigo, a Venetian gentleman who, led on by Iago, is pursuing Desdemona, much against her father's wishes. Iago is exploiting Roderigo, extracting money from him in pursuit of his courtship by promising that Desdemona will be his. Although Iago had been Othello's accomplice in the courtship of Desdemona, he nevertheless encourages Roderigo without compunction. Iago is betraying his superior for reasons that he soon reveals to Roderigo, all of which involve what is, for Iago, unbearable shame: he has been betrayed, he feels, by being passed over for promotion to lieutenant in favor of Michael Cassio, a Florentine of noble birth and bearing. In later soliloquies, he reveals his suspicion that Othello has cuckolded him.

Iago: I hate the Moor,
And it is thought abroad that 'twixt my sheets
'Has done my office. I know not if it be true,
But I, for mere suspicion of that kind,
Will do as if for surety.

(I, 3, 429-433)

And again:

Iago: For that I do suspect the lusty Moor
Hath lept into my seat—the thought whereof
Doth, like a poisonous mineral, gnaw my inwards,
And nothing can or shall content my soul
'Till I am evened with him, wife for wife.

(II, 2, 317–321)

And shortly thereafter in the same soliloquy:
For I fear Cassio with my (nightcap), too.

(II, 2, 329)

Iago's humiliation, his paranoid feeling of sexual diminishment, presumably by Othello, and later, Cassio, is the basis for his attack. We can presume that his fantasies about having been cuckolded by Othello and by Cassio reflect his envious nature and proclivity for domination by paranoid shame fantasy (Lansky, 2005b).

Such fantasies *look,* so to speak, for opportunities to express themselves. Emilia, in another context, and discussing jealousy, comments on the difference between domination by such a fantasied disposition and the adduction of facts to support it:

> Emilia: They are not ever jealous for the cause,
> But jealous for they're jealous. It is a monster
> Begot on itself, born on itself
>
> (III, 4, 181–183)

Iago's paranoid shame fantasies do not arise from a simply dyadic relationship or a preoedipal state of mind. His utterances are full of states of mind involving primal scene fantasies and oedipal shame. They are the results of a strong tendency toward splitting and regression to preoedipal states of mind that are colored, nonetheless, by developmentally later anxieties. It is Iago's shame that keeps him in hiding. We may grasp this clearly and unmistakably from what he says, at the opening of the play. Only a few lines into the play we see Iago as skilled at reading and manipulating others and already engaged in undoing Othello, Brabantio, Desdemona, and Roderigo for his own envious motives of hate, greed, and suspicion of others (both Othello and Cassio) for cuckolding and betraying him.

Iago's soliloquies and interchanges with Roderigo put in words his pervasive envy and sense of diminishment, his hatred of imagined and actual rivals, his paranoia, and his (plausibly inferable) homosexual longings in making hated rivals or opponents of all of the major characters in the play: Othello, Cassio, Desdemona, and Brabantio. He has been passed over for promotion to the post of Othello's lieutenant, and (we may infer [Wangh, 1952] passed over sexually, by Othello's marriage. Iago's paranoid shame fantasies reflect his tendency toward splitting and detachment from intimates within the moral order. It is impossible for him to attach to anyone other than in an exploitative or a vengeful way. Wangh (1952), following Freud (1922), stresses the importance of Iago's repressed homosexuality in his malicious destructiveness. But Wangh does not take into account the centrality of anticipation of unbearable affect and of rejection, the anticipated danger of unbearable shame (in anticipation of devastating judgment from his ego ideal), and the risk of humiliating ostracism, which makes necessary the repression of homosexuality.

Iago is suspicious and misogynous. In some ostensibly playful banter with Cassio, Desdemona, and Emilia, his mistrust and misogyny (envy of women generally and of their sexuality specifically) emerge.

> Iago: Come on, come on! You are pictures out of door,
> bells in your parlors, wildcats in your kitchens, saints

in your injuries, devils being offended, players in
your huswifery, and huswives in your beds.
Desdemona: Oh, fie upon thee, slanderer.
Iago: Nay, it is true, or else I am a Turk.
You rise to play, and go to bed to work.

(II, 1, 114–128)

The centerpiece in Iago's makeup seems to be his sense of diminishment in comparison with lusty men and sexually bold women, his global exploitativeness, and his mistrust of others—in such cases considered clinically, we would infer a projection of his exploitativeness and treachery onto others. Sexual slurs point to his sexual shame and his envy of women. Wangh's (1952) presumption of the presence of homosexual elements in his paranoia helps us understand his attack of Othello's bed partner, Desdemona. When Brabantio is awakened by Roderigo, Iago, in hiding, adds three sexual slurs (indicative of both his jealousy and his envy of Desdemona and of women generally) to provoke Brabantio even further:

Even now, very now, an old black ram
Is tupping your white ewe.

(I, 1, 97–98)

you'll have your daughter covered with a Barbary
horse.

(I, 1, 124–125)

I am one, sir, that comes to tell you your daughter
and the Moor are (now) making the beast with two backs.

(I, 1, 129–131)

Iago's profound misogyny becomes even more evident in the scene in which Emilia gives Iago Desdemona's dropped handkerchief.

Emilia: Do not you chide. I have a thing for you.
Iago: It is a common thing— [a sexual slur
referring to her sexual "thing"]
Emilia: Ha?
Iago: To have a foolish wife. [turning the
slur into a joke, still at her expense]
Emilia: Oh, is that all. What will you give me now /
For that same handkerchief?

(III, 3, 345–351)

The doings of the other with a sexual third are prominent, even preeminent in his envious thinking. Iago's envy is global, directed toward women and their sexuality and their possession of men, as well as to his superiors, Othello and Cassio, with destructive intent toward all. Three times in the play, consummation of Othello's marriage is disrupted by a disturbance instigated by Iago: when he and Roderigo rouse Brabantio after the elopement (I, 1); when he goads Cassio to drink and Roderigo to provoke him (II, 3), and when he instigates Roderigo's attempt to murder Cassio (V, 1).

Iago, apart from his soliloquies and explanatory dialogues with Roderigo, which reveal his inner workings to us, dwells in secrecy and darkness. He does so in my view because of his pervasive sense of shame. That shame remains in hiding, perhaps even from himself, yet it triggers his destructive envy. His shame is not difficult to infer, particularly when he regards women sexually or when he reveals his conviction that he has been cuckolded. That oedipal, sexual shame drives his vengefulness into being, but the shame, although inferable, is not explicit. The play is usually presented showing Iago as separated, standing apart from others. Yet, in the view of others, he is not an outcast—he has a loving wife and an esteemed military rank. He is appreciated by his commander and Venetians of the highest rank. He is trusted and respected. Others do not see him as diminished by Cassio's promotion. Yet within his inner world, he is in a wounded position in which he sees himself as having been betrayed and cheated by a thoroughly exploitative world of betrayers that, he feels, gives him the entitlement to act vengefully beyond any rules and loyalties and without remorse or guilt. He betrays his commander, kills his own wife, exploits and later kills Roderigo, and attempts to kill Cassio whom he quite consciously envies. When he is exposed, captured, and interrogated, he defiantly refuses to speak further, saying, "Demand me nothing. What you know, you know. From this time forth, I will never speak word" (V, 2, 355–356). These statements, beginning very early in the play, locate his envy, the triggering of that envy by a sense of diminishment before others, his paranoia and paranoid shame fantasies, his homosexual longings, and his envious misogyny. These traits are the basis of his envious character, a character of the type about which Klein and her followers have taught us so much.

In the light of these observations on envy in the play, I see criticism of the play that judges it an imperfect tragedy because Iago is an unmotivated malefactor (Coleridge, 1884; Shaw, 1961, to name a few) as psychologically and, especially, psychoanalytically naive. We may question Iago's ascription of causes for his suspiciousness and vengefulness, but not the psychological credibility of his character structure as it reveals itself to us.

Iago's envy is not reducible to a simple affective state or emotion arising from a dyad in isolation. Envy is an evolved psychological complex of shameful and hostile emotions and dispositions, not simply originating from the dyad, but, as Shakespeare so brilliantly portrays it, very much concerned with sexual betrayal and with status, reflecting the developmental influence of oedipal and postoedipal struggles and triggered by oedipal shame conflicts. Iago's envy triggers vengeful and spiteful destructive and self-destructive action. Envy, certainly in Iago, is best seen as involving a complex regression to a state of mind that is an alloy of oedipal and preoedipal traits, jealousy among them, including a sense of admiration for, and perhaps his attraction to, the envied other that exists in conflict with a sense of diminishment in comparison with that other in terms of one's own standards for lovability. The envious state of mind also includes a sense of awareness of the larger community, in Iago's case, his feelings that he has been seen to have been passed over for advancement as well as cuckolded.

JEALOUSY

> Othello: Perdition catch my soul
> But I do love thee! And when I love thee not,
> Chaos is come again.
>
> (III, 3, 100–103)

Othello's grandeur, bravery, and nobility are introduced to us early in the play when, on his way to the urgent nighttime meeting convened by the Duke, Othello and his followers are accosted by the armed and drawn forces of Brabantio, accusing Othello of using magic and enchantment to abduct her. In the face of armed action, Othello, undrawn, stands in the midst of the fierce fighting, exclaiming, "Keep up your bright swords, the dew will rust them" (I, 2, 76–79). The dramatic effect of these lines in a well-directed performance of *Othello* is overpowering. He loves completely and nobly.

> Othello: Speak of me as I am. Nothing extenuate,
> Nor set down aught in malice. Then must you speak
> Of one that loved not wisely, but too well;
> Of one not easily jealous, but being wrought,
> Perplexed in the extreme.
>
> (V, 2, 402–406)

In this regard, Othello does not match the profile of pathological jealousy described in the psychoanalytic literature accompanied by chronic and characterologic doubt and uncertainty, feelings of inadequacy, and suspicion that are described in the psychoanalytic literature (Coen, 1987; Fenichel, 1935; Freud, 1922; Jones, 1929; Riviere, 1932; Wurmser & Jarass, this volume). But his love is colored by a pronounced naivete and idealization that make him prone to pathological jealousy once he has been seduced into doubt. He repeatedly uses the term, "honest Iago," a phrase that highlights his naivete and his inability to read others in sharp contrast to Iago's mistrust, cunning, and stealth. I see this naivete as a significant feature of jealousy reflective of Othello's regression to a strictly oedipal (not postoedipal) state of mind, which hearkens back to a time of ignorance of others' motivations and a proclivity for idealization. Iago, on the contrary, sees things only in exploitative terms, only the dark side of things. Othello's sense of justice does not exclude his own wrongdoings from judgment and punishment. Even in the tragic finale of the play, his conscience judges his own transgressions no less severely than it judges those of others. He punishes himself, killing himself in perfect accord with the standard he deployed for his killing of a Turk who beat a Venetian:

> in Aleppo once
> Where a malignant and a turbaned Turk
> Beat a Venetian and traduced the state,
> I took by the throat the circumcised dog
> And smote him, thus. [he stabs himself]
>
> (V, II, 413–417)

Othello's pathological jealousy finds something of an explanation in the backdrop of his circumstances revealed on the night during which the action of the play opens (I, 1). Othello has eloped with Desdemona on that night after a stealthy wooing, which he has not revealed to her father, Brabantio, and his sudden promotion to head of the Venetian forces deployed to Cyprus. The coincidence of events at the beginning of the play, Othello's promotion and his elopement, pave the way for his subsequent pathological jealousy. He is jealously doubting of the love of a fundamentally forbidden woman—of a different generation, race, and social class, one obtained by stealth, incurring thereby her father's hatred.

The fact that Othello is an outsider has been dramatically offset by his sudden changes in status. He has been elevated by circumstances to a specialness that is confusing: Venice needs him because of the Turkish invasion of Cyprus, and so he is catapulted to an exalted station and made supreme commander in Cyprus. Brabantio's charges against him pale, in part, because he is so central to Venetian security. I see these circumstance of the play as concretizing and symbolizing an omnipotent oedipal fantasy, one of stealing with impunity the beloved older man's woman and going off with her to utterly omnipotent control of a separate world, which is subject to domination by his will alone. By contrast, Roderigo is an insider, young, a nobleman, but not in the true sense of the word jealous, although he is certainly rivalrous for the love of Desdemona. He has no preoccupation with his presumed rivals, Othello and Cassio, nor with personal diminishment. He wants either Desdemona or his money and jewels back.

I consider these opening circumstances of the play as contexts for the emergence of Othello's character, especially insofar as those circumstances symbolize elements of a precarious oedipal victory, one that the victor is utterly incapable of sustaining in reality: The receiving of omnipotent powers and the sudden and stealthy oedipal victory and their dramatic reversals add mightily to the unconscious impact of the play. I am taking the poetic and psychoanalytic liberty of emphasizing the strictly oedipal nature of the wooing and stealing of the forbidden woman and the designation of Othello as omnipotent overlord of the military operation, and, in act II, of the entire world on the island of Cyprus. There, he has been credited with a victory over the Turks, even though no battle has taken place with the Turks, who were defeated by the storms, not by Othello's military brilliance, or even by Venetian troops. He is lord and master over that island in act II until he is replaced by Cassio in act V. I see this as a concretization symbolizing the unconscious omnipotent grandiosity of the pathologically jealous person, who, in fantasy, carries off his beloved to a world where he is in absolute control of a society in which he was hitherto an outsider—but finds himself out of place. Othello has displayed no skill in winning the war or in dealing with the people under his command. The play leaves ambiguous whether or not the marriage has actually been consummated. These features seem to me to warrant consideration of a symbolized regression to early oedipal fantasies, specifically locating Othello's jealousy in the context of such a regression.

This omnipotent grandiosity is shattered in act III when Iago's envious seductive machinations exploit Othello's naivete and undo his peacefulness (and, once more, interrupt the consummation of the marriage). I am emphasizing not only Iago's consummate skill at reading people in his capacity as seducer, but, by contrast, Othello's striking naivete and incompetence in reading people insofar as they reflect his seducibility. Othello's speeches are peppered with the phrase, "honest Iago," a phrase that speaks more to Othello's need to see his ancient and advisor as honest and reliable, and capable of vision that Othello does not possess, than to actual attribution of honesty that Othello has evaluated. Othello's obscurity on this matter marks a childlike naivete, a tragic flaw, and a fatal one, for himself and many others in the hotly political world Othello has been inhabiting and governing. Iago exploits the fact that Othello, especially when he regresses in jealous states to shame-based oedipal states of mind, is painfully aware that he is out of place in his omnipotent position as Desdemona's husband and as military commander of Cyprus. His rapid rise from social unacceptability to ruler and husband has elevated him in a way that sets him up for a humiliating fall. His fulminant jealousy derives in part from his rapid and humiliating fall from exaltation to disgrace following his seduction to jealous vengefulness by Iago. Othello, by being simple himself, does not read complexity in others well and accepts matters on their surface as they appear to him. Iago, in hiding always, is expert in reading others' depths. Othello's naive idealizations cover over the fragility of one who knows that at some level he is naive, out of place, and incapable of reading people accurately. The conviction that he has been cuckolded plummets him into a fragile, shame ridden sense of himself as, again, an outsider: foreign, black, impotent, old, military rather than courtly, and a betrayed husband. He must face his guilt at having "stolen" a forbidden woman—and having been deceived by her as she deceived her father to go with him. He, perhaps, also projects his deceptiveness toward Brabantio onto Desdemona. We are reminded of Brabantio's final words to Othello:

> Brabantio: Look to her, Moor, If thou hast eyes to see.
> She has deceived her father, and may thee.
>
> (I, 3, 333–334)

Othello's seduction to jealousy by Iago consists not simply of an affective response to his presumption of Desdemona's loving Cassio, but a reaction to the specific allegation that he, Othello, has been cuckolded by one who gloats in his triumph. It is Othello's (incorrect and maliciously induced) conviction of having been publicly shamed, not just faced with jealous rivalry—public shame, not just private jealousy, that signal to Othello his loss of (perhaps not yet consummated but) newly found marital bliss and political status and esteem. Unbearable shame, therefore, is prominent in the picture of his turn from jealousy to murderous vengefulness. It is this mortifying shame that is a major trigger to his pathological and murderous vengeful action.

An interesting comparison to Othello's pathological jealousy is provided by Bianca, the prostitute with whom Cassio has taken up while on Cyprus. Cassio is not simply her client, she is jealously rivalrous and possessive regarding the owner of (Desdemona's purloined) handkerchief that Cassio had found after Iago left it in his lodging. Bianca (curiously, "white," as contrasted to Othello's "black") presents an instance of simple (albeit intense) (postoedipally centered) erotic jealousy in contrast to the distinctly pathological oedipal jealousy of Othello that involves splitting and vengefulness. Othello's is the type of jealousy that results in vengeful destructive action—"crimes of passion," as they are appropriately called.

There are many possible interpretations of Bianca's significance in the play; one interpretive line of thinking might contrast her openly promiscuous sexuality—she corresponds rather closely to the type of woman that is the brunt of Iago's sexual slurs—with that of (what I am presuming to be) Othello's doubts and shame over his unlovability and his questionable potency.

CONCLUSIONS

An examination of the play highlights features of pathological jealousy and envy that may be confirmed clinically. Jealousy and envy are complex. Both involve rivalry, hatred, and destructiveness. Both states of mind, in the play, and, I contend, in our clinical work, are significantly influenced by regression in the face of oedipal conflicts and, very strikingly in the play, by primal scene anxieties. Envy involves regression from postoedipal relatedness in the world to states of mind concerned with preoedipal mistrust and paranoid anxiety. The resultant states of mind are preoccupied with explicit primal scene fantasies and anxieties concerning unbearable oedipal shame. These anxieties trigger the "search" for evidence of having been cuckolded. Pathological jealousy as part of a crime of passion, as represented in the play, also involves a regression from postoedipal relationship to the world to specifically oedipal stage anxieties, including the sense of one's omnipotence (Othello as commander of Cyprus); a marked naivete about people's actual inner workings; the sense of the love object as a stolen, forbidden woman and the rival as a deceived older man; and the sense that one is inferior in capacities physically, emotionally, and socially both to the love object and to the rival.

In terms of my overall intent in putting forward these reflections, I contend that Freud tended to conflate jealousy, which I shall take to be a derivative of specifically oedipal intrafamilial rivalry in childhood, with a more sublimated and less regressed type of jealous postoedipal rivalry, say, the type that one might find in athletic competitions or among approximate equals for a mate or for glory in athletic, scholastic, or financial dominance. Klein, in her groundbreaking clinical studies on envy, has tended to ignore the element of simple rivalry in envy, to collapse the distinction between persistence of a preoedipal state of mind and regression to a preoedipal fixation, and to unnecessarily narrow the concept of envy to a catechism involving hatred of the object on whom one intensely depends.

Jealousy centers on the anticipation of loss of a truly loved person to a rival, whereas envy centers on diminishment of the self. As is evident in the play, envy can include elements of jealousy, and jealousy can include elements of envy of the loved one and of the rival. Both involve core feelings of unlovability and mistrust. Although jealousy and envy are both part of human experience, the full-blown pathological features of jealousy, as represented in Othello, and envy, as represented in Iago, highlight the destructive potential of these rivalrous emotions insofar as they become defining characteristics of a personality. Jealousy coexists with a genuine capacity to love and to have concern for the object. Envy, insofar as it is a defining characterological trait, centers on the incapacity to truly love because of a pervasive sense of diminishment and paranoid shame (Lansky, 2005b).

Shame is prominent in the dynamics of both characters, but the shame is not entirely overt. Pathological jealousy is not merely an amplification of even extreme normal jealousy. In this regard, a comparison of Othello's possessive jealousy with that of Bianca's is telling. Othello's murderous jealousy is related to his sexual shame, which is fulminantly activated by the prospect of his being publicly seen as cuckolded and (I am presuming) by his guilt and sense of deserving punishment in kind at having the woman he stole from Brabantio then stolen from him, in turn, by Cassio. Likewise, Iago's pervasive envy is the preeminent and organizing feature of his makeup, not simply an amplification of the envy that is an inevitable part of the human lot. Iago's shame-prone envious personality is devoid of love or moral concern. He is secretive, stays in hiding, works in the shadows, and physically split off from the other characters on the stage, as he is psychologically split off from any love or moral obligation for anyone else in the play.

Apart from its presence in envious and jealous states of mind per se, shame is significant in another important dimension, an understanding of which increases our understanding of envy and jealousy—its role as instigator of vengeful destructive action (Lansky, 2005b, in press; Lewis, 1971). Iago as envious is the stealthy instigator of conflict, destruction, and chaos. Jealous and envious states of mind by themselves are not sufficient explanations of the ensuing destructive vengeful action that is so much at the heart of the play's impact. Only if we assume the prospect of unbearable shame—in both Iago and in Othello, resulting from their convictions that they have been known publicly to have been cuckolded—can we understand the transformational processes between these states of mind and vengeful destructive action. These processes involve detachment of each from the moral order and from their relationships to intimates, that is to say, splitting (Lansky, in press); detachment from and the ensuing diabolical action that has been shaped by the influence of paranoid shame fantasies, omnipotence, and oblivion to consequences to the loved one or oneself, or the fantasied restoration of well-being that would follow vengeful action. Shame fantasies underlie this and other vengeful actions, which should not be confused with the envious and jealous states of mind that both trigger and accompany the split of a destructive vengeful state but do not fully explain it (Lansky, 2005b).

Shakespeare's masterpiece captures and discriminates fully between the chaotic and destructive potential of the rivalrous emotions of jealousy, envy, and simple rivalry as well as the relation between the states of mind per se and the shame-driven instigation of tragic and destructive vengeful action.

ACKNOWLEDGMENT

I thank Professor Herbert Morris for numerous insights into the play and comments on an earlier draft of this essay.

REFERENCES

Aristotle. (1992). Poetics. In H. Adams (Ed.), *Critical theory since Plato* (p. 55). New York: Harcourt, Brace, Jovanovich.

Arlow, J. A. (1980). The revenge motive in the primal sense. *Journal of the American Psychoanalytical Association, 28,* 512–541.

Coen, S. J. (1987). Pathological jealousy. *International Journal of Psychoanalysis, 68,* 99–108.

Coleridge, S. T. (1884). *Letters and notes on Shakespeare and other English poets.* London: Bohm's Standard Library. G. Bell and Son.

Etchegoyen, R. H., Benito, M. L., & Rabih, M. (1987). On envy and how to interpret it. *International Journal of Psychoanalysis, 68,* 49–60.

Fenichel, O. (1935/1953). A contribution to the psychology of jealousy. In *Collected papers of Otto Fenichel.* First Series. New York: Norton.

Freud, S. (1897/1966). Letter to Fliess (letter 71). In *Standard edition* 1:65. London. Hogarth.

Freud, S. (1922). Some neurotic mechanisms in jealousy, paranoia, and homosexuality. In *Standard edition* 18. London: Hogarth.

Hutson, P. (1996), The envy complex: Its recognition and analysis. In M. Goldberger (Ed.), *Danger and defense: The technique of close process attention* (pp. 221–240). Northvale, NJ: Jason Aronson.

Joffe, W. (1969). A critical review of the status of the envy concept. *International Journal of Psycho-analysis, 50,* 533–545.

Jones, E. (1929/1961). Jealousy. In *Papers on psychoanalysis* (pp. 325–340). Boston: Beacon Press.

Joseph, B. (1986). Envy in everyday life. *International Journal of Psychoanalysis and Psychotherapy, 2,* 13–22.

Kilborne, R. (2002). *Disappearing persons.* Albany: State University of New York Press.

Kilborne, B. (2003). Shame dynamics. *American Journal of Psychoanalysis, 63*(4).

Klein, M. (1957). *Envy and gratitude.* New York. Basic Books.

Konstan, D. (2003). Before jealousy. In D. Konstan & N. K. Rutter (Eds.), *Envy, spite, and jealousy: The rivalrous emotions in ancient Greece.* Edinburgh. Edinburgh University Press.

Lansky, M. R. (1997). Envy as process. In M. R. Lansky & A. P. Morrison (Eds.), *The widening scope of shame* (pp. 327–338). Hillsdale, NJ: Analytic Press.

Lansky, M. R. (2004). Trigger and screen: Shame conflicts in the instigation of Freud's dreams. *Journal of the American Academy of Psychoanalysis, 32,* 441–468.

Lansky, M. R. (2005a). Hidden shame. *Journal of the American Psychoanalytic Association, 53,* 865–980.

Lansky, M. R. (2005b). The impossibility of forgiveness: Shame fantasies as instigators of vengefulness in Euripides' *Medea. Journal of the American Psychoanalytic Association, 53,* 437–464.

Lansky, M. R. (in press). Unbearable shame, splitting, and forgiveness in the resolution of vengefulness. *Journal of the American Psychoanalytical Association.*

Lewis, H. B. (1971). *Shame and guilt in neurosis.* New York: International Universities Press.

Mitrani, J. (1993). Deficiency and envy: Some factors impacting the analytic mind from listening to interpretation. *International Journal of Psychoanalysis, 74,* 689–704.

Neubauer, P. (1982). Rivalry, envy, and jealousy. *Psychoanalytic Study of the Child, 37,* 121–142.
Proust, M. (1989). *Remembrance of things past. Swann's way* (C. K. Moncrieff & T. Kilmartin, Trans.). New York: Vintage.
Riviere, J. (1932). Jealousy as a mechanism of defense. *International Journal of Psychoanalysis, 13,* 414–424.
Segal, H. (1973). *An introduction to the work of Melanie Klein* (enlarged ed.). New York: Basic Books.
Shakespeare, W. (1604/1999). *Othello.* New York: New Folger Library. Washington Square Press.
Shaw, G. B. (1961). Othello. In E. Wilson (Ed.), *Shaw on Shakespeare.* New York: Appliance. (Original review, 1897).
Spielman, P. (1971). Envy and jealousy: An attempt at clarification. *Psychoanalytic Quarterly, 40,* 59–82.
Spinoza, B. (1951). Ethics (Elwes, R. H. M. Trans.). In *The chief works of Benedict de Spinoza,* Vol II (pp. 1–277). New York; Dover.
Wangh, M. (1952). Othello: The tragedy of Iago. *Psychoanalytic Quarterly, 40,* 59–82.
Wilson, E. (1929). *The wound and the bow.* Athens: Ohio University Press.
Wittgenstein, L. (1953). *Philosophical investigations* (GEM Anscombe, Trans.). New York: Macmillan.
Wurmser, L. (1981). *The mask of shame.* Baltimore: Johns Hopkins University Press.

3

Toward an Understanding of Womb Envy

Developmental and Clinical Perspectives

CHERYL L. ESCHBACH

> The womb is an animal which longs to generate children. When it remains barren too long after puberty, it is distressed and sorely disturbed, and straying about in the body and cutting off the passages of the breath, it impedes respiration and brings the sufferer into the extremest anguish and provokes all manner of diseases besides.
>
> *Plato, Timaeus (Veith, 1965, pp. 7–8)*

Among the envies, envy of the womb may be considered the most primordial. According to Melanie Klein, "envy implies the subject's relation to one person only and goes back to the earliest exclusive relation with the mother" (1957/1993, p. 181). The mother's womb is the nurturing inner space that encompasses and contains, providing total care to the fetal child within its confines. But the same womb necessarily excludes those who are not inside, and it ultimately expels the one who is. In this essay I consider womb envy to be envy both of the sexuality of this inner space, defined physically by the utero-vaginal-vulvar tissues but metaphorically by the concepts of receptivity and generativity, and of the consequent life-giving and life-denying powers that accrue to the mother. I suggest that this envy of woman as sexual object *and* mother shapes the psychosexual development of girls as well as boys with ramifications into adulthood for both women and men.

The centrality of the womb to female and male sexuality has given rise to a large and rich tradition, following Klein, that stresses the part object, especially the mother's breast, the child's envious and aggressive relationship to it, and the child's subsequent capacity for whole object relations depending upon whether he or she is able to surmount the frustration intrinsic to that initial, envious relation. But the crucial clinical importance of these insights runs up against the legacy of what, as I suggest in the first section of this essay, is Freud's own envious removal of the womb from psychoanalytic theory. As a result, the concept of womb envy has not received the attention that it merits in the psychoanalytic literature. Balsam refers to the "vanished" pregnant body in psychoanalytic thinking, a body that "has actually been omitted in important aspects of theory building to date" (2003, pp. 1153–1154). Freud's unanalyzed envy of female childbearing capacities may bear the imprint of an ancient Western convention, dating to Hippocrates and Plato, of regarding the woman's womb as something that wanders about her body, gets stuck in various places, and in those extra-uterine sites, causes numerous specifically feminine maladies and afflictions. But as I argue in this essay, the issue is not where the womb is in woman's body, but where we—male *and* female—are with respect to the womb. If the womb wanders, it wanders into our imagination and unconscious fantasies, where it can be a source of tremendous creativity or of impoverishment and conflict.

In the second section of this essay I look at female sexuality in association with the maternal functions of pregnancy, parturition, and lactation, not to privilege biological drives but to call attention to a substrate of bodily experience that shapes our fantasies and identities. We must pay close attention to the varied individual meanings of this experience (Chodorow, 1996), while not losing sight of the deep anxiety, found in cultures everywhere (Otero, 1996), that is evoked by female sexuality and the power of woman to give birth to—or to abort—and to nurture—or to neglect—her young. Section three of this essay draws upon the contributions of Kestenberg and others to suggest that a vague, if unconscious, awareness of the womb in both boys and girls shapes an inner genital phase of development. Because this phase tends to precede the phallic phase with its orientation to external surfaces, womb envy is usually submerged by penis envy, which remains closer to consciousness. In the fourth section, I discuss ways in which womb envy may reemerge in the clinical process, in the form of incorporative fantasies that defend against its awareness and projective fantasies in which the aggression associated with the womb-envious impulse is put into external or internal objects. The concluding section returns to Freud to suggest how the analytic situation, the creation of which is arguably his most important legacy, may recapitulate the womblike worlds of pre- and postnatal life, both evoking this primordial envy and offering a venue for its eventual sublimation.

WOMB ENVY IN FREUD: AN INJURY DISPLACED

Freud writes poignantly about the mystery of the origin of babies, which is "the first problem" for children, the riddle that gives birth to the instinct for knowledge (1905/1953, p. 195). Freud's language leaves no doubt that the child's inability to solve this "first, grand problem of life" to his satisfaction is profoundly traumatic (1908/1959, p. 212). Because the child does not know about the fertilizing role of the semen or the existence of the vagina, "his sexual researches are habitually fruitless … [leaving behind] ... a *permanent injury* to the instinct for knowledge. … [and] ... a high degree of ... [alienation] ... from ... [the adults] ... who formerly enjoyed his complete confidence" (1905/1953, p. 197, emphasis added). Freud writes later that the child's "brooding and doubting … [over this question] become the prototype of all later intellectual work directed toward the solution of problems, and the first failure has a *crippling effect* on the child's whole future" (1908/1959, p. 219, emphasis added). Moreover:

> the obscure part played by the father ... [means that the child's] investigation of where babies come from must inevitably come to nothing too and be abandoned as insoluble. The impression caused by this failure in the first attempt at intellectual independence appears to be of a *lasting and deeply depressing kind*. (1910a/1957, p. 79, emphasis added)

Freud also describes a "permanent injury to self-regard in the form of a narcissistic scar" associated with the failure of the child's sexual researches (1920/1955, p. 20).

This injury was one that Freud knew all too well in his own childhood, where the fecundity of his young mother resulted in many displacements for him, as one sibling after another—a total of seven rivals for his mother's attention—arrived on the scene. It is an injury, moreover, that may be especially salient for the boy (Lax, 1997). Although the girl, who may defend against her displacement by identification, assuming that she, too, will someday possess her mother's procreative powers, the boy is usually unable to appreciate his vital if invisible role in procreation until well after he makes the devastating discovery that his internal anatomy differs decisively from his mother's. The affect associated with this discovery, as Freud aptly captures it in the passages cited above, is indeed injurious, crippling, and deeply depressing. The "small bearer of the penis" (Freud, 1924, p. 178) is left to wonder where he fits—indeed *if* he fits—into the reproductive scheme of things. Freud hints at the sense of devastation felt by the boy, whose "own attempt to make a baby himself, carried out with tragic seriousness, fails shamefully" (1920/1955, p. 21).

Rather than exploring the impact of this injury, Freud displaces it entirely onto the girl. This displacement first occurs in Freud's initial presentation of his theories about sexuality. As can be seen in the passage cited below, Freud, after perceptively observing how pregnancy and childbirth may seem like a "threat to the bases of a child's existence," abruptly changes the subject, explicitly adopts the perspective of the male child, and introduces, for the first time in his writings, the concepts of penis envy and castration anxiety:

> It is not by theoretical interests but by practical ones that activities of research are set going in children. The threat to the bases of a child's existence offered by the discovery or the suspicion of the arrival of a new baby and the fear that he may, as a result of it, cease to be cared for and loved, make him thoughtful and clear-sighted. And this history of the instinct's origin is in line with the fact that the first problem with which it deals is not the question of the distinction between the sexes but the riddle of where babies come from. ... On the contrary, the existence of the two sexes does not to begin with arouse any difficulties or doubts in children. It is self-evident to a male child that a genital like his own is to be attributed to everyone he knows, and he cannot make its absence tally with his picture of these other people. ... Little girls do not resort to denial of this kind when they see that boys' genitals are formed differently from their own. They are ready to recognize them *immediately* and are overcome by envy for the penis—an envy culminating in the wish, which is so important in its consequences, to be boys themselves. (Freud, 1905/1953, pp. 194–195, emphasis added)

How can we explain the precipitous shift that occurs in this passage, from the child's profound, existential fear of being displaced by the new baby to the boy's "self-evident" certainty that all people possess a genital like his own? Viewed from the child's perspective (from which, at one level, Freud is writing), one possibility is that the little boy's newfound certainty that everyone has a penis may be a form of hope: If the mother has a penis like the boy then the boy might still have a womb like his mother! Indeed, that the boy may approach the problem in this way is suggested in the clinical material of Freud's own case study, Little Hans, which documents the enthusiasm of the 4-year-old child to have children of his own while he simultaneously insists, over the objections of his father and Freud, that his mother has a penis (1909a/1955, esp. pp. 13, 86–87, 93). But Freud the adult does not comment on this aspect of Little Hans, which is consistent with his denial in other writings of the child's awareness of the vagina and the uterus. Similarly, Freud's dramatic shift from helplessness to triumphant confidence in the text cited above bears the mark of a defensive maneuver.

The defensive character of Freud's argument is also evident in his language describing an immediate change of a sweeping nature that takes place in the girl herself when she sees the penis for the first time. The girl does not *develop* envy of the penis, as one might expect based on the idea of an ego that is shaped slowly over time by more or less consistent inputs from brain, body, and external environment. Instead, she is instantaneously struck by the envy when she sees the male anatomy that is so different from her own. Freud states, for example:

> the first step in the phallic phase ... is ... a *momentous discovery* which little girls are destined to make. They notice the penis of a brother or playmate, strikingly visible and of large proportions, *at once recognize it* as the superior counterpart to their own small and inconspicuous organ, and *from that time forward* fall victim to envy for the penis.

As if she were mutilated by an actual event, the girl knows *"in a flash* [that] ... she is without it and wants to have it" (1925/1961, p. 252, emphasis added).

Freud suggests that the damage caused by this discovery is severe and often permanently disfiguring for girls. It "will leave ineradicable traces on their development and the formation of their character ... which will not be surmounted in even the most favourable cases without a severe expenditure of psychical energy" (Freud, 1935/1964, p. 125). "The discovery that she is castrated" (p. 126) is not merely that she lacks something that she would like to have. It is as if she has, by violent means, suffered the loss of her physical and psychical integrity. She is now *castrated*, in both body and spirit.

The ramifications of this horrible sight are extensive for the boy as well. He realizes that he, too, could be castrated. In boys, Freud argues, the Oedipus complex "is not simply repressed, it is literally *smashed to pieces* by the shock of threatened castration" (1924/1961, p. 257, emphasis added). The shattering violence that ensues from the boy's observation of female sexual anatomy results in the decathexis of the mother, the creation of the superego, and "all the processes that are designed to make the individual find a place in the cultural community" (1931/1961, p. 229).

Closely heeding the nuances of Freud's language, however, we see that the word "to castrate," which means not only to remove the testes or ovaries but also "to deprive of vigor or vitality: weaken by removal of the most effective or forceful elements; to render impotent especially by psychological means" (*Webster's Third New International Dictionary*, 1993, p. 349), describes an act of removing or *taking away*, by surgical or violent means if necessary, of something vital to another person. In this sense, to castrate is to commit a quintessentially envious act. Thus when Freud describes the girl as a "mutilated creature [who is now the object of] triumphant contempt" (1925/1961, p. 252), he can be read as perhaps enviously removing the anatomic and sexual basis of her gender identity.

Freud sensitively detects in the child the narcissistic injury caused by his inability to procreate. This injury is indeed traumatic, but perhaps especially for boys. We may even see stigmata of this injury on Freud himself in his denial of the child's awareness of the vagina and uterus, of the boy's desire for children, and of the wish, persisting into adulthood, for connection with the preoedipal mother.

WOMB ENVY: MATERNAL AND SEXUAL ROOTS

If the breast is seen as an aspect of the womb—a concrete, visible representation of this cryptic inner space—then the notion of womb envy may be understood as crucial to Kleinian theory and practice. Yet outside the literature by Klein and her followers, discussions of womb envy are difficult to find. This relative neglect is in sharp contrast to the extensive discussion in psychoanalytic literature of the notion of penis envy, traditionally considered so central to female development, that no analysis of a woman was regarded as complete unless penis envy was thoroughly explored. Moreover, where the notion of envy of woman's reproductive capacities is discussed, it is rarely, if ever, called womb envy (but see Lax, 1997). Many have used the general term "woman envy" (Jacobson, 1950; Zilboorg, 1944). Others refer to an assortment of envies, such as "vagina envy" (Bettelheim, 1954), "breast envy" (Kubie, 1974), "baby envy" (Kestenberg, 1991), or, more clinically, "reproductive envy" (Boehm, 1930). Almost always, the envy is described in quotation marks, as if its existence is uncertain or requires apology.

Why should we focus on womb envy, and not breast or vagina envy, or perhaps all three? What is it about the womb per se that it should be singled out among the female genitalia? I wish to suggest that the womb is the primary target of envy because it is the childbearing capacity of woman that both differentiates her biologically from man *and* is central to her sexuality. The physiological processes culminating in childbirth are similar to, although more intense than, those that produce female orgasm (Kitzinger, 1985). And sexual intercourse, for both sexes, may be driven in part by the unconscious regressive desire to return to the mother's womb (Ferenzci, 1968).

Although the specific anatomical definition of womb is uterus, womb is also defined as "a place or space where something is generated or produced" (*Webster's Third New International Dictionary*, 1993, p. 2629). By this broader definition, the concept of womb may encompass the vagina; the vulva, including the clitoris; and the breasts as well as the uterus, since all are involved in childbearing. This more encompassing definition of womb reflects the fact that in humans, as in mammals more generally, childbearing entails several types of relationships, copulation, gestation and parturition, and lactation. Although in our culture only copulation is considered a sexual act, in fact sensual pleasure is central to pregnancy and lactation as well. As anthropologist Hrdy has noted, in evolutionary terms:

> Long before any woman found sexual foreplay or intercourse pleasurable, her ancestors were selected to respond positively to similar sensations produced by birth and suckling, because finding these activities pleasurable would help condition her in ways that kept her infant alive. (1999, p. 139)

The womb is centered in the uterovaginal space, a space potentially open to the outside world but with a deep interior that is sealed from it by the sturdy, powerful musculature of the cervix. This interior chamber, the uterus, is itself open to the surrounding abdominal cavity via the ovarian tubes. The womb's openness to external and internal spaces adapts it uniquely to fertilization, enabling both sperm and egg to be sucked in and drawn together, but its enclosure deep inside the larger cavity of the female abdomen allows it to contain, hold, and provide total security to the embryonic inhabitant that matures inside of it. The nestled location of the womb among abdominal and other pelvic organs is reflected in colloquial definitions of womb as "belly," or more specifically, as the stomach or the bowels (*Oxford English Dictionary*, 1989, p. 490). The overlay of gastrointestinal organs, and meanings, on the internal female genitalia not only blurs the boundaries of the womb but also intimately associates it with highly cathected drives that are oral and anal as well as genital.

The female breasts, while physically separate from the uterovaginal space, are functionally linked to the womb insofar as they provide nurture to the profoundly dependent—and in the case of humans, relatively premature—infant after parturition. The same hormone that stimulates uterine contractions, oxytocin, is released from the posterior pituitary gland when breast tissue is stimulated. Once gestation has run its course, lactation begins, and the umbilical connection at the naval is replaced by the oral latching of the infant to its mother's breast. This new bond, although no longer uninterrupted, gives the infant not only optimal nutrition but also, at least in the normal situation of a "good-enough" mother, emotional nurturing in a maternal embrace that contains and holds the child much as the uterus once did. Since the adipose "padding" in breast tissue is superfluous to the functioning of the lactiferous ducts, the physical beauty and sexually arousing appearance of female breasts may be seen as external advertisements for woman's hidden, internal reproductive capacities (Hrdy, 1999, p. 127).

The successive openings and closings of a woman's womb shape both the monthly rhythms and the major events of her life. (And, perhaps needless to say, where access to contraception and abortion is limited, female fertility not only shapes but may powerfully determine her destiny.) The womb of the premenstrual girl is sealed by the thin hymenal membrane. At menarche, and monthly until menopause, the internal cervical os dilates ever so slightly to release the sloughed layers of the uterine endometrium. At mid-cycle, heightened receptivity and ovulation synchronize with a thinning and proliferation of the cervical mucus to reopen the womb for conception (LeVay & Valente, 2006, p. 142). At this time, women are more likely to mate—and to mate promiscuously—than at other times of the month (Hrdy, 1999, p. 222). During gestation, the womb is closed again, fortified by the thick, powerful musculature of the cervix—among the strongest of the muscles in the human body—that holds the fetus securely inside. The softening and relaxation of the pubic symphysis heralds the arrival of parturition, in which the fundus of the uterus contracts ever more intensely while the lower uterine segment and the cervix dilate to allow fetal passage. Immediately after delivery of the placenta, the uterus contracts again to perform a hemostasis as dramatic as the parting of the Red Sea, and the 4 to 5 liters of blood that flowed each minute into the placental bed during gestation are abruptly clamped off and diverted back to the pregestational circulation. No human-made hemostatic device can compare with this instantaneous sealing of uterine circulation to avert, with complete success as much as 99% of the time, massive maternal hemorrhage (Beckmann et al., 1995, p. 211).

Joined to woman's reproductive capacities is a complex sexuality, a center of which is the uterus, in addition to the clitoris. Uterine contractions may be induced externally by the arousal of the lower vaginal, clitoral, or breast tissue, culminating, along with vaginal and clitoral contractions, in orgasm, or internally by the release of prostaglandins from the amniotic fluid in pregnancy, triggering the onset of labor. Initially expectant, diffuse, and in-gathering, female sexuality gathers force, becoming in orgasm as in parturition ever more intense, rhythmic, and propulsive. In lactation, the rhythmic sucking of the infant produces a reciprocally patterned discharge of milk, a gradual shrinking of the uterus, and a deep sense of well-being not incomparable to that which accompanies orgasm. "It would be more nearly correct, then, to refer to the 'afterglow' from climax as an ancient 'maternal' rather than sexual response" (Hrdy, 1999, p. 139).

This sexuality, and the rhythmic cycles that shape it, gives rise to generative yearnings. Women whose life circumstances free them to cultivate these yearnings may or may not have the specific desire for biological offspring. In either case, in evolutionary terms, successful maternity has required highly developed libidinal instincts. Anthropological research suggests that active female sexuality in primates—continuous receptivity, promiscuity, and strategically competitive mating behaviors—may have been selected so that the female could inhibit males from harming her offspring and increase the likelihood her primary male partner would help in child-rearing (Hrdy, 1981).

Similarly, the forging of a mature feminine ego from female libidinal drives may be an intrinsically active and pleasurable process (Mayer, 1985; Richards, 1992, 1996). In infancy, the breast is actively sought after, internalized, and then released by the child. "[T]he infant who was first inside of the mother now has the mother inside of himself" (Klein, 1957/1993, p. 179). In toilet training, as Richards (1992, 1996) has described, the girl learns to flex her perineal musculature to open and close her anal and urethral sphincters, gaining a sense of control and mastery not only over the contents of bowel and bladder but also over her vulvar-vaginal opening. This mastery is reinforced by play in which the girl actively explores interior enclosures such as playhouses (Moore, 1977; Richards, 1992). Early on, therefore, the girl apprehends, however vaguely, the many ways in which her sexuality involves the opening *and* closing of her genitals and the exploration, through external objects, of the boundaries and meanings of her cryptic inner space.

Nevertheless, as Bernstein (1990) argues, in contrast to the boy with his highly visible and easily manipulated genitalia, the girl depends more upon adult caregivers in forming psychic representation for her hidden, internal genitalia. This dependence, if not accompanied by "good-enough" guidance from the adult, can induce anxiety. Does the girl's discovery of her vagina result in the pleasurable secret that she has an opening and potential space inside, as Mayer suggests (1985, p. 334), or in the terrifying revelation that she has a *hole*, "a hole where no hole should be" (Horney, 1933/1967, p. 156; see also Bernstein, 1990)? These early psychic representations of the girl's genitalia may shape her sexual experience in adulthood. In contrast to the more localized sensations in the male sexual experience, in female orgasm, contractions that originate in the clitoris, vagina, and uterus spread as waves of excitement over the entire body (Montgrain, 1983). Although one woman may enjoy the intense pleasure of this experience, for another this letting go may recall *being let go of*—the terrifying independence or unavailability of the mother—and she may recoil in anxiety and unconsciously inhibit herself in order to provide the secure containment of which she may have felt cheated in infancy (Dinnerstein, 1976, pp. 62–63).

These genital anxieties may be reinforced in maternity by the heightened libido associated with second- and early third-trimester pregnancy, the explosive intensity of labor, delivery with its messy admixture of baby with urethral and anal excrement, and the spreading, diffuse sensual sensations associated with breastfeeding. Underlying these experiences are persisting early incest fantasies, which may produce unconscious feelings of sexual pleasure in parturition (Horney, 1926/1967, p. 66). For these feelings the ego in turn exacts its price, so that unconsciously, the pain associated with labor may be regarded as the punishment for this forbidden pleasure, while consciously, women will often feel tremendous anxiety about delivery and anticipate pain in excess of what might otherwise be the case. Parturition as punishment is, of course, an ancient theme dating back to Eve's expulsion, along with Adam, from the Garden of Eden.

Female sexuality is a source of anxiety, even dread, in men as well. Male identity, originally immersed in the "femaleness" of the mother (Stoller, 1968), may be threatened by heterosexual intercourse if it stirs fears of being sucked into a greedy womb. Mature female sexuality may be associated with unconscious ideas of the "vagina dentata," the teeth of which are hidden by the woman's pubic hair (Bettelheim, 1954, p. 233; Otero, 1996). Indeed, clinical material from male analysands not uncommonly reveals fearsome fantasies of the vagina as an "insatiable, cannibalistic organ … [that] threatens not only the man's penis but also his sexual identity and status as a male" (Montgrain, 1983, p. 172). The fear of castration may be displaced, either in fantasy, as in the Freudian boy's raw exclamation of "horror at the mutilated [female] creature" (1925/1961, p. 252), or in fact, as in the widespread cultural practice of female genital mutilation in the Middle East and Muslim Africa (Kulish, 1991). Another defense against castration anxiety is splitting, involving a primitive idealization of the surface of the female body, which in turn protects the man against his fantasied projection of aggression into the interior of mother's body (Kernberg, 1995, p. 39; Meltzer & Williams, 1988)—that is, against his destructive envy of mother's womb.

To this primal anxiety about female sexuality must be added the murky question of paternity. As Freud observes, "the relation to ... [one's mother] is based on an event that is not open to any doubt" (1910b/1957, p. 169), but paternity is so fraught with uncertainty that it is one subject that obsessionals, with their predilection for doubt, will brood over incessantly (1909b/1957, p. 232). Thus the womb that contains necessarily also displaces, including—perhaps especially—the supposed father of the child. "[D]espite all his economic and sadistic and phallic superiority, man could not fail to discover that the woman ... still possessed a unique power over mankind. She could produce children *who always clung to her,* who loved her without stint" (Zilboorg, 1944, p. 288, emphasis added).

The political and cultural importance of woman's womb is captured in the Hebrew language, in which the plural form for the word "womb" or "uterus" is usually translated as "compassion," "mercy," or "love" (Trible, 1978, p. 33). Ideally, compassion and love are the emotions that people who are biologically related feel toward one another; they have "wombs" because, ultimately, they come from the same womb. Nevertheless, as psychoanalysis shows, intimacy and relatedness can generate hostility as well as love and compassion (Freud, 1921, p. 101). In particular, friends and family of the pregnant woman may experience especially intense feelings of greed and deprivation (Lax, 1969, p. 371). And as Klein suggests when she states that envy is rooted in the early, exclusive relationship with the mother, envy of the womb begins at birth with one's forcible expulsion from it.

This envy is inevitable, because the terrifying reality that all children face from birth is that mother, more than anyone else, has the capacity to determine whether the child thrives or even survives. The human female, more than other mammalian mothers, is unable to produce large litters and instead must concentrate her limited reproductive resources on ensuring that a small number of offspring survive. She is, therefore, genetically programmed from millions of years of evolution to make stark choices about whether she has the resources to make the investment in a particular child (Hrdy, 1981, 1999). Although infanticide is not condoned in modern human societies, limited maternal resources often mean that within the same family some children receive less attention and fewer resources than others.

For the neonate, the need to behave in ways that increase the odds its mother will keep it and nurture it is of overriding importance. The child's very genome predisposes its every action to be an attempt to secure mother's favor, to sustain her attentions, and to postpone or prevent the advent of siblings. If the neonate succeeds in these efforts and securely latches onto its mother's breast, it remains in a womblike setting. Its mother continues to secrete the hormone prolactin, which inhibits ovulation. No rivals for its attention are likely to be produced, and the enraged desire to destroy its former home, and the mother that contains it, can subside, at least until the child is better equipped to cope with its primordial envy.

NORMAL WOMB ENVY IN THE INNER GENITAL PHASE OF DEVELOPMENT

For both boy and girl, early understandings of gender are initially undifferentiated and overinclusive (Fast, 1978). Although core gender identity, shaped by constitutional as well as sociocultural factors (Robbins, 1996), begins to form as early as 18 months, this early identity is still bisexually inclusive. Boys as well as girls assume they can bear children *and* that their mothers have penises. These assumptions are prominent aspects of what Kestenberg (1982, 1991) has described as the inner genital phase of development and Parens (1990, p. 745) terms the first, or infantile, genital phase. The importance of this omnipotential genital experience is emphasized by Fogel, who argues that its integration into the adult personality facilitates a character structure defined by "more differentiation *combined* with an ability to 'let go' of firm boundaries, 'take in' and 'open up' to new experiences … and put them all together in their richness and ambiguity" (1998, p. 677).

In this phase, the desire to procreate emerges as an organizing developmental force sometime between the ages of 2 and a half to 4, before the male child knows with certainty that he cannot ever bear children and before the female child realizes that she will have to wait to bear a child. Temporally, the inner genital phase follows from the anal-urethral phase and precedes the phallic phase of development. For boys, this phase is typically of shorter duration than it is for girls (Kestenberg, 1991, p. 31), but many psychoanalytic researchers have documented that young boys in this phase have no hesitation endorsing their wish to be female or to have children (Horney, 1932/1967; Lax, 1997; Stoller, 1964, 1968).

Although the inner genital is cryptic and difficult to conceptualize, multiple developmental drives converge to reinforce in the preoedipal child an awareness of its reality. First, as psychoanalytic writers have recognized since the 1920s, children at this stage begin to experience inner genital sensations (Horney, 1926), often, as Richards (1992, 1996) has described, in association with toilet training and the attendant flexing and relaxation of the sphincters and surrounding perineal musculature. The child is developing the idea that he or she has something inside, something that is neither food nor feces nor urine but that has symbolic, unconscious connections to all three.

Second, cognitively, children are beginning to distinguish between inside and outside. They are especially curious about what is "inside" of their mothers and obtain immense pleasure hearing, over and over again, that once upon a time *they* were inhabitants of "Mommy's tummy." They reveal their newfound capacity to understand inside versus outside in drawings of circles and enclosed shapes.

> It is characteristic for children 3 to 4 years of age that these circles contain a scribble or another circle inside of them. In many instances these "inside" structures are identified as babies inside Mommy. Thus there is a development from what seems a chaotic concept of space to a distinction between inside and outside. (Kestenberg, 1991, p. 28)

Whereas the 4-year-old wants to know how babies get inside of their mother, 3-year-olds, focusing on things from inside out, want to know how they get out.

Third, children during this phase are attempting to cope with the loss of their babyhood. They are increasingly expected to brush their own teeth, get themselves dressed, and deposit their urine and feces in the toilet. They seek to compensate for this loss through an intense identification with their mother. Now little mothers themselves, they are especially gentle with babies (especially if not their own siblings), pets, and dolls. They demonstrate motherliness in their play with dolls. Boys in particular may become preoccupied with moving objects such as trains, which have maternal as well as phallic representations insofar as they carry objects such as people and cargo (Kestenberg, 1991, p. 33).

At the same time, there is an incipient hostility toward mother in both sexes. The child is beginning to differentiate between excrement and other productions of the body, such as babies, although the boundary between the two is still blurred. Its own productions, after all, are urine and feces, and it is usually mother who carries them off and demands that the child start putting them him- or herself in the toilet. The child begins to pay attention to other differences. Mother's breasts are bigger than the boy's penis; and unlike the flat chests of boys and girls, they can produce milk and suckle. Moreover, if mother has another baby at this time, the child may feel profoundly displaced, reacting with the dual desire to destroy the baby inside mother's belly and to want to have a child of its own (Klein, 1928/1992, pp. 189–190).

Toward the end of the inner genital phase, this hostility toward mother is reinforced by the growing, unpleasant awareness that it may not be possible to have babies. The boy discovers that he does not, and never will, possess a womb, while the girl realizes that her own womb cannot "grow" a baby until she herself grows to the size of her mother. The child, until now profoundly identified with mother, begins to feel betrayed. This sense of betrayal may be reinforced if the child's parents have attempted to dissuade him (usually only the boy) from playing at being pregnant or being a mother and to "enlighten" him that he cannot ever have children.

The boy may find this situation especially difficult to understand. The ability to recognize inner genital differences evolves at a time when boys do not yet identify as strongly with their fathers as do girls with their mothers (Chodorow, 2000, p. 38). Although the "boy is struggling with his wish to be like mother and identify with her, he is simultaneously enraged with her for having made him different from her" (Lax, 1997, p. 130). The boy may attempt to undo this narcissistic injury by defensively endowing his mother with a penis. This transitional fantasy of a phallic mother, which emerges earlier than oedipal phase fantasies of the phallic mother that may be motivated by castration anxiety, both preserves the identification with the mother and protects the boy from the punishing envy of her nurturing and procreative powers (Barth, 1990, p. 70; Lax, 1997, p. 131).

The girl may have her own difficulties with this developmental stage. She needs to separate but she still depends on her mother to help her master her genital anxieties (Bernstein, 1990). Klein (1928/1992) similarly suggests that the girl with a healthy identification with her mother may experience strong feelings of pride and joy in her childbearing potential that help to mediate her genital anxieties, but if she does not enjoy such an identification, her envy, combined with aggressive feelings toward mother and fear of retribution, result in anxiety, guilt, and consequent repression of her inner genitality.

As development proceeds into the phallic phase, awareness of the inner space of the womb is repressed in girls and boys, at least somewhat, and the child's aggression increases. Both sexes begin to feel that what is bothering them inside must be expelled rather than figured out. They start to ask, "How did the baby get into mother's stomach in the first place?" And both boy and girl begin to focus on what is outside, and on external surfaces of the body, such that their womb envy gradually is submerged by penis envy, or, in the case of the boy, penis envy mixed with penis pride (Kestenberg, 1991).

Corresponding with the later developmental phase in which penis envy occurs, penis envy usually remains relatively closer to consciousness, in contrast to womb envy which is more completely repressed. The greater degree of repression is facilitated by the earlier age at which it occurs. It is also facilitated by the fact that the womb is hidden and therefore never acquires a concrete visual representation, while the existence of the penis is incontrovertible (Moore, 1968, p. 579). Blos argues that the boy's "'wish for a child' is far more deeply repressed than the girl's 'wish for a penis'" (1962, p. 29), but this argument misses the deep repression of womb envy that occurs in girls as well. Yet for both boy and girl, the repression of the aspiration to bear children of one's own, linked to deeper fantasies and fears of fusion with the preoedipal mother, is never completely successful. Inevitably, these fantasies and fears are mobilized in the clinical process.

WOMB ENVY IN THE CLINICAL PROCESS

Achievement of adulthood stirs generative strivings in men and women alike (Erikson, 1968). These yearnings may activate latent conflicts in which womb envy is a salient affect. The intolerable envy is defended against in various ways.

Klein makes a basic distinction in this regard between envy, which she defines as largely projective, and greed, which is more introjective:

> Greed is an impetuous and insatiable craving, exceeding what the subject needs and what the object is able and willing to give. At the unconscious level, greed aims primarily at completely scooping out, sucking dry, and devouring the breast: that is to say, its aim is destructive introjection; whereas envy not only seeks to rob in this way, but also to put badness, primarily bad excrements and bad parts of the self, into the mother, and first of all into her breast, in order to spoil and destroy her. In the deepest sense this means destroying her creativeness. One essential difference between greed and envy, although no rigid dividing line can be drawn since they are so closely associated, would accordingly be that greed is mainly bound up with introjection and envy with projection. (1957/1993, p. 181)

As Klein admits, greed and envy have much in common and are often difficult to distinguish from one another. Both the introjective mode of "taking in" and the projective mode of "spitting out" represent the earliest, oral mechanisms for dealing with the outside world (Blos, 1962, p. 234). Both modalities are important to understanding womb envy, for introjection may be a defense against the awareness of separation and loss, and the consequent experience of envy, which can be as unbearable to the adult as to the child (Spillius, 1997, p. 144). Below I provide some clinical examples of introjective and projective defenses against womb envy.

INCORPORATION: FANTASIED INTERNALIZATION OR FUSION WITH THE WOMB TO WARD OFF AWARENESS OF ENVY

The earliest form of introjection or internalization is incorporation. According to Meissner, incorporation may be seen as "the primary and most primitive form of internalization related to primitive oral fantasies as an aspect of primary process functioning" (1971, p. 286). Similarly, Bettelheim states, "The most archaic method of acquiring the desired qualities of an object, if not the desired object itself, is oral incorporation" (1954, p. 199). Incorporation is unequivocal only in certain severely regressed psychotic patients. Freud's patient Dr. Schreber, for example, was so disappointed by his inability to have children that he developed a delusional paranoia, the core of which was his transformation into a woman who would be God's wife. By incorporating the divine womb, he could now people the world with "a new race of men" born, like Athena from Zeus, from his own head (Freud, 1911/1958, p. 58).

In nonpsychotic states, incorporation serves as the prototype of all later identifications. The objects that are first incorporated are, by definition, part-objects, including the uterus, the breast, and the penis. Where conditions exist for the child's healthy and adaptive maturation, incorporation gradually gives way to more complex modalities of internalization based on whole object representations and identification. Indeed it is the loss of the part-object that precipitates the infant's first appreciation of its mother as a separate, whole person.

But if this loss and the depression that attends it are intolerable, then a regressive yearning for the nourishing, sheltering womb may emerge. Nasio (1998, p. 55) describes a "fundamental fantasy" of identification with the uterus as both a sheltering womb and as an internal organ that itself is sheltered, deeply protected within the maternal body. I have selected the clinical material discussed below to highlight both aspects of this fundamental fantasy. In the first aspect, the womb is incorporated as a hollow life-giving organ so that it is possible to give birth by oneself. In the second, the womb is reentered, or merged with, in order to claim this primordial, protected, and exclusive space for oneself.

Incorporation Fantasies

Mr. A sought treatment shortly after the birth of his first child. He resented the change that had come over his wife. "D. says she's a feminist, but now, with our baby, she is using motherhood as an excuse to give up her career. I'm afraid she'll never go back to work and that I'm going to be the only breadwinner in the household. I feel exploited." Mr. A also described a sense of feeling excluded from the new mother–daughter dyad. He began to put in long hours at work, and he began to drink heavily.

One morning, Mr. A described the fantasy he had while in the waiting room, in which he was lying on his side next to me with his torso curled around my back, in a "Lima bean position, with me encompassing you, or protecting you." He added, "I don't really like the way that Lima beans taste, but it felt good, and natural, to encompass you like that." In exploring this fantasy, it turned out that the opposite image, of me curled up around him, was not what Mr. A had in mind. "That didn't feel comfortable—it's not comfortable being the object of being protected," which recalled his mother's undependability and his wife's emotional lability. The idea of lying down face-to-face with me also felt unsettling to Mr. A.

I commented that his fantasy evoked an arresting image. "You are in a mothering position, as if you're pregnant and I'm inside of you." He replied, "The way I felt I was, early on, with D." He characterized D. as "a lost soul" when they met in their early 20s—"I took her under my wing, she was suffering from panic attacks, and she was very fearful in general. I wanted to protect her and nurture her; it was a very strong desire of mine." He added, "Now, I feel displaced, and deadened inside. I feel relieved only by my work, because by staying away, I can protect both my wife and daughter from the gloom that I feel within." I remarked that perhaps the gloom came from feeling excluded from the household that he was working so hard to establish and provide for. Mr. A became animated, "I am definitely envious and pissed off! I am providing the house, and, at the same time, wanting to be inside of it!" I replied, "You defend yourself from that envy here with me by insisting on providing the house, or the womb, by way of the Lima bean position where I am the protected one and you are locked into the role of protector." He paused, then said, with a sigh, "You're right. It's an either-or position. I never contemplated lying down with you in a face-to-face position. The idea of that would make me feel extremely uncomfortable."

By putting me inside of his womb, Mr. A could keep his envy at bay, as I was now the one in need of his nurturance. But it was, at this relatively early point in the treatment, still an insecure internalization. Several sessions later, he reported a dream of looking out the window before going to sleep and noticing a teddy bear on the sidewalk below. When he looked again the next morning, all that was left of the teddy bear was a button. He associated the teddy bear to a woman—"perhaps you"—and the button left over to a belly-button. "Somehow that button seems like my connection to you ... I wish I *could* consume you in order to keep you inside of me."

Over the years in his treatment since this episode, Mr. A continued to talk openly of his envious feelings toward his wife for getting to be the mother who stayed at home while he had to work. He and his wife had a second child, which made him more aware of his wife's need for his help at home. He stopped drinking and increasingly found ways to make his work schedule fit around family events. And he frequently used his sessions with me to talk about the importance, to him, of being a father and of his feelings of satisfaction in his own growing emotional connection to his children.

Ms. B's fundamental fantasy is not of nurturing me but of giving birth to a new self, with me in a supportive or peripheral role. Her father was prone to frequent angry outbursts, which he directed at her mother and, among his four daughters, at Ms. B. Ms. B's mother did not intervene to protect her. At age six, Ms. B had a history of meningitis, requiring a lengthy hospitalization. Her illness brought about a dramatic if temporary cessation in her father's rages, and she remembers the uncharacteristic warmth and affection that her parents showered on her at the time.

As a young adult, Ms. B developed bulimia, and although she no longer purges she does ruminate constantly and unhappily about her weight, her diet, and her body image. Ms. B's persisting, unrealistic experience of her body as enormous in size leads to a relentless self-persecution that both displaces and defends against her immense anger toward the abandoning mother and the enraged father.

In one session, Ms. B described her sister's hospitalization and surgery the previous week for acute cholecystitis. "I was so envious! She lost 10 pounds just lying there in the hospital bed for 4 days. Now all I can think of is how I want to get sick and be hospitalized and strapped to my bed. While the nurses take care of me, and without doing anything at all, I lose weight." I asked Ms. B why she would need to be strapped to the bed, particularly since she presumably would want to be there. She replied, thoughtfully, "I really don't know. I know only that I just want to become a part of that bed, a part of the hospital itself, and not move or be moved, until I am finally thin."

For the next several months, Ms. B continued to fantasize about being tethered to the hospital bed, a bondage that, while not involuntary, reflected the sheer urgency and intensity of her identification with the idealized object—the literally sterile, institutional space of the hospital-womb. "In the hospital you don't have to think about what you eat. You don't have to deal with the stress of wanting food and constantly fighting off the desire and constantly fearing that you'll succumb. You don't have to deal with the guilt of finally succumbing and then binging and then feeling worse about yourself than ever before." In losing weight, Ms. B finally would shed the bad internal object that has persecuted her in the form of constant obsessing about food. But at this point in her treatment, she felt she could do so only in the state of being strapped to the hospital bed, where loss could take place effortlessly and without pain or awareness of anxiety, separation, or guilt.

Merger Fantasies

The wish to greedily devour may be seen in merger or fusion fantasies, which hearken back to the intrauterine state. They are aptly characterized in Chasseguet-Smirgel's words as "a primary wish to rediscover a universe without obstacles, rough edges or differences, identified with a mother's smooth belly rid of its contents—the father, his penis and babies" (1988, p. 511). Particularly illustrative of this wish are apocalyptic dreams and fantasies of a devastated, deserted, and barren Earth. Chasseguet-Smirgel describes these fantasies in a patient, Franca, who had the following dreams:

> "The whole world has been devastated. Everyone has disappeared but for 34,000 people. (She was to associate this figure with her bill for analysis in that month: 3400 francs.) The earth has returned to the ice age. I am with a few survivors on a sledge, on a road that goes all round the world. The feeling is extraordinary, marvellous and rather idyllic. We are thrilled. It is like skiing on soft, smooth snow." She had another dream that same night. She

> was with her friend, Lewis. They were climbing a staircase. They reached the top of a cliff overhanging the sea. He wanted to push her into the sea. She was frightened and fascinated. Then the scene changed. They were in an apartment. She was to introduce him to her mother. Lying in a bath, someone was stretched out in the water. She wondered how this person managed to breathe. (p. 511)

Chasseguet-Smirgel interprets the first dream as showing "the desire to return to the smooth belly of the mother-analyst by destroying all the obstacles (the catastrophe of the end of the world, leaving her alone with 34,000 people who represent the analyst, identified with Mother Earth and now totally accessible. It is possible to go all round it on a sledge with a feeling of perfect elation)" (pp. 511–512). The second dream, involving falling into the sea and the person in the bathwater, again evokes the idea of a return to the intrauterine state. Of note is the devastation and frigidity of the Earth in the first dream, underscoring the infertility of this regressive union. As Franca seems to know, in reality this kind of fusion with the maternal object can never be a satisfying or productive one; like Persephone who descends into the earth to Hades, bringing on endless winter, Franca's regression to the womb has brought on an ice age.

PROJECTIVE DEFENSES AGAINST ENVY: ATTACKS ON PROCREATIVITY AND GENERATIVITY

In contrast to greed and the incorporative fantasies that it generates in order to repress the sense of loss, envy is likely to be experienced most acutely in the context of awareness of loss or of the separateness of the object (Spillius, 1997, p. 150). This unwanted awareness is particularly likely when the capacity to tolerate the frustration associated with such loss was not well developed in infancy and childhood. To revisit Klein's definition cited above, the response to such loss is the envious impulse "to put badness, primarily bad excrements and bad parts of the self, into the mother, and first of all into her breast, in order to spoil and destroy her" (1957/1995, p. 181). Such naked aggression is, of course, unbearable to the superego, which splits the badness off such that it is now experienced, as implied in Klein's definition, as being *in* and coming *from* the mother. Below I analyze the projective aspect of womb envy in two settings: (a) as it emerges for the child in the context of the mother's subsequent pregnancies, and which may be reactivated in adulthood by one's own or one's spouse's pregnancy, and (b) in the context of the mother–daughter relationship.

Attacks on the Mother's Pregnant Uterus

One of the most potent sources of the envious impulse, as suggested in the discussion of Freud above, comes from the child's suspicion of the mother's pregnancy. In response to this potentially catastrophic event, the child may seek, in fantasy, to destroy the baby in the mother's belly and reclaim that primordial territory for him or herself (Volkan & Ast, 1997). Since the fantasied murder of the fetus might also harm the mother, the child often becomes extremely anxious. His or her anxiety is bound by displacement of the womb onto specific concrete representations, such as closed spaces. The child then develops a fear of closed spaces, or claustrophobia. As an adult, the neurotic conflict associated with the claustrophobia may be exacerbated by one's own or one's spouse's pregnancy, insofar as it recalls the childhood trauma.

In this fantasy, both incorporative and projective defenses against envy are at work. By staying away from the closed space, the claustrophobic child avoids the womb with the fetus that is now the source of the child's projected aggression. This displacement and projection, and the associated avoidant behavior, permit the fantasy of greedily or incorporatively repossessing the womb to live on in the unconscious mind. Another important feature of this fantasy is the interplay between envy and jealousy. The intrusion of a potential third party in the form of the mother's pregnancy evokes an intense incipient jealousy, such that the reoccupation fantasy may represent both an oedipally driven attack on the third object as well as the more preoedipal attempt to reacquire or fuse with the sheltering space of the womb.

The case of Stewart, described by Volkan and Ast, is illustrative. Stewart had severe sibling rivalry with a 3-year younger brother, rooted in early neglect by both parents. Stewart did not have claustrophobia as a child but developed it in adulthood at the time his wife gave birth to their second son, their first child being 3 years old at the time. He developed homicidal thoughts about killing the 3-year-old, and he became very afraid every time his 3-year-old touched the infant. After a pleasurable day in the park with his son, Stewart daydreamed of the son swimming in a pond and having fun; but this daydream was followed by a second daydream in which he pushed his son into the pond and then dove into it to rescue him.

> [I]t was Stewart, as a 3-year-old child, who wanted to swim—in his mother's belly ... and not allow his brother to enter it. He felt guilty and the pleasurable feelings gave way to his directing murderous aggression toward his son, who represented himself as a murderous youngster.

In this example, Volkan and Ast represent the murderous aggression as a jealous rivalry with the brother displaced onto the son, but one wonders if that aggression was not also directed, enviously, at his mother herself, for daring to disturb Stewart's exclusive claim to her by becoming pregnant, and in the displacement, at his wife, whose pregnancy stirred up the original trauma. At this point in the analysis, Stewart began to dream of a closet covered with vines. One night, Stewart in his dream actually entered the closet-womb, finding it dark and moist inside. He found something that looked like a fetus in the water, but when he picked it up, it turned into a hand that grabbed his own hand. Stewart, in the dream, felt that the hand belonged to Robert Redford, an association that recalled the Redford directed movie, *A River Runs Through It*, which is about the relationship between two brothers and the death of the younger one. (Moreover, Stewart's younger brother was nicknamed Red, and drove a red Ford.) Stewart had directed both his envious attack on his mother's procreativity and his jealous rage toward his brother onto his mother's (and wife's) womb and the fetus within it. In his dream, he carried out both of these attacks. Through his analytic work, Stewart was able to reintroject this aggression and come to terms with both his envy and his jealousy. His claustrophobic symptoms disappeared (Volkan & Ast, 1997, pp. 36–39).

Attacks by the Mother on the Daughter's Fertility

Envy rooted in fears and fantasies about the womb may be an underlying dynamic shaping the relationship between mother and daughter. The young girl who has for so long envied her mother's capacity to bear children often becomes a pubescent young woman just as her mother enters menopause. That she now possesses the fertility, and increasingly, the beauty that accompanies it, may be a source of confusion to the girl-woman who still carries within her the envious sense of lack in comparison to her mother. This lack gets projected into the mother who, as fairy tales show, is now experienced as the womb-envious one. (And the mother, needless to say, may be all too willing to step into that role.) In the story of Snow White, when the queen's mirror tells her that her stepdaughter is now the "fairest of them all," the queen becomes narcissistically enraged and dispatches a hunter with orders to kill Snow White. As proof that she is dead, the hunter is ordered to cut out Snow White's lungs and liver—organs that are anatomically very close to the real source of threat, Snow White's now fertile uterus—and bring them back to the queen (B. Seelig, personal communication, 2003). In some versions of the fairy tale, the wicked queen *eats* the dissected organs, attempting to incorporate into herself the envied fertility of the younger woman (Bettelheim, 1977, p. 207). Seelig draws on Greek mythology, in particular the competitive relationship between Athena and junior female rivals for the attention and patronage of Zeus, to stress the triadic dimension of this envy between mother and daughter (2002).

This dynamic emerged in the transference with Ms. C, a woman in her mid-30s with a history of severe anorexia and bulimia. She had one

3-year-old child, with whom she and her husband had a very loving relationship, but efforts to have a second child had resulted in a series of miscarriages. Now she and her husband had decided to divorce, and in one particularly emotional session, she confessed that she had recently begun to purge again, three to five times per day. As she was describing her relapse, I raised the issue of hospitalization, not for the first time, but more emphatically than before. Ms. C's initial response was a firm refusal. She had her child to care for, professional obligations, and a prior hospitalization for anorexia in her adolescent years that was associated with humiliating memories. Moreover, her mother, who had bipolar disorder, had been in and out of psychiatric hospitals since Ms. C's early childhood. Ms. C returned to the next session with a dream featuring a woman doctor, represented by her father's new girlfriend, E., who in reality was a physician who was only a few years older than herself. In the dream the doctor was attempting a novel cure for a "detached backbone" by literally stringing her young female patient up, at her umbilicus, "the center point," on a chandelier, "which shone light into the patient's belly and showed all these diseased parts that needed to be cut out. … I could see this doctor's hands, hanging the little thing up, and everyone was really proud of her, telling her what a great doctor she was," Ms. C stated.

Among her many associations to the dream, she said, finally, "you remind me of E." She had talked much about E., a detested rival, and I had anticipated her identification of me with E., but for some reason, at this moment, I felt mildly anxious about the aggression in the dream and did not know what to say. Although it was the end of the session, it was uncharacteristic of me not to comment immediately and directly on a negative transference. I thought about my own conscious and possible unconscious identifications and, in the next day's session, we began to explore her feelings about me as E. Interpretation of the dream, in particular her fear that her father would give me all the credit for her cure, became the point of departure for further discussion of hospitalization. It led in subsequent sessions to deeper analysis of her identification with and rage toward her mother. Eventually, Ms. C made the decision to be hospitalized.

THE SUBLIMATION OF WOMB ENVY IN THE ANALYTIC SETTING

Yet another manifestation of womb envy is its sublimation into scientific and cultural achievements. Among these achievements, certainly, is the scientific work of psychoanalysis, above all the discovery and exploration of the most internal and hidden aspect of the human mind, the unconscious. Freud understood the primitive, instinctual forces within the unconscious as urges that press *"to restore an earlier state of things"* (1920/1955, p. 57, emphasis in original). His fascination with and compulsion to understand the unconscious, *inside* of things, as well as the conscious mental apparatus that "must lie on the borderline between inside and outside" (1920/1955, p. 24), was the driving force behind his career.

Of particular importance clinically is Freud's re-creation of the womb in the analytic situation. The essence of this situation is the provision of an interior space for the analysand, which the analyst is at once directly connected to and yet unequivocally on the outside of. "To have created such an instrument of investigation may well be looked upon as the most important stroke of Freud's genius" (Macalpine, 1950, p. 526).

Several aspects of the analytic situation recapitulate the womblike worlds of both pre- and postnatal life. First, the analyst's office itself may be regarded as a protective womb, isolated from the external world. This environment is constant, and it is spare, creating a soothing ambience that stirs the analysand's fantasy of rediscovering and having free access to a "smooth universe without obstacles, roughness, or differences, identified with a mother's insides" (Chasseguet-Smirgel, 1986, p. 30). Second, the analytic couch, an extension of the analyst's lap, is a kind of umbilical connection. Sitting behind the couch, the analyst literally sees the patient protruding into the foreground at the level of the abdomen. Indeed, the analysis itself may be regarded as a prolonged gestation. The analyst as well as the analysand must wait and watch the relationship slowly unfold.

Third, the analyst's interpretations can be regarded as functioning as a sort of placenta through which the analysand's experiences are filtered. This communication is only formally created by the explicit verbal content of the analyst's comments. Its structure grows out of the analyst's "evenly suspended attention" and is enriched and defined emotionally by intonations and a multiplicity of preverbal and subverbal exchanges. As Chasseguet-Smirgel asks about the communication between analyst and analysand, "is it not the umbilical cord, the prototype of every immediate and absolute relationship?" (1986, p. 33).

The womblike setting of analysis is not an inoculation, however, against womb envy in the countertransference. The transference may at times be, as Anna Freud stated, an "intrusive foreign body" for the analysand (A. Freud, 1937/1966, p. 19), especially in the acute phases of the transference neurosis, but it will also inevitably feel that way in the countertransference for the analyst who is uncomfortable with his or her deepest infantile wishes. No matter how diligent the analyst is, he or she may unconsciously resent and sabotage the inhabitants of the analytic "womb" unless his or her own analysis has dealt with the primordial envious urges alternatively to destroy or to seek to fuse with the maternal imago (Chasseguet-Smirgel, 1986, p. 40). By contrast, the analyst who has worked through his or her own womb envy has achieved the psychological equivalent of the immunologic suppression of the pregnant mother, enabling the "intrusive foreign body" to be accepted and worked through, such that the analytic gestation itself is much less likely to be aborted.

ACKNOWLEDGMENTS

I would like to acknowledge the helpful comments of Beth J. Seelig, M.D., Burness E. Moore, MD, and Nancy Kulish, PhD, on an earlier version of this essay as well as time generously afforded for its research during a psychiatry rotation at Emory University under the directorship of Beth Seelig. Earlier versions of this essay, which won the runner-up Affiliates' Council Scientific Paper Prize of the American Psychoanalytic Association (APsaA) and the Julian Gomez Award of the Atlanta Psychoanalytic Society (APS), were presented in meetings of the APsaA in San Francisco in June 2004 and the APS in Atlanta in May 2003.

REFERENCES

Balsam, R. (2003). The vanished pregnant body in psychoanalytic female developmental theory. *Journal of American Psychoanalytic Association, 51,* 1153–1179.

Barth, B. (1990). Die Darstellung der weiblichen Sexualitat als Ausdruck mannlichen Uterusneides und dessen Abwehr. *Jahrbuch der Psychoanalyse, 26,* 64–101.

Beckmann, C., Ling, F., Barzansky, B., Bates, G., Herbert, W., Laube, D., et al. (1995). *Obstetrics and gynecology* (2nd ed.). Baltimore: Williams & Wilkins.

Bernstein, D. (1990). Female genital anxieties, conflicts and typical mastery modes. *International Journal of Psycho-analysis, 71,* 151–165.

Bettelheim, B. (1954). *Symbolic wounds.* Glencoe, IL: Free Press.

Bettelheim, B. (1977). *The uses of enchantment.* New York: Vintage Books.

Blos, P. (1962). *On adolescence.* Glencoe, IL: Free Press.

Boehm, F. (1930). The femininity-complex in men. *International Journal of Psycho-Analysis, 11,* 444–469.

Chasseguet-Smirgel, J. (1986). *Sexuality and mind.* New York: New York University Press.

Chasseguet-Smirgel, J. (1988). From the archaic matrix of the Oedipus complex to the fully developed Oedipus complex—Theoretical perspective in relation to clinical experience and technique. *Psychoanalytic Quarterly, 57,* 505–527.

Chodorow, N. (1996). Theoretical gender and clinical gender: Epistemological reflections on the psychology of women. *Journal of American Psychoanalytic Association, 44* (Suppl.), 215–238.

Chodorow, N. (2000). *Feminism and psychoanalytic theory.* New Haven, CT: Yale University Press.

Dinnerstein, D. (1976). *The mermaid and the minatour: Sexual arrangements and human malaise.* New York: Harper & Row.

Erikson, E. (1968). *Identity: Youth and crisis.* New York: Norton.

Fast, I. (1978). Developments in gender identity. *International Review of Psycho-analysis, 5,* 265–273.

Ferenczi, S. (1968). *Thalassa: A theory of genitality.* New York: W. W. Norton.

Fogel, G. (1998). Interiority and inner genital space in men: What else can be lost in castration. *Psychoanalytic Quarterly, 67,* 662–697.

Freud, A. (1937/1966). *The ego and the mechanisms of defense.* New York: International Universities Press.

Freud, S. (1905/1953). Three essays on the theory of sexuality. In *Standard Edition* (Vol. 7, pp. 135—243). London: Hogarth Press.

Freud, S. (1908/1959). On the sexual theories of children. In *Standard Edition* (Vol. 9, pp. 209—226). London: Hogarth Press.

Freud, S. (1909a/1955). Analysis of a phobia in a five-year-old boy. In *Standard Edition* (Vol. 10, pp. 5—149). London: Hogarth Press.

Freud, S. (1909b/1955). Notes upon a case of obsessional neurosis. In *Standard Edition* (Vol. 10, pp. 155—249). London: Hogarth Press.

Freud, S. (1910a/1957). Leonardo da Vinci and a memory of his childhood. In *Standard Edition* (Vol. 11, pp. 63—137). London: Hogarth Press.

Freud, S. (1910b/1957). A special type of object choice made by men. In *Standard Edition* (Vol. 11, pp. 165—175). London: Hogarth Press.

Freud, S. (1911/1958). Psycho-analytic notes on an autobiographical account of a case of paranoia (dementia paranoides). In *Standard Edition* (Vol. 12, pp. 12—82). London: Hogarth Press.

Freud, S. (1920/1955). Beyond the pleasure principle. In *Standard Edition* (Vol. 18, pp. 7–64). London: Hogarth Press.

Freud, S. (1921/1955). Group psychology and analysis of the ego. In *Standard Edition* (Vol. 18, pp. 69—143). London: Hogarth Press.

Freud, S. (1924/1961). The dissolution of the Oedipus complex. In *Standard Edition* (Vol. 19, pp. 173—179). London: Hogarth Press.

Freud, S. (1925/1961). Some psychical consequences of the anatomical distinction between the sexes. In *Standard Edition* (Vol. 19, pp. 248—258). London: Hogarth Press.

Freud, S. (1931/1961). Female sexuality. In *Standard Edition* (Vol. 21, pp. 225—243). London: Hogarth Press.

Freud, S. (1935/1964). Femininity. In *Standard Edition* (Vol. 22, pp. 112–135). London: Hogarth Press.

Horney, K. (1926/1967). The flight from womanhood. In H. Kelman (Ed.), *Feminine psychology* (pp. 54–70). New York: W. W. Norton.

Horney, K. (1932/1967). The dread of woman. In H. Kelman (Ed.), *Feminine psychology* (pp. 133–146). New York: W. W. Norton.

Horney, K. (1933/1967). The denial of the vagina. In H. Kelman (Ed.), *Feminine psychology* (pp. 147–161). New York: W. W. Norton.

Hrdy, S. (1981). *The woman that never evolved*. Cambridge: Harvard University Press.

Hrdy, S. (1999). *Mother nature: A history of mothers, infants, and natural selection*. New York: Pantheon Books.

Jacobson, E. (1950). Development of the wish for a child in boys. In *The psychoanalytic study of the child* (Vol. 5, pp. 139–152).

Kernberg, O. (1995). *Love relations: Normality and pathology.* New Haven, CT: Yale University Press.

Kestenberg, J. (1982). Inner-genital phase: Prephallic and preoedipal. In D. Mendell (Ed.), *Early female development* (pp. 81–125). New York: Spectrum.

Kestenberg, J. (1991). Two-and-a-half to four years: from disequilibrium to integration. In S. Greenspan & G. Pollock (Eds.), *The course of life: Middle and late childhood* (Vol. 3, pp. 25–51). Madison, CT: International Universities Press.

Kitzinger, S. (1985). *Woman's experience of sex*. New York: Penguin Books.

Klein, M. (1928/1992). Early stages of the oedipus complex. In *The writings of Melanie Klein: Love, guilt, and reparation and other works 1921–1945* (Vol. 1, pp. 186–218). London: Karnac Books.

Klein, M. (1957/1993). Envy and gratitude. In *The writings of Melanie Klein: Envy and gratitude and other works 1946–1963* (Vol. 3, pp. 176–235). London: Karnac Books.

Kubie, L. (1974). The drive to become both sexes. *Psychoanalytic Quarterly, 43,* 349–426.

Kulish, N. (1991). The mental representation of the clitoris: The fear of female sexuality. *Psychoanalytic Inquiry, 11,* 511–536.

Lax, R. (1969). Some considerations about transference and countertransference: Manifestations evoked by the analyst's pregnancy. *International Journal of Psycho-Analysis, 50,* 363–372.

Lax, R. (1997). Boys' envy of mother and the consequences of this narcissistic mortification. *Psychoanalytic Study of the Child, 52,* 118–139.

LeVay, S., & Valente, M. (2006). *Human sexuality* (2nd ed.). Sunderland, MA: Sinauer Associates.

Macalpine, I. (1950). The development of the transference. *Psychoanalytic Quarterly, 19,* 501–539.

Mayer, E. (1985). "Everybody must be just like me": Observations on female castration anxiety. *International Journal of Psycho-analysis, 66,* 331–347.

Meissner, W. W. (1971). Notes on identification–Ii. Clarification of related concepts. *Psychoanalytic Quarterly, 40,* 277–302.

Meltzer, D., & Williams, M. H. (1988). *The apprehension of beauty: The relationship of aesthetic conflict in development, violence and art.* Old Ballechin, Strath Tay: Clunie Press.

Montgrain, N. (1983). On the vicissitudes of female sexuality. *International Journal of Psycho-analysis, 64,* 169–186.

Moore, B. (1968). Psychoanalytic reflections on the implications of recent physiological studies of female orgasm. *Journal of American Psychoanalytic Association, 16,* 569–587.

Moore, B. (1977). Psychic representation and female orgasm. In H. Blum (Ed.), *Female psychology* (pp. 305–330). New York: International Universities Press.

Nasio, J. (1998). *Hysteria from Freud to Lacan: The splendid child of psychoanalysis.* New York: Other Press.

Otero, S. (1996). "Fearing our mothers": An overview of the psychoanalytic theories concerning the *vagina dentata* motif F547.1.1. *American Journal of Psychoanalysis, 56,* 269–288.

Oxford English Dictionary(2nd ed.). (1989). Oxford: Clarendon Press.

Parens, H. (1990). On the girl's psychosexual development. *Journal of American Psychoanalytic Association, 38,* 743–772.

Richards, A. K. (1992). The influence of sphincter control and genital sensation on body image and gender identity in women. *Psychoanalytic Quarterly, 61,* 331–351.

Richards, A. K. (1996). Primary femininity and female genital anxiety. *Journal of American Psychoanalytic Association, 44* (Suppl.), 261–281.

Robbins, M. (1996). Nature, nurture, and core gender identity. *Journal of American Psychoanalytic Association, 44* (Suppl.), 93–117.

Seelig, B. (2002). The rape of Medusa in the temple of Athena. *International journal of Psycho-analysis, 83,* 895–911.

Spillius, E. (1997). Varieties of envious experience. In R. Schafer (Ed.), *The contemporary Kleinians of London* (pp. 143–179). Madison, WI: International Universities Press.

Stoller, R. (1964). A contribution to the study of gender identity. *International Journal of Psycho-analysis, 45,* 220–226.

Stoller, R. (1968). *Sex and gender: On the development of masculinity and femininity.* New York: Science House.

Trible, P. (1978). *God and the rhetoric of sexuality.* Philadelphia: Fortress Press.

Veith, I. (1965). *Hysteria: The history of a disease.* Chicago: University of Chicago Press.

Volkan, V., & Ast, G. (1997). *Siblings in the unconscious and psychopathology: Womb fantasies, claustrophobias, fear of pregnancy, murderous rage, animal symbolism, Christmas and Easter neuroses, and twinnings or identification with sisters and brothers.* Madison, WI: International Universities Press.

Webster's Third New International Dictionary of the English Language. (1993). Springfield, MA: Merriam-Webster.

Zilboorg, G. (1944). Masculine and feminine. *Psychiatry, 7,* 257–296.

4

Of Woman Born
Womb Envy and the Male Project of Self-Creation

PETER SHABAD

FROM PRIVATE TO PUBLIC: MEN AND THEIR SYMBOLIC RE-BIRTH

For a long time now, I have been intrigued by how the biblical account of Eve emerging from Adam's rib is a blatant reversal of the biological facts. In the history of humankind we can only imagine how many Adams were born of Eves—not to mention Matthews from Sarahs and Johns from Marthas, and so on. On the basis of the prima facie evidence, man is born of woman and not the other way around.

It is not a simple task for men to face the fact that in the most elemental, procreative sense, as sons, they are mere creatures who are indebted for their emergent life to their mothers, woman the creator. Although, of course, men, too, contribute to the procreative process, it is also true that most immediately, most viscerally, and most visibly for all eyes to see, the miracle of creation has its source in woman. Slater (1968) put it this way:

> A woman holds her immortality within herself; who impregnates her is of little importance in this respect. She need not guess whether something of herself continues on in a new organism—she can see the child emerge from her own body. (p. 234)

Lax (1997) points out that boys do not usually learn of the father's role in procreation until after they discover that they do not possess a womb with which to produce babies. In his narrative of the case of Little Hans, Freud (1909/1955) recounts Hans's poignantly doomed wish to be included in the procreative drama by becoming pregnant instead of his mother. Years later, Freud (1920/1955) notes again how the boy's "own attempt to make a baby himself, carried out with tragic seriousness, fails shamefully" (p. 21).

It is often said that men have far more power than women. I would qualify that statement by saying that men have always had more *public* power, whereas women, in their role as mothers, wield an enormous amount of private power. Even in the most patriarchal of households, when the father "cat" is away, the mother "mouse" will play. While fathers are away from home, mothers exert an unacknowledged, yet profound, influence on their children. Indeed, if we were to take Freud's thinking on the unconscious truly seriously, we would say that this maternal influence on the child is profound precisely because it is unacknowledged, that is, unconscious. Inasmuch as the mother insinuates herself into the child's psyche unconsciously, she wields a power of demonic intensity, untamed by the child's consciousness. In this most private of realms, the mother reigns as the queenly creator and shaper of human worlds. Bettelheim (1954/1962) thus declares "We are hardly in need of proof that men stand in awe of the procreative power of woman" (p. 10).

Perhaps it is this procreative power of the mother that prompted Klein (1957), in part, to posit the infant's primary envy of the contents of the mother's breast. Although Klein suggests that the infant's envy is provoked by its inevitable dependence on the life-sustaining contents of the mother's breast, the child's sense of helplessness and smallness contributes more generally to an awe of the mother's power to give or to take away life. Whereas both sons and daughters may feel initially dwarfed by the mother's procreative power, girls may already sense early in life that the creative potentiality of motherhood is open to them in the future. Sons, on the other hand, are left to emerge from under the biological insecurity of being a mere creature, born of someone unlike themselves. In order to find a transcendent place within the cosmological scheme of things, men must struggle restlessly in their search for creative meaning.

A major thesis of this essay then is that the existential fact of being born of a woman has had a primary psychological and cultural impact on the male quest for significance in the eyes of the cosmos. From Otto Rank's (1941) perspective, men have always sought to deny that they are born of woman in order to keep their mortality at bay. He states:

> Man born of woman never accepted this basic fact of being mortal, that is, never accepted himself. Hence, his basic psychology is denial of his mortal origin and a subsequent need to change himself in order to find his real self which he rationalized as independent of woman. (pp. 248–249)

Mead (1949) suggests that boys become men through initiation rites in which the original birth of a woman is undone by a symbolic rebirth that is provided by older men. Bettelheim (1954/1962) also asserts that in preliterate cultures, boys who have previously lived within the maternal domain are given a symbolic death via initiation rites, so that they can be given a symbolic rebirth that has been effected by men. Lederer (1968) notes how the members of innumerable male societies from around the world do not

> consider a man properly born until he be reborn from a man, and his womanish origin superceded. The rebirth occurs at initiation ceremonies or rites of passage, some of which clearly imply not just the rebirth of the boy into the world of men, but a prior undoing of his birth from women. (p. 155)

Often, this transition from the maternal to the man-made is also a journey from the private realm (where the mother reigns supreme) to the public sphere (where everything can become potentially *man-made*). The creations in the public sphere of culture, far away from the rival creative influences of motherhood, may be viewed as man's attempt to compensate for his biological lack and create an enduring monument of creative significance in his own right. Rank (1941) states:

> Herein is to be found the dynamic drive for man's religious, social and artistic creativity through which he not only proves his supernatural origin (religion) and capacity (art) but also tries to translate it into practical terms of social organization (state, government). (p. 236)

Rank (1941) suggests that whereas once there was a universal veneration of female creativity, increasingly, man's need to eternalize his own personality makes him render woman evil, dangerous, and less valuable. Indeed, Lederer (1968) states that "men always claimed that both sex and death were initiated by the mother (Eve), and thus the earthy, biological, sexual cycle-of-life-and-death immortality was a feminine scheme" (p. 167). In what he calls "The Great Reversal," in which the supremacy of female goddesses gave way to male gods, Lederer speculates that there was a "turning away from the needs of sexual reproduction and life, and the turning towards an absorbing preoccupation with individual immortality" (p. 159).

REWRITING ONE'S BEGINNINGS: THE CAUSA-SUI INTERPRETATION OF THE OEDIPUS COMPLEX

The need to become a self-perpetuating creator in one's own eyes and to deny one's creaturely beginnings in the mother's womb is illustrated by the *causa-sui* (self-creation) interpretation of the Oedipus complex. Whereas Freud emphasized the sexual needs of the son as primal in and of themselves, the causa-sui interpretation of the Oedipus complex suggests that the little boy has a fantasy of being a self-created immortal superman of heroic proportions. This view of the Oedipus complex as a project with the aim of creating oneself was first described by Norman O. Brown (1959) in his book *Life Against Death*. According to Brown, "the essence of the Oedipal complex is the project of becoming God—in Spinoza's formula *causa-sui* (self-creation)" (p. 118). Becker (1973) extended this concept when he suggested that a primary goal of the causa-sui fantasy is to turn the helplessness of being a small, mortal creature into the active potency of a godlike creator by becoming father to oneself. Freud (1910/1957) himself was alert to this aspect of the Oedipus complex when in speaking of the small boy, he wrote, "All his instincts, those of tenderness, gratitude, lustfulness, defiance and independence, find satisfaction in the single wish to be *his own father*" (p. 173, emphasis in original).

The aims of causa-sui are bred in fantasy precisely because in order to straddle two generations and thus defeat one's finitude, one must magically transcend one's physical limitations. In this sense, the fantasized quality of causa-sui is also an attempt to combat the helplessness of remaining imprisoned in a body hurdling toward a destined appointment with its death. And because the hour of one's birth is also the hour of one's death, one must somehow rewrite the story of one's beginning in order to alter the course of one's destiny. Like Freud's (1908/1959) concept of the family romance, Rank (1909) points out how in various myths of the birth of heroes like Moses, Romulus, Oedipus, and Gilgamesh there are certain themes that repeat themselves: the infant often is exposed and abandoned, and there are always two sets of parents: the ordinary parents who are present and a set of more noble, and sometimes divine parents, who are hidden and waiting to be discovered.

The causa-sui project can then only take on validity if the rival story of being born of one's ordinary parents is discredited. The little boy must tear asunder the image of the primal scene and recast the relative contributions of its characters. In this causa-sui version of the oedipal drama, by eliminating the father, the boy casts himself as *both* father and son. In the imagined role of father, the boy can then impregnate the fertile material (*mater*) of mother and become creator of his own life.

This rewriting of the origins of one's life may be viewed as a form of reconceiving oneself, whereby one gives oneself a new identity and new name. This sort of phenomenon is especially evident in professions that are constructed in the refracted image of the public eye, such as show business and politics. For example, Cary Grant was originally Archibald Leach, Tony Curtis was Bernie Schwartz, and Kirk Douglas was Issur Danielovich Demsky. During the 1984 Democratic primary campaign for president, there was a political controversy when it was discovered that Gary Hart's real name had been changed from his given name of Gary Hartpence. In all of these examples, public figures have attempted to reinvent themselves by transforming the creaturely shame of an ordinary identity into the extraordinariness of a self-created public persona.

However, from the little boy's perspective, the journey toward self-creation is only initiated by the elimination of his father. After all, once his father is out of the way, looming before him is the imposing omniscient figure of a mother who holds within herself the mysteries of creation he wishes to claim as his own. In order to change this mother creator into what the Jungian analyst Erich Neumann (1954) calls a "magic vessel" of fertile material, he must embark on a journey of conquest. The would-be oedipal hero must find a way of taming the fiery passions of the mother-dragon who jealously guards the secrets of her power and of rendering her active creative majesty into an accessible receptivity. Here, Lederer (1968) suggests that in various rites of passage, in order for men to undo being born of a woman and to achieve their own heroic rebirth, they must confront the intimidating source of their own beginnings. In referring to these initiation rites, Lederer states:

> These are the ceremonies which force the boy to enter the gaping mouth of a dragon, to be swallowed, killed and digested—as if the boy, by way of the *vagina dentata* of the mother through which he was born, were re-entering the womb and reversing the whole process of his gestation. (p. 155)

THE RIDDLE OF THE SPHINX: COMING TO "KNOW" THE MYSTERY OF CREATION

This dilemma of facing down the powerful creator-mother throws the riddle of the Sphinx, an often-neglected aspect of the Oedipus complex, into bold relief. Whereas Freud placed the problem of incest at the center of the Oedipus story, Thass-Thienemann (1973) suggests that if the riddle is taken into account, the story centers around the theme of knowledge of one's own identity. I would add that the chronology of the story, whereby Oedipus solves the riddle of the Sphinx before marrying his mother, is significant to its understanding. Oedipus's ability to solve the riddle enables him to achieve sufficient self-respect and confidence in his own creative potency as a male so that he dares to have incest with Jocasta. Instead of just being content with a symbolic penetration of the Sphinx/mother, however, Oedipus literally breaks the incest taboo by having sexual intercourse with his mother. In turning the orderly progression of generational perpetuation topsy-turvy, he is tampering with the divine power of the gods. For that Promethean crime he strikes himself blind. Ultimately, Oedipus's self-blinding becomes a means of forcing himself to look inside and achieve insight into the mortal limitations of his human condition.

The Sphinx is a man-eating monster with the hybrid features of a female upper body and an animal lower body. Various sources have viewed the Sphinx as a sitting Mother Earth figure jealously guarding the treasures of her creative mystery that lay deep within the bowels of the Earth. In the Sophocles version of the Oedipus story, the whole land has been brought to a standstill because each man who has attempted to solve the Sphinx's riddle in order to get past her well-guarded gates has failed, and then has lost his life to her. Thass-Thienemann (1973) points out that Sphinx is a derivative of the Greek *sphingo*, to "bind tight, bind fast," which he believes refers to her "strangling" attribute.

I am reminded here of some pregnant mothers who "jealously guard" the treasures of new life that lie within and may be reluctant to release that life to the outside world. There have been some recent incidents in the news in which mothers such as Susan Smith and Andrea Yates, while suffering from postpartum illness, drowned their children. One might speculate that these women were attempting to live out a fantasy in which they, by "strangling" the budding lives of their children, attempted to tuck their "possessions" back into the watery womb where they believed they rightfully belonged. Interestingly enough, I have found in my research on the Evil Eye that the fear of the envious Evil Eye often entailed a fear of the strangulation of infants (Shabad, 2001). Oedipus's exposure to danger as an infant also dramatizes this vulnerability to the Sphinx/mother to give and to take back life.

In this sense, Bachofen (1861/1967) suggests that the Sphinx represents the dark aspect of the feminine as an inexorable law of death. Just as from dust we come and to dust we return, the feminine as a personification of nature sends matter from dark to light, but then will consume it again. It is significant that the Sphinx's victims are young men whom she seduces and then devours. Perhaps as long as the Sphinx holds on to her mysteries, men resemble unindividuated, impotent little boys who are always in danger of being reincorporated by the powerful mother. In order to undo the shame of being an inferior creature born of woman and attain some sense of dignity as creative human beings in their own right, men must find a way to modify their feelings of awe with respect to that power.

With this in mind then, here is the riddle of the Sphinx: "What walks on four legs in the morning, two at noon, and three at evening?" The answer to the solution to the riddle is *Man* because as an infant he crawls on all fours, then as an adult walks on two feet, and as an old man leans on a staff. As Child is Father to the Man, this solution to the riddle points to the equivalence of each generation in the fact of their passing. Bachofen (1861/1967) notes that "man is considered only in his transient aspect, mortality" (p. 181).

For Freud (1905/1953), the riddle reflects the question of where babies come from and thus gives birth to the instinct for knowledge. More generally, I would suggest that the riddle not only addresses the question of where babies come from, but also concerns the mystery of creation and the nature of being human. Perhaps fittingly then, from a Freudian viewpoint, it is only through the raising of Oedipus's consciousness, that is, by using his "male" rationality to solve the riddle of a biologically determined fate, that he can transcend the intergenerational code of man as creature, at least in fantasy. Shengold (1963) believed that Oedipus's response to the riddle related to the theme of locomotion and separation from the mother. Perhaps we can say that it is precisely Oedipus's inability to "walk away" from the mother, due to the fact that his ankles were pierced and bound together in infancy, which forced him to use his wits to master the threat of being strangled by the Sphinx.

To solve the riddle of the Sphinx is to pry into the forbidden, sacred knowledge of creation. Roheim (1934) suggests that this secret forbidden knowledge of the Sphinx represents the primal scene that, of course, culminates in biological creation. In my view, however, the Sphinx does not represent the primal scene as much as she implicitly contains the primal scene as an intrinsic aspect of the created, new life inside of her.

Thass-Thienemann (1973) notes that "the Greek verb *oida* 'to swell,' to become swollen, refers to the specific character trait to be inflated" (p. 85). Rudnytsky (1986) writes that in addition to meaning "swollen foot," the first syllable of Oedipus also suggests the Greek word *oida* (I know), so the whole name can be read as "know-foot." He suggests that Oedipus's entire tragedy can be compressed in the double meanings of his name, in which "his pretensions to knowledge are mocked by the reminder of his identity as an exposed infant" (pp. 266–267). Oedipus, the solver of riddles, becomes inflated by his knowledge in both mind and body.

The ambiguity of whether we interpret Oedipus to mean swollen-foot or know-foot itself refers to the double meaning of acquiring carnal knowledge. For at one and the same time that Oedipus gains "swollen" entry to the Sphinx-mother, he is also swelling his head with knowledge of her inner mysteries. In this regard, Thass-Thienemann (1973) asserts that the genital act has been perceived primarily as a cognitive act throughout history.

These intertwinings of what it means "to know" already are apparent in the story of Genesis, where the wording in Hebrew connotes that Adam knew Eve his wife, and she conceived. Nikolova (1994), too, points out that the Greek verb *gignosko* means both "to know" and "to come in connection with somebody, to copulate" (p. 106). This meaning, however, is late Greek (New Testament) and probably derived from the Hebrew double meaning. An interesting corollary to the Oedipus story, a Sudanese proverb states: "A man who thinks he knows everything will finally marry his mother."

If we view Oedipus not merely as a story of incest and parricide, but as a causa-sui fantasy of self-creation, then we would view Oedipus's solving of the riddle of the Sphinx as nothing less than his Promethean attempt to dispossess her of her creative soul. Oedipus's envy of the Sphinx's womb is expressed in his attempt to turn her concealed mysteries inside out, thus rendering them impotent through their revelation. Perhaps significantly, once the riddle is solved and the power of her mystery is stolen, the Sphinx throws herself over a cliff.

TRANSFORMING MADONNA INTO WHORE: NAMING AND USURPING THE POWER TO CREATE

Through the use of reason rather than of sexual prowess, Oedipus's naming of the solution "man" in all his evolving phases of life breaks the stranglehold that the Sphinx has on the male creatures who serve her. By causing her to let go of her secret, to "give birth" as it were, he liberates the prisoners of the Sphinx's riddle from their immobilized state of constriction. In Shengold's (1963) words, this Sphinx/mother, "instead of devouring the weak, defeated challenger (re-establishing the symbiosis) ... hurls herself to her death and the child is rid of the symbiotic incubus" (p. 728).

The suicide of the Sphinx in reaction to the correct solution of her riddle is reminiscent of the Brothers Grimm fairy tale of "Rumpelstiltskin" (1847/1992). There, too, Rumpelstiltskin vanishes in a tantrum of mortification after his name is guessed correctly. To name something is not just a neutral act. On the contrary, the namer, by articulating the inchoate, is able to capture, define, and re-create the essence of that mystery in his own image. Freud (1913/1955) thus declares that "if one knows the name of a man or of a spirit, one has acquired a certain power over the owner of the name" (p. 81). Cassirer (1946) also adds that "the name does not merely denote but actually *is* the essence of its object" (p. 3, emphasis in the original).

In the talking cure of psychoanalysis, this same process of naming is used to profoundly constructive effect to dissolve the demonic power of the unconscious. By transforming what is part of a private space into something exposed and conscious, the analysis demystifies the potential destructiveness of an unconscious whose power depends on its anonymity. But can we take this instrument of naming and truth-seeking, even truth-creating, too far? Is there a risk of losing an awe or deep respect (*aidos* in Greek) for the sacred? In many religious traditions it is considered sacrilegious to represent the sacred too familiarly. In Hebrew the unspeakable represented by the tetragram "YHWH" was pronounced *Adonai* or my Lord. Did Oedipus learn that when he tampers with the creative mysteries of nature, all hell may literally break loose?

The riddle's solution of the "man" of different generations exposes the sexual need hidden in the lower animal half of the Sphinx's body. As Bachofen (1861/1967) stated, "each generation of men fecundates the maternal matter of earth" (p. 180). Bachofen thus views the meaning of Oedipus's swollen foot to be an embodiment of the male fertilizing principle. Oedipus exploits this opening to the Sphinx's secret weakness, her need of everyman to procreate, in order to gain knowledge and power over the riddles of creation.

Once the idealized mysteries of the madonna/mother have been solved and her creative extraordinariness has been rendered into the exposed ordinariness of a whore who will consort with the everyman of her riddle, she is subject to the will of man. In this sense, the technology-inspired unearthing—turning inside out—of the mysteries of Mother Nature parallels the reversal of Eve being born of Adam in the book of Genesis. Thass-Thienemann (1973) suggests that the biblical term "fruit of womb" identifies woman with the Tree of Knowledge. In biting into the forbidden fruit, man attempts to conquer woman by incorporating the power of creation. In Greek mythology, when Kronos eats his children and then regurgitates them, perhaps we can see man's attempt to forge the illusion of reconceiving creation in such a way where now he is the creator of his own progeny from the orifices of *his* body. Zeus, too, creates a number of the Olympian gods from his head, the seat of rationality.

In this regard, man uses his rationality as a means of reconceiving himself as creator in the public domain. The hubris of man's narcissistic inflation thus is reflected in the triumph of the causa-sui fantasy over the limits of the biological, in the victorious reversal of man the creator and woman his creature, and ultimately in the transcendence of the lasting symbols of scientific rationality over the naked transience of nature. Marie-Louise von Franz (1981) thus viewed the Greek cultivation of philosophy as an attempt to escape the concrete reality of the power of the mother. Von Franz's argument is buttressed by Slater's (1968) study of the Greek family, in which he suggests that Greek sons were both preoccupied with and fearful of the power of Greek mothers.

Psychoanalysis, too, has been based in the triumph of reason over passion and self-awareness over emotive action. In a scene that could have been lifted from the film *My Fair Lady* when Henry Higgins sings "Why can't a woman be more like a man?", the prototypical analytic dyad may be viewed as one in which the obsessional male analyst attempts to lift the consciousness of the histrionically emoting female analysand in order to create her in his own image of greater rationality. Bachofen (1861/1967) thus states that "In Oedipus, the male principle takes on independent significance side by side with the female" (p. 182).

Roheim (1934) suggests that by gaining knowledge into the mysteries of the Sphinx, Oedipus makes the transition of being a little boy born of woman to man as sexual conqueror. In this same regard, Shengold (1963) concludes: "By his deed Oedipus is awarded the city and his mother—symbol and the symbolized; that is, he can now have his mother, and need no longer be (part of) her" (p. 728). Neumann (1954) puts it this way:

> The hero's incest and the conquering of the Sphinx are identical, two sides of the same process. By conquering his terror of the female, by entering into the womb, the abyss, he weds himself triumphantly with the Great Mother who castrates the young men and with the Sphinx who destroys them. His heroism transforms him into a fully grown male. (pp. 162–163)

Although Nikolova (1994) asserts that the Sphinx and Jocasta are two sides of the same maternal essence—Jocasta is the genital aspect of the mother, whereas the Sphinx is the pregenital mother—we should not completely collapse the differences between the Sphinx and Jocasta. Whereas Oedipus conquers the Sphinx symbolically by use of his wits, thereby making the transition from little boy creature to self-respecting rational man, he then proceeds onward with the causa-sui project of becoming father to himself by having sexual relations with his mother. Perhaps in this sense, Oedipus's tragedy can be read in part as a cautionary tale about the corrupting, hubristic exploitation of the power of knowledge in its double meaning.

Looked at this way, the Oedipal victory of committing sublimated incest with one's mother in fantasy is an important initiation rite from boyhood to manhood. It marks a transition from the little boy's sense of bondage to the mother's powers to a life of creative self-determination in his own right. By sublimated incest, I mean an erotic and romantic tension between mother and son that is not terrorized out of imaginative existence by an excessively harsh incest taboo. This romantic tension is one in which the mother is accessible and receptive enough for her son to be able to emotionally penetrate her and derive some form of sustenance from the treasures that lay within her. The son's accessibility to the mother allows him to partake of her creative gifts and alleviates his shame of being only her creature, thereby reducing his envy of her womb.

SYMBIOTIC ANXIETY AND THE CONCEPT OF THE SUPERMAN

This need for access to the mother's insides highlights the importance of her generously sustaining her son's life. By sharing her inner space, she enables her son to partake in and identify with her creative power, thereby reducing womb envy. As Klein (1957) has pointed out, if she withholds that sustenance, she accentuates her son's greed, thus increasing his womb envy. This, in turn, can lead to rape fantasies in which the little boy wishes to forcibly penetrate and pillage her insides and grab what he believes is rightfully his.

Further, if the little boy is subject to the chronic humiliation of oedipal loss in which he is dwarfed by the father's stature in his mother's eyes (as is communicated in "wait 'til your father gets home"), his attempts to get inside the mother are blocked by the powers of the patriarch. Later in life, it is especially these humiliated men, stuck in unindividuated boyhood, who must find or invent whore women to overcome their sense of inferiority and feel like they are sexual conquerors. Or alternatively, if there is no father at all who is present to safeguard against the son's incorporation by his powerful mother, then the son may flee from the terror of feminine identification and have problems in intimacy with women. He may scrupulously avoid his own curiosity and any sublimated attempts to penetrate her mystery.

In this sense, if the mother remains inaccessible to the boy's fantasied causa-sui attempts to symbolically penetrate her insides and give birth to his own individuation, he may become filled with the symbiotic anxiety that he will never escape the shadow of a mother that dwells within. This anxiety may lead to compensatory attempts of narcissistic self-puffery in ever-more desperate and violent attempts to overcome the shame of the "parasitic" woman from whom one cannot separate. When men cannot overcome their sense of cosmic smallness by symbolically penetrating the mother, they may remain masochistic in relation to women who are perceived as madonna-like figures, and/or are ever-more desperate to invent whores and other displaced sexual and aggressive objects with whom they can feel larger than life.

With the causa-sui illusion of a self-manufactured oedipal victory, we see the narcissistic fantasy par excellence: a fantasy in which the young boy usurps his father's role and transforms his mother into the objectified conduit for his own self-perpetuation. He does not need the cycle of generations to transcend death, he has no need to yield a sacrificial toll to the previous generation via tradition; he is sole creator of his own life. Rudnytsky (1986, p. 265) thus notes that the effect of Oedipus's incest is to arrest the passage of time.

This self-styled superman has severed his biological dependency on woman and continues to prove his independence of her by not adhering to the ordinary laws of conscience. He who has dared to eat from the Tree of Knowledge of Good and Evil can now move to the beat of his own drummer, beyond good and evil. Nietzsche's (1885/1954) notion of a self-created *Ubermensch* (Overman) who is not bound by the "weakness" of Judeo-Christian morality also may be viewed as a defensive male attempt to move beyond the ever-lurking presence of woman the creator who shadows one's existence. Indeed, it is interesting to speculate with regard to the symbolism of the crucifixion, whether the symbiotic binding of Christ to the cross/mother was a sacrificial atonement to her Sphinx-like appetites for the "sin" of separation, thereby enabling others to separate from her and go on with their lives. For Nietzsche, this sacrifice and its accompanying Judeo-Christian morality is unnecessary for the self-creating superman because he does not acknowledge the symbiotic tie in the first place. As a biographical aside, it is interesting to note that Nietzsche grew up as the only boy in a family of women.

OF DOTING MOTHERS AND MURDEROUS SONS: FROM RASKOLNIKOV TO ANTI-SEMITISM

Dostoevsky's (1866/1993) character Raskolnikov in *Crime and Punishment* transforms the fantasy of a self-created superman who is beyond good and evil into murderous action. Not coincidentally, Raskolnikov is oppressed by the doting qualities and neediness of his mother and sister.

Early in the book we are introduced to the mother's intense feelings for her little boy in a letter she writes to her son:

> Rodya, you are everything to us—all our hope, and all our trust. If only you are happy, then we shall be happy. Do you pray to God, Rodya, as you used to, and do you believe in the goodness of our Creator and Redeemer? I fear in my heart that you have been visited by the fashionable new unbelief. ... Remember my dear, in your childhood, when your father was alive, how you prattled out your prayers sitting on my knee, and how happy we all were then! (p. 39)

It is clear from these lines how Raskolnikov's mother links her nostalgic memories of her innocent little boy "sitting on his mother's knee" to a moral sense of goodness. Did Raskolnikov feel he had to turn his back on his mother's Judeo-Christian morality and become an extraordinary self-made man to prove he was free of her? Perhaps a primary function of the concept of a "superman," like that of little boys dressing up in superhero outfits, is to imagine oneself as an extraordinary, self-created being who is not merely born of a woman. Conversely, we can discern the mother's suspiciousness of change and separation, her loss of control of her son, and that Raskolnikov is no longer her little Rodya, in her mistrust of the "fashionable new unbelief."

We see clearly in Raskolnikov's reaction to the letter that his feelings for his mother are not nearly so straightforward as his mother's seem to be for him: "Almost all the while he was reading, from the very beginning of the letter, Raskolnikov's face was wet with tears; but when he finished, it was pale, twisted convulsively, and a heavy, bilious spiteful smile wandered over his lips" (p. 39).

As part and parcel of his causa-sui project of creating himself anew, Raskolnikov fashions for himself a philosophy of being a superman who is beyond the laws of good and evil. This philosophy then serves as a justification for the murder of an old woman who is a pawnbroker (which significantly coincides with the image of the Jew as moneylender), and the pawnbroker's sister, who as witness to his crime, embodies the conscience he wishes to eradicate. Desperate to escape once and for all from his indebtedness to a symbiotic mother who clings to him for dear life, he murders a withholding, greedily parasitic pawnbroker (bad mother), ostensibly so he can steal money to give to his own "good" mother. The killing of the pawnbroker may be viewed as a displaced attempt of finally annihilating and escaping the haunting shadow of a mother he cannot seem to shake in any other way.

There are interesting echoes of this theme of mothers and murderous sons also in Alfred Hitchcock's film *Strangers on a Train*. Robert Walker's homicidal character calculatedly offers to swap murders with the lead character, which is rejected, but he cold-bloodedly proceeds with his part of the bargain by murdering the lead character's wife. In another fascinating scene, he becomes so overcome with rage at a babbling old woman he has never met before, he nearly strangles her before he faints. Significantly, when we are introduced to this murderer's mother, we meet an empty-headed chatterbox who seems blind to her son's dark side, and who like Raskolnikov's mother, is primarily attuned to the little boy in her adult son.

Indeed, when Raskolnikov struggles to reveal his crime to his mother, saying "I only wanted to say that I ask your forgiveness, mama," she replies: "Ah Rodya, there's no need; I'm sure everything you do is wonderful." He responds, "Don't be sure," as his mouth twists into a smile. After a few silent moments, he thinks to himself, in referring to his mother and sister, "I seemed to love them so much when they weren't here" (p. 227). Whereas Raskolnikov can idealize his mother and sister from a distance, when they get up close and it becomes clear to him that his mother is not attuned to the grown-up reality of his dark side, he finds their presence oppressive.

In another scene, Raskolnikov thus says to them:

> Whatever happens to me, whether I perish or not, I want to be alone. Forget me altogether. It's better. ... Don't make inquiries about me. When need be, I'll come myself, or ... send for you. Perhaps everything will rise again. ... But for now, if you love me, give in. ... Otherwise, I'll start hating you, I feel it. (p. 313)

Raskolnikov's need for his mother to take off her rose-colored glasses of denial and accept him as his own man, murderous warts and all, *not* just as her little boy, comes out clearly in the following exchange near the end of the book:

> "Mama, whatever happens, whatever you hear about me, whatever they tell you about me, will you still love me as you do now?" he asked suddenly, from the fullness of his heart as if not thinking about his words or weighing them. She then replies: "Rodya, Rodya, what's the matter with you? How can you ask me that! And who is going to tell me anything about you? No, I won't believe anyone at all, and whatever comes to me I'll simply chase away." (p. 514)

In many ways, Raskolnikov's murder of the old pawnbroker woman—perhaps because he was not able to penetrate her stubborn inaccessibility—ingeniously anticipates the attitudes of Nazi ideology toward the Jews many years later. Hitler, himself, slept under a portrait of his idealized mother wherever he went. Again, someone else—other whores and their symbolic equivalents—had to pay a heavy price for his whitewashing of his mother of all sin. Given that Jews were forced into the job of usury throughout European history and, as a result, took on the image of parasitic moneylenders, we may be able to see a symbolic equivalence in the perception of symbiotically clinging mother and money-lending Jew. Not coincidentally, Raskolnikov's superman ideology anticipates the Nazi concept of the Aryan superman, who in his idealized racial purity, has also freed himself of all contaminants.

In his book *Male Fantasies*, the German writer Klaus Theweleit (1978/1987) examines the fantasies of right-wing German storm troopers immediately following World War I. He suggests that the overflowing, soft, fluid liquid of the female body was viewed as a negative other that the storm troopers feared existed inside themselves. These men, who Theweleit insightfully refers to as the *not fully born*, were hell-bent on transforming the feared softness of their bodies into the hardness of a bodily armor. This fascistic idealization of hardness thus defends against the threat of being devoured by the symbiotic mother who forever lurks within. As in *Crime and Punishment*, the danger of this symbiotic mother is externalized; now in the image of the alien, parasitic Jews who live off the German host nation and in the flooding contagion of Judeo-Bolshevism, as well as in the "mongrel" mix of male and female in the male homosexual.

In this regard, it is worth speculating whether homophobia has less to do with the image of two men having sex and more to do with the fear of effeminacy. Effeminacy is embarrassingly manifest proof that one has not been able to separate from the mother of whom one was born and give rebirth to oneself as a man. Here, one's worst fear, that one will finally be overtaken by the mother of whom one can never be free, comes to nightmarish life as she eats away at one's "maleness," exposing the shame of one's womanish origins for all to see. The fear of being flooded by the contagion of Judeo-Bolshevism also recalls the ever-lurking threat of strangulation that the Sphinx held over the males in the Oedipus story. Hitler thus played on the fear of the underlying symbiotic mother to spur a reinvented, self-created Aryan superman whose firm musculature and moral hardness delineated rigid boundaries that armored him against the constant threat of the parasitical mother, Jew, and homosexual.

In sum, when a boy cannot symbolically penetrate the mysteries of his mother and become a self-respecting man, he remains forever stuck in shame and inferiority in relation to the inaccessible madonna/mother. Inasmuch as the boy's attempts to emerge from under her creative shadow are "stillborn," the humiliating fallout of his frustrations may be displaced eventually onto the sexual accessibility of the whore whom he can turn inside out, and thus he attempts to conquer his womb envy by means of sexuality. Sometimes more desperately and more ominously, however, his anxiety and shame may cause him to devise a compensatory ideology for his inferiority toward women that then serves as a justification to turn others into creature "things" and annihilate displaced images of the suffocating, strangulating mother who lurks within.

Perhaps then there is a final cautionary lesson in this male attempt to compensate for the shame of womb envy by excessive displays of hubristic pride and power. Is there a way for men to achieve some modicum of dignity in the creative significance of their manhood without having to depreciate the female source of their earthly origins? As Raskolnikov discovered, he could not and did not ultimately wish to escape the goodness and vulnerability he associated with his mother. He found that it is a grand self-deception to think that one can use the causa-sui fantasy of self-creation to escape one's mortal destiny.

Oedipus, too, was punished for his hubris of defying divine law. Instead of just being content with a symbolic penetration of the Sphinx/mother, however, Oedipus literally breaks the incest taboo by having sexual intercourse with his mother. Nikolova (1994) states: "As a violation of human taboos, incest is also a violation of the boundaries between human and divine realms—that is, an act of self-divination" (p. 107). In turning the orderly progression of the cycle of generations topsy-turvy in his attempt to perpetuate himself, he is tampering with the divine power of the gods. For that Promethean crime he strikes himself blind. Nikolova declares: "The self-blinding of the blindly seeing Oedipus makes him into a blind seer, and transforms surfaces into essences" (p. 107). Ultimately, Oedipus's self-blinding forces him to limit the expanding horizons of the grandiose and look inside himself to achieve *insight* into the origins and ultimate destiny of being an earth-bound mortal.

REFERENCES

Bachofen, J. J. (1861). *Myth, religion and mother right.* Princeton, NJ: Princeton University Press. 1967.

Becker, E. (1973). *The denial of death.* Glencoe, IL: Free Press.

Bettelheim, B. (1954/1962). *Symbolic wounds.* New York: Collier.

Brown, N. O. (1959). *Life against death.* Wesleyan, CT: Wesleyan University Press.

Cassirer, E. (1946). *Language and myth.* New York: Dover.

Dostoevsky, F. (1866/1993). *Crime and punishment* (R. Pevear & L. Volokhonsky, Trans.). New York: Vintage.

Franz, M-L von. (1981). *Puer aeturnus.* Santa Monica, CA: Sigo Press.

Freud, S. (1905/1953). Three essays on the theory of sexuality. In *Standard edition* (Vol. 7, pp. 135–243). London: Hogarth.

Freud, S. (1908/1959). Family romances. In *Standard edition* (Vol. 9, pp. 237–241). London: Hogarth.

Freud, S. (1909/1955). An analysis of a phobia in a five-year-old boy. In *Standard edition* (Vol. 10, pp. 3–149. London: Hogarth.

Freud, S. (1910/1957). A special type of choice of object made by men. In *Standard edition* (Vol. 10, pp. 163–175. London: Hogarth.

Freud, S. (1913/1955). Totem and taboo. In *Standard edition* (Vol. 13, pp. 1–161). London: Hogarth.

Freud, S. (1920/1955). Beyond the pleasure principle. In *Standard edition* (Vol. 18, pp. 7–64). London: Hogarth.

Grimm, J., & Grimm, W. (1847/1992). *The complete fairy tales of the Brothers Grimm.* New York: Bantam.

Klein, M. (1957/1997). *Envy and gratitude.* New York: Vintage.

Lax, R. (1997). Boys' envy of mother and the consequences of this narcissistic mortification. *Psychoanalytic Study of the Child,* 52, 118–139.

Lederer, W. (1968). *The fear of women*. New York: Harcourt Brace Jovanovich.
Mead, M. (1949). *Male and female*. New York: William Morrow.
Neumann, E. (1954/1962). *The origins and history of consciousness*. New York: Harper.
Nietzsche, F. (1885/1954). Thus spake Zarathustra. In *The portable Nietzsche* (W. Kaufmann, Trans.). New York: Vintage.
Nikolova, V. (1994). The Oedipus myth: An attempt at interpretation of its symbolic systems. In P. Rudnytsky & E. H. Spitz (Eds.), *Freud and forbidden knowledge* (pp. 96–108). New York: New York University Press.
Rank, O. (1909/1964). *The myth of the birth of the hero*. New York: Vintage.
Rank, O. (1941). *Beyond psychology*. New York: Dover.
Roheim, G. (1934). *The riddle of the Sphinx*. London: Hogarth.
Rudnytsky, P. (1986). *Freud and Oedipus*. New York: Columbia.
Shabad, P. (2001). *Despair and the return of hope*. Northvale, NJ: Aronson.
Shengold, L. (1963). Parent as Sphinx. *Journal of the American Psychoanalytic Association*, 11, 4, 725–751.
Slater, P. (1968). *The glory of Hera*. Boston: Beacon.
Thass-Thienemann,T. (1973). *The interpretation of language* (Vol. II). New York: Aronson.
Theweleit, K. (1978/1987). *Male fantasies* (Vol. 2). Minneapolis: University of Minnesota.

5

"The Burned Hedgehog Skin"

Father's Envy and Resentment Against Women Perpetuated in the Daughter's Superego

HEIDRUN JARASS AND LÉON WURMSER

> I am suggesting ... that our case studies, while conveying the disinterested scrutiny of a psychoanalytic process, also should communicate its experiential truth, by marshalling the craft and thereby the aesthetic power of fiction.
>
> *(Schwaber, 2006)*

In this essay we present some excerpts from a long-lasting analytic therapy of a severely traumatized young woman where what we infer to be the father's womb envy manifested itself in an extremely destructive attitude toward his daughter. We show how in the course of the therapeutic process with one of us (HJ) the patient gradually succeeded in finding access to her femininity and to liberate herself from the paternal introject reflecting his womb envy, which had been "lodged" in her superego. In the treatment the analyst allowed herself to be guided above all by her countertransference feelings as a woman. It was essential in the encounter with her that she put at the patient's disposal her own female inner space, which resulted in the gradual relinquishment of her protective pseudomasculinity by discovering and developing her own inner feminine spaces.

Moreover, we encounter in the material an intertwining of the personal pathology of the patient's father with the then ruling Nazi ideology. Because of this phallic orientation with its destructive goals, the development of the individual and particularly its maternal and creative possibilities are put under phallic control and reduced to secondary functions. These conditions prevailed in the background of the father of Nora, the patient to be presented, with the result that he was unable to react either to the femininity of his wives or of his daughters in a constructive and specifically supportive way. To the contrary, his (birth)-envious and hateful attacks upon their femaleness and creativity were, from the beginning, manifestly present. On the other side, Nora's "responses" to them were only revealed during her long analysis—a treatment still not concluded now (after 15 years, with interruptions). The main interest in this presentation is directed at the particular destructive dynamic occurring between father and daughter, especially because of their different genders and leading to its destructive precipitate in the psychological structure of the patient.

CONSEQUENCES OF SEVERE EARLY TRAUMATIZATION

We start out with some considerations of Joachim Küchenhoff (1990). In regard to early trauma, he writes:

> in contrast to later trauma, it does not remain external to the psychical apparatus, but becomes part of it. In other words, the *traumatic experience becomes a transcendental part of the categories of experience, a subjective a priori of all possible experience.* In this regard, the early trauma poses an entirely different psychodynamic problem. Its assimilation is so total that the trauma becomes the image of self and world whereas later trauma remains a foreign body for experience which could still infect all other forms of experience. It is the early trauma that is therefore used for the formation of identity. (p. 18, emphasis added)

We should, therefore, rather speak of "traumatic identity or traumatic identity formation," instead of "early trauma," Küchenhoff says, manifest in a basic sense of unpredictability.

> Dependent upon the development of identificatory ego-functions, this identity formation will vary. Due to a trauma in the first months of life, the development of basic trust may be interrupted; no memory image of a good breast arises that could form the background for any possible experience; the trauma becomes incorporated like a bad and unpredictable breast, leading to the basic conviction that life unfolds within a basic unpredictability. (p. 18)

This early trauma can be defended against by "personification in the traumatic object," the bondage to an evil object as fundamental to life and perpetuated in the archaic superego (with the alternating solutions of submission to it or triumph over it), or by "rejection of the relationship to the traumatic object," the "attacks on linking," and the establishment of *"the phantasma of the empty space"* p. 25, or in the parlance of André Green (1993), again as a defense, "the *disobjectalizing function* leading to an *absence of representation* rather than to depression," p. 127, "the pathological negative" or "void" (p. 130; Reed & Baudry, 2005).

Also quite relevant to our case presentation is Küchenhoff's talking of the splitting off of the libidinous object relation:

> When he [the analyst] tries to maintain some positive interpretative activity in its beginnings she [the patient] reacts by blaming the therapist that he does not permit any closeness, that he is disinterested in her and only plays with her. Not only are here positive and negative aspects split from each other, but this destructive side is placed by projective identification into the therapist; he is now experienced as destructive, and thus she has to ascertain that there cannot be any good relationship. (p. 25)

We, as analysts, often see ourselves confronted with hatred and spite, as we witness in the case to be presented. This hate and defiance seemed to be a kind of substitute object relation—what Valenstein (1973) called "an attachment to painful feelings": "I believe that such affects are emphatically held to because they represent the early self and self-object" (p. 376), and "the negative affect state represents the primary object, i.e. the mother" (p. 387); "attachment to pain signifies an original attachment to painfully perceived objects and inconstant objects at that" (p. 389). In another metaphor, Ernst Morgenthaler (1987) spoke of a "lead seal" or "plug" ("Plombe"): these affects may have served Nora as a substitute, covering the lack of an early securely supporting relationship.

Küchenhoff's (1990) considerations contribute to a deepened understanding of this process:

> One attempt of a psychological processing of early traumata consists in binding them into an object relation. In this way the *trauma becomes personified.* With that, the fateful, traumatic burdens are attributed to a harmful, cruel object, as it were, to an evilly acting breast that keeps striking … this evil early object should be called *traumatic object.* … The defense by the ego is directed toward the goal to escape the annihilation by the traumatic object. At the same time, the escape by flight is blocked; the traumatic object is by its ubiquitous presence the only available, emotionally cathected object. Because no other vitally important object exists it has to be held fast by various means. (pp. 23–24)

Added to this first observational and theoretical pillar is a second one: the introjection of the traumatizing object into the superego.

THE MASSIVE INTROJECTION OF THE TRAUMATIZING OBJECT INTO THE SUPEREGO

In our context some thoughts from Mathias Hirsch's (2005) article "About Vampirism" appear to be relevant. In his dealing with the mythological meaning of vampirism, he invokes Le Couteux. After naming the forms of vampire figures listed by Le Couteux (1999), like "caller, knocker, visitor, devourer, nine-killer, nightmare, strangler, one who eats afterwards, and Dybbuk (Rufer, Klopfer, Besucher, Verschlinger, Neuntöter, Alp, Würger, Nachzehrer, Dybbuk)," he also mentions "incubus" (*Aufhocker*):

> A ghost that at certain places throws himself upon people … that sits on their backs and lets himself be carried by them for a good stretch of the way. … It is only told that the victim of this *Aufhocker* remains in a state of great exhaustion as if a vampire had sucked out his life force and that he is only one inch away from death. (p. 128)

In the continuation of his essay, Hirsch demonstrates how these myths link with modern conceptions of psychoanalytic traumatology, according to which the traumatic relationship leads to a "sucking out of vitality," as already remarked by Ferenczi (1932). Hirsch then quotes Pohl (1985, p. 188):

> The motive of the vampire, this crude mixture of murderous aggression, guiltless guiltiness (*nicht verschuldete Schuld*), consuming love, sadomasochistic sexuality, fatal orality, symbiotic fusion, cannibalism, and necrophilia, was a favorite motive both of the serious and of the trivial literature of the nineteenth century. (p. 129)

Hirsch writes that Dettmering (2003) had talked, in regard to "the early screening of the vampire theme in a movie by Murnau ("Nosferatu") about a blood circulation between mother and child," and he continues:

> Whereas in that situation it is the flow of blood from the nourishing mother to the child, in the vampire myth one has to see much rather the reverse flow: from the innocent victim enjoying life to the powerful but needy perpetrator. In such a scenario, it would be about robbing the life of a child by the adult, i.e. the transition of a vital substance of a really needy object to the other who by rights should be the nourishing one, and this exactly corresponds to the image for which Bollas (1987) coined the notion of the *"extractive introjection."* (p. 134)

Hirsch gives examples for these interpersonal traumatizations:

> [D]epriving the child of the self-critical faculties by constant scolding about small acts of clumsiness, in the assumption that the child itself is unable to recognize that it has made a mistake; robbing the child of playfulness. … According to Bollas, the ability of thinking, affectivity, mental structures,

> parts of the self, could all become objects of such robbing. Britton [see Kennel & Reerink, 1997] calls "vampire" the destructive container that keeps the child captive in "the interior of the mother" whom it has to live for. (p. 137)

We are reminded of Ferenczi's (1932) statement: the abused child "feels enormously confused, innocent and culpable at the same time—and his confidence in the testimony of his own senses is broken" (p. 519).

Furthermore, Hirsch mentions an article by Stolorow and Stolorow (1989) that describes very graphically the robbing of the child's identity, and continues: "It becomes very clear how this robbing opens up an empty space into which something foreign, i.e. the fantasy of the parents, can flow. ... According to Bollas (1987, p. 177), the reaction to such robbing may be a deep seated vindictiveness, a vengeful recapturing of what has been stolen by a violent penetration into the other" (Hirsch, p. 142).

The question arises if this vengefulness might also be understood as an aspect of the male birth envy studied in this essay. Similarly, the reversal of the nourishing circulation and of the mother's nursing the child might be viewed as an expression of the male envy of the procreative functions of the woman.

Some thoughts of Derrida (1976), also quoted by Hirsch, play a particularly crucial role in Nora's further treatment: "The traumatic introject is alive (effective) by being dead (cryptical, hidden) and it can only come to rest if it becomes alive (actualized)" (Hirsch, p. 136).

HOSTILITY AGAINST FEMININITY

Hostility against femininity would be the third theoretical pillar for our case study. Talking about the conflicts and debates engendered by the differences between men and women and about the resulting anxieties, we sometimes speak colloquially about "gender tension." In such disputes about the differences, we conjointly need to keep struggling and striving for creative solutions if we want to avoid the failure of this dialogue. If this endeavor succeeds, it leads to integration and overcoming of the mutual anxieties. This creative solution is the basis for the joint creation of a shared fantasy of the relationship as a mediating bridge. This process presupposes that both participants can tolerate their loneliness based in their gender identity. As Margaret Mahler (1975) described it, "psychological birth" is tied to a series of separation experiences; the mourning over these losses is decisively important for the development of the individual. The little boy's giving up the fantasy to be like his mother, the little girl's renouncing the fantasy of being like her father, are experienced as losses, and they need to be mourned. This work of mourning underlies the creation of some mediating third that builds a bridge between the two poles of "male" and "female." The way in which this mediating bridge is already preformed in the relationship between the maternal figure and the baby in their mutually attuned interaction is elucidated by the concept of the "inner space" of the Finnish couple Hägglund (cf. Benz, 1984).

The Hägglunds describe how the child gradually, during the oral, anal, and genital stages and thanks to sufficiently satisfactory experiences with the mother and her "inner space," succeeds to identify with her "inner genital space" and her motherly participating and caring attitude.

> The experience of the oral inner space means introjection of the object in total, devouring the object, keeping it in the inner space, etc. The object of love, hate or ambivalent emotions is incorporated into the oral inner space. The object then no longer exists outside the subject as a separate part or entity. ... In the oral phase the mutuality is experienced in the shared emotion of melting together, in the "ocean fusion feeling," and in mother's warmth, in her milk and in her loving care which have all become fused with the child's existence. (p. 61)

In this way, this mediating third arises, something like a symbolic transitional object. By trying to communicate, with the help of words, her feelings to the child, the mother contributes to this process. If this interaction fails, however, the male child might react with phallic defenses to his being excluded from his mother's inner space. This phallic mode of processing stands in the way of the mourning process and may cause a destructive kind of dealing with self and/or object representations, manifested by aggressive actions toward her- or himself or the other.

They continue:

> [T]he question can be asked whether such a stubborn inability to conceive of the existence and the meaning of the vagina bases itself only on psychosexual immaturity of the child in the phallic phase, or are there possibly other factors to be accounted for. A child does have phantasies of pregnancy and of impregnation in this phase which are in no way related to his psychophysical possibilities at that age. Could it be reasonable to suppose that a child, by means of his phallic phantasies, defends himself not only against the incomprehensibility of new sexual impulses, and the castration anxiety following misconception of these impulses, but also against consciousness of the vagina, the womb and the female inner space with all the problems included? ...
>
> When a small child, or even a somewhat older child, instead of sharing motherhood through identification, becomes only its object and dependent on the mother, then motherhood leads to emotions of envy from which it is difficult to find the way out. ... When a small child contemplates the bliss of motherhood and the creative elation in the relationship between mother and the baby, or when he observes *the sublimated inner space qualities of mother,* his envy encompasses both the object of motherly care and mother

> herself. *The envy raised by motherhood is the first and the strongest emotion of envy experienced by a child, and it is aimed at the very person the child is dependent upon.* Through identification with mother, both boys and girls are able to participate in what, to a certain degree, they envy. (pp. 60–61, 62–63, emphasis added)

On the other side, the identification with the "inner genital space" of the mother prevents, during the little boy's further development, a splitting between his genital libidinous tendencies (sexuality, especially of a phallic nature) and the strivings tied to the inner space (the attitude of caring). If the little boy can share, in creative illusion, the inner genital spaces of mother and/or father, and thus can participate in them and not feel excluded, his birth envy may gradually be integrated. "*The goal of inner space function is always the well-being of another person.* Orgastic gratification, on the contrary, is accomplished in the personal psychophysical system regardless of the well-being of another person, or even in opposition to it" (Hägglund & Hägglund, 1975/1976, p. 64, emphasis added).

Birth envy arises in the little boy out of the insight that he is different from the gender of his mother and from her capability to give birth to children. If such a solution by identification and creativity is thwarted and the mother, for inner or external reasons, excludes the child from her inner space, the child feels he is made into a dependent object of his mother's impulses and turns his aggressions against the envied mother and later, in a resentful attitude, against women in general. This entails the need to act out the feelings of envy and to castrate and destroy the triggering object. At the same time, it is only indirectly possible for the child to express those feelings of resentment because he feels existentially dependent upon the maternal object.

> Phallic ethos has both an active and a passive component: power, force and honour—submission, sacrifice and veneration. Its opposite is identification with the good, gentle giver and carer. The phallic structure has probably been formed mainly as a protection against the envy felt by the child towards the genital inner space and its derivatives. (Hägglund & Hägglund, 1975/1976, p. 66)

The Hägglunds add that the phallic defense organization is only then really detrimental for the child if it coincides with an ideal of the parents or of the surrounding culture.

This is an arresting thought insofar as we shall encounter in the following material a presumable intertwining of the personal pathology of the patient's father with the then ruling Nazi ideology. Because of this phallic orientation with its destructive goals, the development of the individual and particularly its maternal and creative possibilities are put under phallic control and reduced to secondary functions.

FIRST ENCOUNTERS

When Nora first sought my (HJ) help, she presented herself as an attractive, sporty, and slim young woman (she was 30 years old at the time) and claimed that, although usually able at first to get involved with men, she was unable to keep long-term relationships:

> I have so much anxiety about closeness. I come with a lot of hope and a lot of anxiety—hope that there will finally be somebody who can put up with me, anxiety that the relationship could fail because of me. And at the same time, I am also afraid of what would happen if it did not fail because of me.

Nora showed very much her masculine identification. Her external appearance reminded me of a "rocker bride": she wore jeans, black leather stiletto boots, and a black leather jacket. Shaking her hand, I felt my own caught as if in a vise; it relayed to me, in a quite physically imposing fashion, besides the pain, also her ability to strongly grasp at something. She let me know that she was a karate fighter, and I felt queasy at the thought that there could be any differences of opinion between us.

In my counter-transference at the time, the unrestrained violence that broke in over me during this first meeting did not make it easy to keep track of my thoughts. Physically as well as nonverbally and verbally, she exerted a strong pressure upon me to be exactly the way she wanted to have me, and to be always and immediately able to offer her solutions because she could not wait. I felt very controlled by her and cornered again and again. I was afraid of the extent of her narcissistic rage. Her judgment, polarizing, sharp, and merciless, let me infer a very cruel superego. Contrasted to it was her long, wonderful hair that spoke to me very much. Already in the first meeting I learned that in her childhood her father had always cut it short and partly (in the back of her head) shaved it off. I vented my shock by a spontaneous expression—which was picked up in my supervision at the time with the critical remark: "You are an analyst, not a hairdresser!" She apparently was startled by my emotional "acting-out," although this was for the patient important and comforting. However, my experience that the supervisor seemed identified with the judgmental superego side of the patient could not change the fact that the male attack on the female child was communicated to me on a physically very close and deep level and was leaving its traces in me.

At the time, I could not yet grasp fully in fantasy the emotional content of what she was telling me, but I understood that her phallic behavior was very important for her survival. I was preoccupied by this lacuna in my fantasy space that I had not encountered in other circumstances, and I observed how I was tempted to fill this hole with content. Now I understand that what was very clearly communicated to me was her inner state of a split and of the lack of an inner space, of a "transitional space" necessary to be able to think, to fantasize, and to give meaning to things.

Thus, already in the first encounter, the central themes were palpably present: intrusion, violation of boundaries, her splits, and the tension between "male" and "female," most of all, however, that in her object fantasy I *was* her father: that she could have only such a notion of a close relationship. Her self-representation entailed being hateful and phallic because she needed this in order to save herself from her father; being soft vis-à-vis him and opening herself would be a mortal peril. This was her primary transference.

Nora tried in the encounter with me to intrude in my inner space and to control it. She appeared with a phallic attitude. In my concordant counter-transference, she let me sense her great anxiety about being overwhelmed. The initial naive utterance of my counter-transference feelings about the assault upon her femininity permitted me to sense a first hint of what was, in the later course of our work together, to play a big role: that I as a woman let myself be touched by what had been inflicted upon her. Its effect was that in the long process of our work we were slowly succeeding to work through her traumatic past and to mentalize it through the work in our relationship. It was essential for the treatment that in the encounter with her, I made my own inner space available to her so that, little by little, she succeeded in giving up the defensive masculinity she had built up as a protection for her femininity and for her survival and was able to discover and develop her own female inner space.

HISTORY

Nora is the only surviving biological child of her father. Before her, there were three other sisters. The oldest died 24 days after her birth, allegedly from sepsis. The mother took the next two sisters (5 and 3 years older than Nora) with her in a murder-suicide when she drowned herself in the Danube; the sisters were 4 and 6 at the time. Nora survived only because on the day of the drowning, fatefully on the day of her first birthday, she was hospitalized for an attack of croup. She remained for several weeks in the children's hospital because her father's possible participation in her mother's death was investigated by the police. Nothing could be proven against him, and Nora was therefore allowed to return home to him. Not long afterward, a housekeeper moved in with her own children; she took care of the household and Nora.

Nora describes her father as being very much tied to his own mother, as restrictive and unreachable, with little tenderness toward his daughter: "He was inclined to extreme reactions." For instance, he shot roving cats and forced Nora to bury them as punishment for her having eaten his strawberries against his prohibition. He also shot her own favorite cat when it was sick.

Nora's mother had been born out of wedlock; her own mother had died right after the child's birth, so that she (Nora's mother) was raised in an orphanage and very early had to become independent. Nora believes that she was artistically gifted and a faithfully caring mother. I was very touched by this yearning for an idealized, good mother.

Now some biographical details about Nora's father: In Nora's memory, no emotional relations were noticeable between her father and his mother, although it was very important for the father to care for his mother's needs. The grandmother allegedly was a beautiful, well-groomed, but nonsensual woman who showed little interest in men, but was very close to her own sister. There was very little that connected her with her own husband. In her marriage she wished for female children and was very disappointed about the birth of her two boys; she did not know what to do with them. Nora's father was the firstborn. Ten years later, the second son was born. In contrast to his little brother, who presented himself as girlish, wrote poetry, and on the surface was able to adapt himself very well to his mother's expectations, Nora's father was allegedly a vivacious little rogue who was often beaten by his mother and presumably never felt accepted in his gender identity. As a child, although taken care of, he never felt any warmth or love. The brother married, but never had children of his own; to the contrary he hated children altogether. Originally, Nora's father wanted to become an architect, yet he was not allowed to study because early on he had to earn money independently. Therefore, he chose, as a compromise, civil service in the city. He manifested his identification with his mother's hostile regard in his effort during the Third Reich to be inducted as a volunteer parachutist in the Wehrmacht. He saw the resulting danger to his life as a punishment of his parents. During the war, he became a prisoner of war in Russia. After many unsuccessful attempts to flee, he finally succeeded in marching home, where, shortly after the war's end, he arrived completely undernourished and deathly ill. He was very paranoid and for a year after was unable to leave the apartment. Even later on, he slept with his gun at the ready under his bed cover. With every movement of Nora, who had to sleep with him in the same room, he startled and grabbed his weapon. He thus reenacted his captivity by holding Nora in his thrall.

These descriptions let us surmise that the father continually experienced the interaction with the grandmother as an attack upon his gender identity and that the inability of the grandmother to let him participate in her own feminine interior space had the effect that the father developed a very phallic and hostile attitude toward everything "weak," foreign, and feminine. The question imposes itself: What role was played *here* by the father's intolerance of utterances of neediness and his own envy and jealousy of the relationship between mother and baby? Partly this appears as a self-destructive attitude, but also in externalized form when his personal mindset joined up with the Nazi ideology and continued to be expressed in his destructiveness against everything that is feminine and generative.

In Nora's third year of life, her father married the housekeeper. During her marriage, she at first developed an addiction to drugs, then in addition an alcohol dependency. Allegedly, the father did not notice anything of this development, and he blamed the children for having kept it secret from him. In Nora's 18th year of life, the stepmother tried after a family fight to kill herself, and soon thereafter committed suicide in the same way as Nora's mother had done, by drowning herself in the Danube.

Nora noticed that in her perception of the past there was something like a double reality. Until entering school she officially did not know that her stepmother was not her real mother, while subliminally sensing that there were a lot of things that could not be named, talked about, and clarified. This situation gave her a feeling of unreality so that she could not learn in school and not open herself in relationships. Permanently, she experienced *diffuse shame*. Due to her learning difficulties, her father had her intelligence tested, and she turned out, according to his statements, to have a below-average IQ. Also after the revelation of the real family situation by a woman teacher, she did not dare to confront her stepmother with her knowledge and with questions about what had happened, "in order not to hurt her." Her father indicated to her, however, that the disappearance of her biological mother had something to do with her: "After your birth, your mother went downhill because you cried so much and were a 'spitting baby.'" The mother, therefore, needed to go away several times to recover, and thus Nora already during her first year of life repeatedly had to be sent away to a baby nursery.

COURSE OF TREATMENT

At the inception, Nora did everything to attack the setting because she had no idea of the possibility that a relationship to someone else could be different from one where the other would intrude into her and would seek to control and destroy her from within. Although maintaining the limits and the analytic frame, I was often afraid that I would put her to flight by doing so. In turn, I also understood how much she was afraid that I too would be put to flight by the extent of her rage. The opportunity to induce in me her feeling states and conflicts on a very deep and "body-near" (*körpernahe*) level by projective mechanisms and my readiness to accept them within myself, to process them with my emotional resources, and also to survive them, and then to give them back to Nora in a worked-through, mentalized form, gradually allowed Nora to use my inner space.

One example stands for many others: Nora was one of my first "analytic children." Each patient could select for the couch his or her own pillow, and she had a wide choice. She selected the color blue, but could not inform me at that time that she would have liked much more to take the lilac pillow. In a part of herself, she experienced my offer that she could express her wish to be dangerous and seductive, and thus this pillow became for a very long stretch of her analysis a projection screen for the most diverse conflicts: namely, that what is essential (*das Eigentliche*) always was and is withheld from her, that forever in life she is the excluded one, that she never was and is really acknowledged in her desire. A genuine mother/analyst would immediately have recognized this wish and cared for its fulfillment. Here the conflict between her *longing* for an intimate encounter with another (*einem Gegenüber*) and the *dread* of it became very clear. Only slowly she recognized that there was behind her immense hatred and defiance some other feelings.

Nora used her first analysis to free herself from the constricting external entanglement with her father. Originally, she had followed in his footsteps professionally in order to avoid conflicts around envy and the fear of separation in the relationship with him. Now she started using the analysis to dare leaving her father's outer sphere of power and to develop her own autonomous life plans. Defying her father's insistence on her lack of intelligence she decided to make up her high school graduation on the so-called second path of education, while simultaneously working professionally.

The analysis helped her to achieve her high school equivalency, to establish for the first time in her life a friendship built upon trust and intimacy with a girlfriend, and finally to enter university studies. This exposed her to her father's annihilating resentment. With all available means, he attempted to thwart Nora's development, and she terribly dreaded her father's envy and revenge for her successes. Eventually, she was able to conclude her finals as the second best of her class. During this time, she increasingly realized how difficult it was for her to separate herself effectively in real life from her father because he could not enjoy any of her successes nor any autonomy of hers and thus refused her the permission to separate. She was not yet conscious then of how a part of her was still identified with him, in particular with his conflicts about birth envy and revenge. She was still assuming that an external separation from him would solve her inner conflicts. Her paternal object representation was then still largely externalized.

Why birth envy? We infer that because he had been so painfully excluded from the inner space of his mother Nora's father harbored very deep resentment against the abilities of women; they reminded him of the original hurt. Therefore, he had to persecute everything that was particularly feminine.

Her defensive fantasy of becoming, thanks to the analytic treatment, the wished-for son of her father became more conscious. The analysis nearly broke down because of her insistence that she would indeed become a son. She staunchly maintained the doubleness of acknowledgment and denial of her gender—a true splitting in Freud's sense (the Yes and No of character perversion).

During my own pregnancy Nora dreamt that her father emerged as a butcher who dismembered the bodies of women. Another dream sequence had her intrude into my womb in order to tear out the growing child from my body. In my counter-transference I sometimes felt as if paralyzed by anxiety about the destructive part of her, fearing that I could not maintain my body boundaries and protect my unborn child against her hatred so that I would suffer a miscarriage or premature birth. In her primitive regressive fantasies, the man's "poisonous" semen destroyed the woman from within, and in a condensation, she equated the baby with the stick of stool, but she also experienced it with another part of herself as belonging to her *own* self. Another part of herself was identified with the dangerous baby within me.

In the transference I changed from the mother of symbiosis, prior to the separation by suicide, into the disappointing mother and into the unreliable addictive stepmother after her mother's death, and I saw myself exposed to annihilating envy and hatred, just when she had begun believing that she had found something like a substitute mother. She felt violent and from one day to the next catapulted out of the dyad of the analytic relationship, terrified that she was losing everything, namely her place within me. She gained access to her jealousy of her siblings who could remain united in death with their mother while she was excluded from that union. The stepmother also ultimately felt closer and more attached to her own biological children than to Nora. Finally, she said good-bye to me as I prepared for my delivery with the words: "If we survive this separation it could be very valuable for me." Then I understood the remark under the aspect of her lacking object constancy, and that parts of her self and of her conflicts were somatized and projected upon my baby. Only much later did I recognize that I may have reacted in my counter-transference to the birth-envious paternal introject within Nora, but also that she could make valuable experiences for her gender identity because I did not let myself be destroyed in my female potency by this introject.

She was afraid that she would poison everything by her envy so that she would ruin the relationship with me (and her boyfriend) and that ultimately she would again remain alone with her guilt for her destructivity in her dead world. Nora said:

> *It is so unfair.* Many people had something from the start, and I had to fight so strongly for everything. I ruin my happiness because I have not learned to accept it. I can be so truly poisonous just when something is truly good. Now I can only be sad. I know I become venomous as soon as somebody tries to approach me. This is also the case with you, and I find this so horrible. I want so much to live differently, to experience what is beautiful with others, and that is just what I cannot do.

We understood that her inability to experience my pregnancy in any other way than by identification pointed back to the early relationship with her mother. When she lost her at the end of the first year of life she was still in the midst of the process of separation and individuation from her mother. This intimate contact was abruptly and traumatically disrupted by her suicide, so that developmental steps were deeply disturbed according to their phase specificity, steps like increasing ability to symbolize, the development of expanding ego functions, and the integration of genital anxieties, which would lead to a stable gender identity. For now, the only living object that remained after that traumatic loss was the soul-blind, cold, and functionalistic father.

As many of her dreams did, all this also reflected to what extent the merciless aspects of her earlier reality had become intertwined with the traumatizing attitude of the early object and how both had turned into a "precipitate" within, in the form of an *absolutely cruel superego*. To put it briefly: The content during the future course was work on her belief that everything good would be destroyed anyway and that she therefore would have to destroy it first herself, in the sense of turning passive into active.

In a dream she visited her grandmother (father's mother): "She has two pure-bred cats (*Rassekatzen*, with the double *entendre* of the Nazi ideology) and I realize: 'I cannot count on her either.'"

I said: "There was nobody who would have perceived and confirmed your pain." Now she remembered, for the first time with much emotional participation, how her father beat her up so that she would go into the bathing water and how he forced the food that she had repeatedly vomited back into her, with the reason that she "was too thin"; how he beat her often also at other times, and how very difficult it was to reconcile this side of her father with the other side of him that was competent and received public recognition: "Nobody would have believed what I was going through with him at home!"

A CENTRAL FAIRY TALE

Nora dreamt about two tiger cats:

> One of them was running around freely while the other was locked up in a cage. Then they [people] let the cats go. I did not see that. Two lionesses pursued a bear. I saw that on TV. I closed my eyes: Right now they will mangle him (*zerfleischen*). But instead, they licked the bear's snout. Then I played with a hedgehog. Nothing can happen to him because he has spines. With the lionesses, you and I came to my mind. And with the tigers it occurred to me that we both have (in reality) the same skirts (tiger-like miniskirts). Then I ask myself: How is that for you that I come in with that skirt? Can you bear that? I can also call forth so much envy. This is the mangling struggle (*der zerfleischende Kampf*). With a protective garment (i.e., the hedgehog's spines), nothing can happen to you.

At this point I would like to mention that Nora had talked some time ago about the Brothers Grimm's fairy tale of "Hans mein Igel" (Johnny my hedgehog), and that it had been a favorite story of her childhood. I was not familiar with that fairy tale, and when I read it I could not at first make much with it or see the connection to her. Because from time to time it did play a role in the course of the treatment, I would like to narrate it freely and insert my interpretations in brackets of the story as it also pertains to my patient.

"Hans mein Igel"

A peasant couple was materially blessed but something was missing in their happiness. [In the world of things they could function well, yet they were unable to have loving relations with each other and could not together be creative and procreative—something that was also true for Nora's father. In my view, what is indicated here is the soul-blindness of Nora's surroundings and of the people closely related to her, especially her father, and her lacking "feminine inner space."] The pair could not have any children. Often the peasant was shamed and ridiculed for this by other peasants so that he finally said in anger: "I want to have a child, even if it is a hedgehog!" [Here it becomes very evident how big a role shame and the defense against it play in this fairy tale. Thus the wish for children could here be understandable more under the aspect of avoiding shame than as a wish for a child as a materialization of a loving relationship, and thus as an independent third.] Immediately afterward, they had a child that was in the lower part a boy, but above that a hedgehog. [Nora's prickly pseudo-masculinity. Yet also the aspect of a cruel and archaic superego should be considered: The desperate and fervent prayer: "Even if it is a hedgehog!" is followed at once by the punishment, without that it would be "metabolized" and "detoxified" in some inner space. This was Nora's very problem: Everything always returned according to the talion principle.] The wife said: "Look! You have cursed us." Because of his misshape, he did not get a godfather, but he was baptized under the name "Hans mein Igel." [Here we see, as I perceive it, the entire tragedy of an existence as hedgehog: because of his spines, he cannot cuddle and have close and tender contacts. Speaking more generally: Out of fear of the pain of touching, everybody avoids direct contact and remains isolated in his world. Thus the soul-blindness of the parents brings about the deformation of the child and, due to the lack of inner space, no creative transformation can take place. Everybody stays within his own world; there is no deeper meaning behind the external appearance, and there is no touching.] Because of his spines he could not be nursed and for the same reason was also not allowed to sleep in a small bed, but instead behind the oven on a little straw. The father wished him dead, but Hans mein Igel lived. [We guess that Nora's father too had such death wishes against Nora, particularly when she was little and very needy and that Nora's defiance (her spines) had, among other things, also the function of facing up to those wishes.] One day the father had to run some errands in town, and he asked wife, maid, and child what he should bring them from there. Hans mein Igel wished to get a bagpipe, and when the father returned with the gifts, Hans mein Igel asked him to shoe a rooster so that he might go out into the wide world. The father was hoping that in this way he could get rid of him. Hans mein Igel rode on his rooster, together with pigs and donkeys, out to the forest where he let his rooster fly onto a tree. There he remained sitting on his rooster for some years shepherding his animals. One day, a king lost his way in the forest. He heard the beautiful music of the bagpipe and through his servant contacted Hans mein Igel so as to ask him if he could show him the way out of the forest. Hans mein Igel was willing to do this if the king for his part would sign over and promise him (*verschreiben und versprechen*) whatever first came across his way upon his return home. The king thought that Hans mein Igel could not write nor understand what he wrote, so the king jotted something down and signed it. As he arrived at home his daughter joyously ran up to meet him. The father told her the story, and she replied that he had done well by writing something false because she would not have been ready to go along with Hans mein Igel. [This whole sequence seems to me like a repetition of Hans mein Igel's experiences with his parents: He is not really recognized by the king, but rather dehumanized and betrayed. On a different level, we might understand this also as equivalent to a very cruel superego. Hans mein Igel, however, carries the hope within that there could be something else besides what he had gotten to know in his relationships, and also that he could implement these ideas by showing care, a behavior that could correspond to milder and more adequate superego aspects. Applied to Nora this could mean: Although she felt in her relationships time and again deeply disappointed, shamed, and betrayed, she carries within the hope for a good relationship with an important other. This hope shows already in that she chose as her favorite this fairy tale of Hans mein Igel that finally comes to a good and hopeful end. Her readiness to dare to engage in the "horror movie" of her psychoanalysis also testifies to this hope.]

In the meantime Hans mein Igel was doing quite well on his tree. He was making music and watching over his animals. Again, another king came along who had lost his way in the forest. As with the first king, Hans mein Igel was willing to help the king if he promised to give him what he encountered first upon his return home. This time the king signed his pledge, and when he also first met his daughter she agreed out of love for her father with the deal. [In a counter-image, a world appears here where inner values do play a big role, where there is contact and exchange so that development and growth can be initiated and creativity becomes possible.] In the meantime, the animals had so multiplied under Hans mein Igel's watch that he decided to ride back home on his rooster with his animals so that the village could be provided with food. His father was disappointed that Hans mein Igel was still alive. He had believed that he had been long dead. In the village, Hans mein Igel had the animals slaughtered: "Hu! What carnage that was, what chopping, so that one could hear it two hours away!" [Perhaps what finds expression in the fairy tale is how Hans mein Igel succeeds, by leaving home, in developing his latent potencies so that by returning home he can bring something new, something different into the parents' reality. Hans mein Igel would then be in the position of a transitional object for the world of the parents, a world of cruelty and archaic assaults. In my view, the parents resemble a traumatic introject, whereas Hans, reentering their world and bringing a milder and more caring experience with him, transcends the trauma. At the same time, it seems important for Hans mein Igel to "work through" those fantasies of massacres.

Also for a long time, there prevailed in Nora's inner world these primitive fantasies and notions that any encounter would lead to terrible carnage. Like Hans in the story, she dared, under the protection of the therapeutic relationship, to get in touch with the archaic and cruel fantasies of object relations within her and celebrated in her own way some kind of "slaughtering feast." Yet she increasingly separated from her father on the outside and tried to base her life upon the hope of a real relationship.] Afterward, Hans mein Igel had his father shoe the rooster once more, promised him that he would never in his life come back home, which made his father very glad, and he rode to the first kingdom. [Hans mein Igel had by his trip home integrated something so that he did not need to enter into the relationship with the first king, but could reach for other goals.] The king had issued orders that when Hans mein Igel appeared in his realm they would have to shoot, to beat, and to stab at him in order to block him from getting to the castle. But Hans mein Igel flew with his rooster over the castle gate, set down on one of the window sills, and demanded that he be given what he had been promised. If not, he would kill the king together with his daughter. The king asked his daughter to go along with him in order to save both their lives. She dressed in white, the father gave her a coach with six servants for the journey, and money and property. Hans mein Igel sat, with rooster and bagpipe, by her side. The father was sure he would never see her again. But they had hardly left the city in the coach when Hans mein Igel took away the princess's white clothes and pierced her with his hedgehog skin until she was bloody all over and told her: "This is the reward for your falseness. Go away! I do not want you!" Marked for the rest of her life, she returned home. [Here the shame motive reemerges and with it the revenge theme. Because of her treachery, the king's daughter is marked for life. Hans mein Igel sees very clearly that treachery is something terrible that one has to be punished and shamed for. He manages somewhat to externalize the negative introject and to liberate himself from it. This sequence may mirror Nora's anxiety about betrayal that has been crucial both in her life history and in the transference. From the beginning of my encounter with Nora, I was very conscious of the *absolutely central significance of clarity and authenticity.*]

Hans mein Igel continued riding on his rooster to the second kingdom where the king had already prepared his subjects with exact instructions:

they should present their rifles, lead him around freely, call Vivat!, and then bring him to the royal castle (i.e., not to shame him, but to meet him with respect, recognition, and love). Although the princess was shocked by Hans mein Igel's exterior she stood by her promise, and he was wined and dined and married to her. Before going to sleep, however, the king's daughter was very frightened of the spines of Hans mein Igel. He calmed her fears and begged her father to send four guards to light a big fire in front of the bedroom door. While preparing for bed he slipped off his hedgehog skin for them to throw into the flames. This they did, and Hans mein Igel changed into a normal human being and was delivered from his curse. Yet he was black as coal. The king called upon his physician, who then washed him and treated him with ointments, whereupon he grew into a very handsome young gentleman. [After the loss of his defense, Hans mein Igel is very vulnerable and very dependent on loving care. There are allusions here to the healing and transformative effect of real human encounter and love.] Many years later, he traveled to his father and told him he was his son, but the father replied that he had no son. Yes, he had had one, but he had been born with spines and had gone out into the world. "At that he made himself known, and the old father was delighted and went with him to his realm." [After Hans mein Igel had undergone the outer and inner metamorphosis he had to return home once more, perhaps referring to the circular movement by which psychological growth occurs. In this way he succeeds in neutralizing and integrating into his personality those parts of his own cruel superego that had been projected onto his father.]

Nora loved this story so much because it has, after all, a happy ending: father and son find their way to a loving relationship. In the analysis, there was much material showing that Nora was ashamed about continuing to yearn for a warm affectionate relationship with her father. Among other things, the shame was also that great because she was seeing ever more clearly how brutal he was toward her.

Returning now to the session where she had reported the dream with the lionesses, the bear, and the hedgehog, I remarked that this reminded me of her favorite fairy tale about "Hans mein Igel." She responded: "Yes, it means that I need a great deal of courage to take off the spines, and that somebody has to be there who does not injure me again when I am without spines." I interpreted to her that there was in her a great anxiety that we might tear each other to pieces in the fight and in the rivalry about the man/the father, and that she was afraid that my envy at her attractiveness could be bigger than my pleasure about it, and that out of her big fear of being hurt she could not take off her hedgehog dress.

BEING THE EXCLUDING FIRST INSTEAD OF BEING THE EXCLUDED THIRD

In the relationship with me she was afraid that during the vacation breaks she would not leave behind any traces in me, that I would simply replace her within myself with other things, whereas she felt so very much dependent on me, and she was very jealous of my baby. Turning this from passive to active she therefore made her boyfriend jealous of her and made him feel excluded, and she also wanted to make a baby with him so that I then would be the one who was excluded. In this way she tried to circumvent the work of mourning and to act it out in its stead. Because her feelings of jealousy were still so hard to tolerate she tried to get rid of them by externalizing them and by an intellectual acknowledgment of the conspicuous realities. She dreamt she was holding in her hand a mussel but which then turned into mud. Her association to this was:

> The thing with the aggression is not so much at issue right now. Rather it is about that what is positive grows and does not have to be ruined by the poison from without. ... I cannot be your child; the old things cannot be repeated and repaired, and I cannot yet build up something new. I feel so homeless and as if I belong nowhere.

In the continuation she now gradually gained insight into how, in her original family, separations were denied by replacing one person with another and how the process of grieving was aborted. She now recognized how important it was on the one side to acknowledge the reality, but also on the other side how rapidly this could turn traumatically cruel.

With her girlfriend, her boyfriend, and me, there occurred now a number of constellations that could be put under the motto: "*If you do or say this or that you are dead for me.*" For our sessions this meant that she let me know: "Either this *pillow* disappears during my session, or I break off the therapy!" That lilac pillow was assigned to another patient and served her, on the face of it, as a symbol for the other patients; as earlier explained, lilac had been her wished for color, but she herself had chosen blue. On a deeper level it functioned as a correlate for all the intolerable and overwhelming feelings whose upsurge she tried to avoid by the omnipotent control of her objects. I interpreted the conflict that she imparted to me and also to her boyfriend: "If I [the analyst] stay with my feelings I endanger my relationship with you [Nora]. If I save our relationship I betray myself and my interests, and I signal to the hopeful part in you that there is no contending with the destructive part in you." Again, the fact that she now had the courage, like a child at the "age of spite" (*in der Trotzphase*), to test the boundaries in the relationship with me testifies for the increasing trust in it.

Subsequently, the stepmother became once more a topic, and I gained a much clearer picture of the oedipal triangle. The stepmother appeared to have been very affectionate toward the father whereas he mostly just used her. She now also remembered casual remarks of her father about her as a little child, according to which she had been alone in her crib, banging her head against the wall and gnawing on the crib bars. She was plagued by guilt feelings that there had been a part in her that had been in solidarity with her father and wanted to eliminate the stepmother, that she, Nora, had been so unempathic toward her suffering, so identified with her father's contemptuous, cold look at the woman who loved him. She started understanding that because of these severe feelings of guilt she allowed herself only so little joy. At the same time, she deepened her understanding of herself as a little girl, that she rejected the surrogate mother because she longed for the real mother, and that she had not been asked whether she really wanted this stepmother. She was now mourning many personal encounters where she had behaved very coldly, harshly, and "soul-blindly."

The triangle and her attempt to deal more effectively with her feelings of envy, jealousy, and exclusion also played a big role in her outside life. She had acquired a pair of cats she tenderly cared for and loved. The female cat took on the role of a self-object, whereas the tom-cat was seen by her as "the other, strange, third." Against the foil of her experiences with the cat pair she could increasingly open up her primal scene fantasies and make them a theme in the sessions. It was particularly the closely experienced sexuality of the she-cat that confronted her very strongly with her own genital anxieties. The cat did not simply disembark from the sexual encounter, and Nora had to bear that, especially during her heat, the cat just came and went as she pleased. Because of the uncontrollable vitality of her cat, Nora also had to tolerate and suffer her sadomasochistic fantasies that she connected with sexual contacts. But the cat did not become a victim of the sadism of the love-crazed tom-cat, but she reappeared after her love night very much alive and eventually pregnant. Also the pregnancy and the delivery of the little kittens did not destroy the cat. Quite to the contrary, Nora experienced their birth as something very intimate and uniting: "During the delivery she was looking for my closeness, and during labor she kept looking into my eyes. I believe she felt consoled by my presence."

What is manifested here is how Nora tries to defend against feeling excluded from my own procreative and giving capabilities, and with that against all the attending affects of envy, hatred, jealousy, and resentment, by turning passive into active and excluding now me and other people. Moreover, she is identifying with *my* motherly and generative attitude, by directing it now toward the cat.

Triangularity is experienced as betrayal. This is only to be understood in that two unite against a third, because it seems so dangerous and forbidden to be an independent, separate subject: being separate is equated with being malignantly excluded from the symbiotic unity, which is the only thing that can give safety. This perhaps implies that subjectivity presupposes an inner space; a subject that has felt excluded from this inner space in his or her primary relationships cannot fantasize that this inner space can be filled with a valuable substance, but rather that it must be replete with the subject's own projected aggression.

In regard to treatment technique, I intuitively understood our work on the extra-transference relationships as extremely important and valuable, with the (preconscious) intention to separate the traumatic introject from the more authentic part of her self. The aim was to enable her gradually, as a second step, to free her self from those foreign elements that had been imposed on her by intrusion.

MOURNING AND DEALING WITH THE VAMPIRE

In my relationship with Nora, Nora expected that I would completely empathize with her view of things, that I in fact would see the world through her eyes. She reacted to the slightest touch of subjectivity on my side with hatred. Working on these sequences, we comprehended that *the other's subjectivity was for her identical with the devaluation and shaming of her self.* Only in being the same was it possible to be protected against these attacks.

She decided for the first time to confront the murder-suicide of her mother: She asked in the city archives for the newspaper reports from that time. She also brought copies to her sessions and addressed the perverse dynamics of her parents' relationship: "The children were used in a brutal battle between the parents." We tried to comprehend the impulsive act of her mother. Was it a response to the shame of having been involuntarily impregnated, of having submitted to the father, and of having been functionalized by him? In this context, I was compelled to think of Melvin Lansky's (2005) considerations about Medea and her unbearable shame as motive for the murder of her children.

Nora, however, did not want me to see her pain. I interpreted that there was a strong conflict in her between the wish to share these horrible things with me and the anxiety about what would then happen in that closeness with me. I added that she herself was very shocked about that cold part within herself that could not admit any "weakness" and hurt, and that she feared I would condemn it just as much as one part of her did. At this point it became very clear to her how her experience and feelings had in the past been misunderstood, wrongly named, and reinterpreted, and that there was one part within her which did the very same thing now with her own experience, and also time and again with the experience of the others.

At the end of her effort to deal with the murder-suicide, she threw flowers in a symbolic act at the suspected place of the suicide in the river and bade in this way farewell to her mother and sisters. She could reconcile herself with her mother. She believes now that on the day of that dreadful event her mother must have been desperate and that her action had nothing to do with Nora's worthlessness and guilt: "She did not have the support in her crises which I have received in the meantime."

Time and again it is evident how great her fear was of the envy and the hatred coming from the negative introject in her (i.e., her superego laden with resentment). She gets hold of a document of her father's descent (i.e., genealogy for the Nazis, *Abstammungsurkunde*). She finds out that during the time of Nazism, her paternal grandfather functioned as a block leader: "Actively collaborating, that must cause an incredible guilt, and this guilt was transmitted. It is so difficult because it is not only a thing of *one* generation. I would like so much to have a child and transmit something good." She gets stuck on one sentence in the document: "It has to be burned into the brains of the young people how essential Aryan descent is. I always thought that I was something better. This Aryan descent! This pure race stuff! Such a strange form of pride!" This transmitted guilt is also part of her tormenting superego.

She adds:

> I want to get rid of the father within me, and I do not know what I can do to succeed. Simply throwing him out of me does not work. He would always return because he cannot live without me. He needs my energy. I imagine I throw him out of our house and slam the house door. But he keeps standing there and is waiting for me. ... This morning during breakfast, I watched a fly get caught in a spider web. It was gruesome to watch. The spider was simply squatting in its corner and waiting. When the fly had gotten in its web it came and wrapped up and enmeshed the fly. The fly was still living but she could not move anymore. This is like a living reserve. ... It is the same with my father. Time and again he has ensnared me by hopes that turned into their opposites and then wrapped me up. He has sucked out my life. ... And I argue with myself so much: in spite of everything I still hope that before his death, he will wake up and notice what he has done to me, that shortly before his death he will say: "Nora, I know I have done much to you," that we can reconcile.

She is able to approach the vampire-like part in herself, and I tell her: "This summer we were very much thinking about how you felt yourself to be the victim of your father's attacks, which were sucking out your life. Now you have come to recognize that part of you is also identified with this aspect. This insight is certainly very painful and very hard to bear."

Commenting on the dream about decline and death of an idolized singer, the traumatic introject in her superego, Nora says: "Now I know why I dreamt of Freddy Quinn. My father wanted to have me as a boy, not as a girl. As a girl I always felt like dirt. I always had to deny and hide my femininity."

She had only known sadomasochistic forms of bonds. Therefore, she was unable to gain any trust because she had never gotten to know any love in a true sense and had only learned to exert control and to expect violence. She was familiar with this sadomasochistic universe of omnipotence and impotence, of power through suffering, of sexualized victimization and sadistically used intimacy.

Slowly, however, during our treatment, a counter-image started emerging, the notion that there could be loving attachments, that there could be closeness without power and control. It meant trusting that the other will return after separation: She says that deeply imprisoned within herself there is a core self with feelings of love, trust, and genuineness. She had been so attached to those tormenting relationships because "if there is so little love, you can also not separate from the other. Sensing love you can accept boundaries." Sobbingly she says before the Christmas break "Ach, how beautiful it would be if you were my mother! Then I would have one! Then I would belong to your family, and we could celebrate together."

DISCUSSION

One of the many relevant elements in this long lasting and complex treatment deserves some special consideration: the complementarity and possible opposition of psychoanalytic technique and psychoanalytic relationship.

Lipton (1977a, 1977b) made us aware of the importance in analytic treatment of the real relationship besides the transference aspects. Of course, it is always possible to understand these also "technically," to reduce them, for example, to early aspects of the relationship to a trusted mother. Still, there seems more to this. Especially in the treatment with so severely and chronically traumatized patients as Nora we may have to resort to a different framework than the one that is based on the theory of technique, and hence on the "analysis of transference." It is a difference of the philosophical vantage point: One goes out from the a priori assumption that inner life can best be understood by seeing all the inner processes as incessantly standing in conflict with each other and continually also complementing each other in spite of their contradictions. Without this philosophical presupposition, psychoanalysis would be unthinkable. It is being used and is useful in every moment of our work.

But it is not the only one. There is a second a priori presupposition: that all these insights are only truly mutative if they occur in the matrix of an emotionally intimate relationship, a deep trustful togetherness that far transcends intellectual insight. Here Buber's philosophy of dialogue appears to us particularly helpful. In no way should it supplant the understanding by conflict, it should only complement it. In other words, the intrapsychic and the interpersonal or relational way of understanding are dialectically bound to each other. One without the other does not do justice to the complexity of our work.

This is an inescapable conclusion from the work that is as difficult and demanding as that described here, a conclusion, by the way, in a literal sense that it came to us in this philosophical dimension only toward the end of this very long treatment.

We try to summarize Buber's thought in a few sentences (following in this the formulation in Dan Avnon's book [1998]). Buber attempts to capture the essence of his conception of the interpersonal by devising the "basic words" I-You and I-It.

> The "I" of I-You indicates a quality of presence that considers self and other as elements of one, inclusive reality: when one addresses the other from an inclusive state of being that is present to the unity of creation and of being, then the interpersonal is permeated by an I-You mode of existence. This "I" is not sensed as singular; it is the "I" of being present to being. Such a relation to being … establishes in the interpersonal sphere a quality of relation that Buber refers to as the Between. In contradistinction, in an I-It attitude to being, the person tends to distance himself from the other, to create in the interpersonal a quality of relationship characterized by the person's desire to distinguish him- or herself by accentuating differences, by emphasizing the uniqueness of the "I" in contrast to the other. The "I"of I-It indicates a separation of self from what it encounters. (Avnon, 1998, p. 39)

In the former, in the "relation" (*Beziehung*) in this specific sense, the other is a person, "not a thing among things nor consisting of things,"[1] whereas the I-It relationship, what Buber calls "experience" (*Erfahrung*), is "distance from you" (*Erfahrung is Du-Ferne*) (Buber, 1947, pp. 20–21).

What the analyst in our presentation felt so strongly was this deep inner relatedness as having a curative effect over a very long period. There were innumerable such "Now-experiences" (Stern, 2004) that formed part and parcel of the enduring dialogue, the lasting relation, a very deep emotional participation by the therapist in the suffering of the patient while again and again finding the necessary distance. It was both a continuous dialectic between an I-You intimacy and an I-It separation, a back and forth of closeness and distance in delicate balance. Many times the search for such a balance failed, but, all in all, the right way of dialogue kept being reestablished.

Perversion is, as we know, dehumanized sexuality and sexualized dehumanization. The extent of sadomasochistic bonds and of moral masochism witnessed in this case is a form of character perversion. To put it now also in the terms just introduced: Character perversion changes everything that is personal and could partake in the I-You relationship into something used, functionalized (i.e., into an I-It). Life turns into that hole about which Küchenhoff and Green speak, into that abyss about which Nora repeatedly dreams; it becomes utterly empty.

Where there is no dialogue, power and thus possessiveness replace love, and with that envy and jealousy rule the relationships with everyone. The transference becomes filled with all the emotions that go with this, not only envy and jealousy, but rage and revenge, and very much also resentment. The vampire vested in the superego threatens to suck out not only the vitality of the patient, but that of the therapist in the relationship as well. This was the huge burden that the analyst had to bear in Nora's case. But an analyst can do this only if he or she opens up to an entirely different form of living, namely to that of a deep relatedness. Technique is important, but it is not all-important. It is a means to an end. The end, however, is a different way of being: where the other is more than a thing among things.

It is a way of being beyond envy and jealousy, beyond furious self-condemnation and shame, and beyond the sadomasochistic functionalizing and dehumanizing of the self and of the other.

ACKNOWLEDGMENTS

We are grateful for the help and suggestions we received in the writing of this study from Mrs. Annemarie Sandler, London, Dr. Irja Kantanen in Helsinki, Dr. Friedrich Eickhoff in Tübingen, and Dr. Elke Natorp-Husmann in Hamburg and Bremen.

NOTE

1. "Stehe ich einem Menschen als meinem Du gegenüber, spreche das Grundwort Ich-Du zu ihm, ist er kein Ding unter Dingen und nicht aus Dingen bestehend."

REFERENCES

Avnon, D. (1998). *Martin Buber—The hidden dialogue*. Lanham, MD: Rowman & Littlefield.

Benz, A. E. (1984). Der Gebärneid der Männer. *Psyche, 38*, 307–328.

Bollas, C. (1987). *The shadow of the object: Psychoanalysis of the unthought known*. New York: Columbia University Press.

Buber, M. (1947). *Dialogisches Leben*. Zürich: Gregor Müller.

Derrida, J. (1976/1979). Fors. Die Winkelwörter von Nicolas Abraham und Maria Torok. In N. Abraham & M. Torok (Eds.), Kryptonymie. Frankfurt: Das Verbarium des Wolfsmannes Ullstein.

Dettmering, P. (2003). Der erste der Vampirfilme. Zu F. W. Murnaus Film "Nosferatu." *Psyche 57*, 551–554.

Ferenczi, S. (1932). Sprachverwirrung zwischen den Erwachsenen und dem Kind (Die Sprache der Zärtlichkeit und der Leidenschaft). In V. Kovács (Ed.), *Bausteine zur Psychoanalyse* (pp. 511–525). Bern, Switzerland: Huber. [Translated in: (1933/1949). Confusion of tongues between adult and child. *International Journal of Psychoanalysis, 30*, 225–230.]

______ (1933/1949). Transl. of previous entry: Confusion of tongues between adult and child ..., *International Journal of Psychoanalysis, 30*: 225–230.

Green, A. (1993). *Le travail du negative.* Paris: Edition de minuit.

Hägglund, T. B., Hägglund, V., & Ikonen P. (1975–1976). On the defensive nature of phallicity. In *Dying. A psychoanalytical study with special reference to individual creativity and defensive organization.* Monograph 6, Psychiatric Clinic, Helsinki University Central Hospital.

Hirsch, M. (2005). Über Vampirismus. *Psyche, 59,* 127–144.

Kennel, R. & Reerink, G. (1997). Klein-Bion. Eine einfurhung. Tübingen (Edit. Discord).

Küchenhoff, J. (1990). Die Repräsentation des frühen Traumas in der Übertragung. *Forum der Psychoanalyse, 6,* 15–31.

Lansky, M. R. (2005). The impossibility of forgiveness. Shame fantasies as instigators of vengefulness in Euripides *Medea. Journal of the American Academy of Psychoanalysis, 53,* 437–464.

Le Couteux, C. (1999/2001). *Die Geschichte der Vampire. Metamorphose eines Mythos.* Düsseldorf: Artemis & Winkler.

Lipton, S. D. (1977a). The advantages of Freud's technique as shown in his analysis of the "ratman." *International Journal of Psychoanalysis, 58,* 255–274.

Lipton, S. D. (1977b). Clinical observations on resistance to the transference. International Journal of Psychoanalysis, 58, 865–898.

Mahler, M.S., Pine F., & Bergman, A. (1975). *The Psychological Birth of the Human Infant: Symbiosis and Individuation.* New York: Basic Books.

Morgenthaler, F. (1987). *Homosexualität, Heterosexualität, Perversion.* Frankfurt: Fischer.

Pohl, H. (1985). Die Gruselgeschichte—ein Beitrag zur Psychoanalyse von Horrorliteratur. *Zeitschrift fur Psychosomatische Medizin und Psychotherapie, 31,* 187–199.

Reed, G. S. & Baudry, F.D. (2005). Conflict, Structure, and Absence: Andre Green on Borderline and Narcissistic Pathology. *Psychoanalytical Quarterly,* 74: 121–156.

Schwaber, P. (2006, June 16). *Plenary Address: "Hamlet and Psychoanalytic Experience."* American Psychoanalytic Meeting, Washington, D.C.

Stern, D. N. (2004). The present moment in psychotherapies and everyday life. New York: Norton.

Stolorow, D. S., & Stolorow, R. D. (1989). My brother's keeper: Intensive treatment of a case of delusional merger. *International Journal of Psychoanalysis, 70,* 315–326.

Valenstein, A. F. (1973). On attachment to painful feelings and the negative therapeutic reaction. *Psychoanalytic Study of the Child, 28,* 365–392.

6

Envy of Maternal Functions in Sacrifice Rituals

NAOMI H. JANOWITZ

Over two decades ago Jeffrey Andresen (1984) challenged analysts to pay more attention to themes of sacrifice appearing in their clinical work. According to Andresen, Freud's insight into this issue has been unduly neglected. Freud recounted throwing a slipper across the room and breaking a statue as a "sacrificial act" directed toward his daughter's recovery (Freud, 1901/1960, p. 169). He saw this as one among many everyday activities that acted out sacrificial fantasies.

Andresen is no doubt correct that sacrificial fantasies appear often in clinical material; sacrifice traditions are so central in most religious traditions it is hard to imagine otherwise. Yet, Andresen proposed a fairly limited set of sacrificial fantasies. He presents several clinical vignettes in which something of value was given up or destroyed by a patient in hopes of restoring a relationship with a loved one. He thereby highlights his patients' wishes to compensate for fantasies of having harmed loved ones. Consideration of other notions of sacrifice might lead analysts to additional fantasies.

If analysts have neglected sacrifice, scholars of religion have not. Theories of sacrifice and initiation constitute the vast majority of theorizing about ritual, with sacrifice weighing in with more ink.[1] Much modern scholarship replays old interpretations, from Plato's gift theory to Hume's concept of meritorious loss. This essay follows Andresen's call for analysts to focus on sacrifice, while simultaneously arguing that scholars of religion should make better use of analytic theories. I will argue that a central role of sacrifice rituals, too often overlooked by both analysts and scholars of religion, is expression of unconscious envy of maternal functions.

Among these functions, the focus here is on the ability to give birth and to nurse.

The unconscious wish to take on these roles is acted out by men in numerous rituals, which represent manic denials of dependence on women by taking on their birthing/nursing roles. In Kleinian terms, the first object of envy is the feeding breast, "for the infant feels that it possesses everything he desires and that it has an unlimited flow of milk, and love which the breast keeps for its own gratification" (Klein, 1975, p. 183). Although all babies envy the breast, she also states that for men "excessive envy of the breast is likely to extend to all feminine attributes, in particular to the woman's capacity to bear children" (p. 201). Although Klein discussed individual patients, this envy is also manifest unconsciously on a societal level in religious myths and rituals. Sacrifice rituals are golden opportunities for men to acquire, if only for a short time, both the birthing and nurturing roles of women.

SACRIFICE RITES AS REBIRTHING EXPERIENCES

Sacrifice rituals, as some of the most exciting recent scholarship argues, represent powerful social mechanisms for articulating and sorting out gender roles. Nancy Jay's (1992) seminal research, for example, drew attention to the gender-skewed aspects of sacrifice. Examples as widely diverse as ancient Israel, Rome, modern West Africa, and Islam all converge in a stunning moment of cross-cultural agreement that men sacrifice animals and women do not. In the few instances where women are closely associated with sacrifices, the women are either postmenopausal or young virgins. Therefore, it is not simply their status as females that is so central to their exclusion from sacrifice, but their status as women capable of having children.

Robertson Smith (1894) noted long ago the close connection between sacrifice and clan membership, but it was Nancy Jay (1992) who outlined the various ways in which sacrifices establish and maintain patriarchal practices. Sacrifice is "male child-birthing," to use a phrase from Hawaiian sacrifice, since sacrificial rituals establish the social identity of the child (Valeri, 1985, p. 114). Birth by women is overcome in the various sacrificial rituals that attribute the social "birth" of a child to the father, even in matriarchal societies.[2] The person born from a woman is mortal, "but the man integrated into an 'eternal' social order to that degree transcends mortality" (Jay, 1992, p. 39).

In Greek society, a newborn was admitted into a family by a sacrifice at the hearth; without it, the baby would be left to die or at least excluded from the family line. In the case of the Hawaiian king, "in his sacrifices, especially those of his installation, the king ritually controls his divine genealogy and reproduces himself and the god without dependence on women's reproductive powers" (Jay, 1992, p. 83).

A dramatic example of the gendering of sacrifice can be seen in the juxtaposition of the near-sacrifice of Isaac (Genesis 22) with the completed sacrifice of the anonymous daughter of Jephthah (Judges 11:29–40). The life of the eldest son is said to "belong" to the deity, and the son's life is given back to him by the divine father when he returns Isaac to his father. The sacrifice of the son, which appears to threaten any chance of Abraham having descendants, turns out to be a male generative act. For his willingness to sacrifice Isaac, Abraham is given the blessing of descendants, as the deity states, "I will bless you, and I will make your offspring as numerous as the stars in heaven and as the sand that is on the seashore" (Genesis 22:17).

Jephthah vowed that he would sacrifice the first living being who came out of his house if he was given victory in battle. When he returns, his daughter comes out to meet him, learns of his vow, and acquiesces to his vow.[3] Before she is killed she asks to go out into the mountains with other young women to mourn her virginity (Judges 11:37). She is unable to offer her generative power via a husband, which would not help her father anyway with his line of descendants, but is able to offer her life to her father instead. The story ends by recounting that this practice is still carried out by the daughters of Israel, who go to the mountains to mourn the daughter's lost virginity but not, we note, her life.

As Susan Sered (2002) has outlined, the cultural death of an animal valorizes the male and makes the female the carrier of everything negative (impurity, mortality, lost virginity, and so forth). The particular manifestation of the gendering power of sacrifice varies from culture to culture. In some cultures women do not sacrifice because they are associated with death, while in others they do not sacrifice because they are associated with life.

For all her brilliant analysis, Jay does not outline any basis for the striking cross-cultural similarities she describes. Alan Dundes' (1984) study of myth is helpful here, as he tries to explain another example of an obvious, yet overlooked, gender-skewed theme found in innumerable religions: a male god creating the first humans from dirt. This theme is specifically based, according to Dundes' Freudian interpretation, on the widespread appearance of (a) a cloacal theory of birth (childbirth via bowels) and (b) male envy of pregnancy. Beyond this bare plot, the full creation stories vary widely, since they are dependent in their details on culturally specific elaboration of the very general common theme.[4] His explanation points to both the cross-culturally fixed part of the theme (the envy of childbirth and common childhood confusions about childbirth) and that the motivations behind the stories are unconscious. Thus it is possible to set Jay's findings in this larger context of aspects of religious expression that unconsciously express envy of maternal functions.

Part of this larger context is the myths Dundes has brought to our attention.[5] In one of the central creation stories of the ancient Indian Vedic traditions, found in the Rig Veda, the world is created by a sacrifice of the cosmic figure called Purus a (Rig Veda 1.10). His body is dismembered and social roles (castes) fixed depending on which part of his body was used in their formation. The sacrifice story, and then all enactments of sacrifices modeled on it, reverses the reality of birth by making people literally out of the body of a man. The text states explicitly that the female principle was born from Purus a as part of the primary work of creation.

It is possible to argue that the entire philosophical system of transmigration of souls, so central to Indian philosophy, solves not only the problem of death but also that of birth from a woman. Rebirth takes place at the time of death through a series of rituals controlled by men. The Hindu upper castes are distinguished as "twice-born," that is, as men who have already overcome the stigma of birth from a woman. The death/rebirth ritual of cremation is a structural parallel to the consuming and transforming sacrificial fire.

Female birthing power is displaced not only by animal sacrifice, but also by martyrdom traditions that emerge as the practice of animal sacrifice is rejected in early Judaism (Janowitz, 2006). In the earliest extant Jewish martyrdom text, the Apocryphal Second Maccabees,[6] a mother exhorts her seven sons to die rather than obey the king and break a food taboo. In the modified self-sacrifice of martyrdom, the mother gains agency and participates much more than she would have in the animal sacrifice system, but the agency is basically her ability to die like a brave man. The mother dies encouraging her sons to reject the life that she gave them for another life given by the male god-father, substituting "rebirth" from the divine father for human birth from females. The martyr-son is offered the hope of an eternal merging with the mother in the afterlife, and at the same time, protection by the divine father (and his law) from a helpless dependence on the mother.

MEN MAKING MALE FOOD

In addition to animal sacrifice and martyrdom displacing the human mother, another fundamental role of females, that of nursing mother, is also displaced unto men by sacrifice traditions. Although many theories have stressed the violent aspects of sacrifice (Girard, 1977), the roles of feeding and being fed have received much less attention. Robertson Smith (1894) placed the communal feast at the center of his theory of sacrifice, but did not note the gender implications at all. No matter what the role of women in the daily preparation of food, the making of sacred food via sacrifice is a male prerogative (for exceptions see Sered [1994]).

The notion of "sacred food" is left somewhat vague here on purpose because the particular examples differ widely from tradition to tradition. In some cases it is possible to point to a specific set of food items, such as the bread and wine of the Eucharist. In other instances, an entire system might produce special sacred food, as the system of *kashrut*, which is controlled by male rabbis (until very recently). Within this general system, specific items such as *matzah* can represent yet another level of sacred food.

These sacred foods stand at the other end of the spectrum from mother's milk. Although it is not necessarily always labeled impure in purity systems, mother's milk cannot have saving power per se. Instead, the value of mother's milk is transferred to male sacred food metaphorically, as we will see in a number of instances below. Sacrificial food far outweighs the natural food of the mother. That is, sacrifice traditions establish the male-produced food as the most important food for humans, often in explicit opposition to female nourishment.[7]

Female participation is denied at every step of the process, since the officiant (priest) who produces the male food for the male deity from the male body must himself be male. By excluding women from making the sacred food of sacrifice, they are excluded from generative roles as well. That is, male-only feeding and begetting go hand in hand. Thus the food rituals reinforce the genealogies in the priestly source of the Hebrew scriptures, which list male offspring as if they were spontaneously generated from their fathers (Genesis 25:19). It might even be possible to argue that female exclusion from making sacrifices is in part demanded by the wish to negate their generative power.

Not only do men produce the sacred food, but it is also possible to make food out of men's bodies. Male flesh and blood can become sacred via sacrifice and can then function as sacred food. Food made from the male body is positively associated with other dimensions of the religious system, such as the divine teachings. The literal eating of the bodily food seems to anchor the metaphorical taking-in of the divine teaching. Male supernatural figures can offer followers either teachings or their bodies, both of which in some fundamental way protect or save the followers.

Can we see this as a denial of the ambivalence felt toward the mother's breast? The male leader produces and distributes perfect food, endless in supply and always there for the taking. Eating the food carries no threat if the person who takes it in is good. In some instances, eating the food absolves the person from guilty feelings, again the opposite of the experience of the breast, which elicits guilt.

One obvious example of this is the institution of the Eucharist as Jesus' body and blood.[8] In 1 Corinthians 11 Paul distinguished between a normal meal and the special meal set in motion by Jesus. The meal is done to remember the actions of Jesus before he died, when he recited "This is my body which is for you; do this as a memorial for me" (1 Corinthians 11:24; Luke 22:19). Beyond being a memorial of the events from Jesus' life, the food has tremendous power. If eaten in the proper context with the proper attitude, it protects the person who eats it. Eating this food makes a person part of the body of Christ, destined for rebirth into an eternal afterlife. Those who do not eat it are literally condemned by death since they will not achieve immortal life.

Some surprising examples of male body-food appear in stories where the Buddha offers his body to his followers to eat. These Buddhist texts shift back and forth between presentations of the Buddha's teachings (dharma) and much more dramatic stories where the Buddha literally turns himself into food for his followers to save them from starving.

These stories, described and analyzed by Reiko Ohnuma (1998) in his article "The Gift of the Body and the Gift of Dharma," seem to embarrass scholars of Buddhism who do not expect such bloody stories in Buddhist circles. The Buddha suffers, sometimes quite dramatically, as he willingly offers others his flesh. The theme appears in the Jataka tales, which recount stories of the Buddha's previous lives where he often appears in the form of an animal.[9] In one of these stories an ascetic is forced by starvation to consider returning to a village where he might fall into temptation. The Buddha, who appears in the story as a hare, willingly throws himself into the fire in order to supply the ascetic with food (Avadanasataka 37 cited by Ohnuma, 1998, p. 328).[10]

In another story from the Sutra of the Wise and Foolish, a human prince comes upon a starving tigress that is about to eat her cubs (Ohnuma, 1998, pp. 329–330). The prince kills himself next to them so that they may drink his blood. Thus he saves both the cubs from their ravenous mother and the mother herself. The prince turns out to be none other than the Buddha. It is hard to imagine a story that more fully displaces the mother. It is a reverse nursing story, where instead of mother's milk, male blood is the fluid that saves the cubs from none other than the devouring mother herself.

Dharma, the Buddha's teaching, then is interpreted based on these stories as a metaphorical image of the body. It too can be "incorporated" so as to save the followers from suffering and death. Ohnuma concludes "The bodhisattva's body is not only a symbol for the Buddha's dharma; it is also that entity that seems to have become the Buddha's dharma" (1998, pp. 358–359).

An even more explicit replacing of mother's milk by Buddha milk is found in "Gotami's Story," part of the Apadana collection of moral biographies written in the last two centuries B.C.E. This text is the autobiography of Gotami, Buddha's aunt, who stepped in as wet-nurse for the Buddha when her sister died while the Buddha was still an infant. Just before her death Gotami recounts how she reared the Buddha and contrasts her milk with the milk the Buddha gave her in return. "I suckled you with mother's milk which quenched thirst for a moment. From you I drank the dharma-milk, perpetually tranquil" (Lopez, 1995, p. 121).

No doubt further study will offer us numerous other examples of male blood functioning as a substitute for female milk, and numerous variants on this theme. For example, in his article on the origin of circumcision, James George Frazer (1904) recounts a number of rituals that employ male blood for what he calls its "fertilizing virtue," yet makes no comment on gender issues (p. 210). Among the Australian aboriginals, men slit their arm veins and let some of their blood fall on the ground as a way of increasing the fertility of the emus (pp. 205–206). Here the male fluid functions as a sort of combined mother's milk and perhaps the uterine blood as well.

These stories seem like male fantasies of nursing stories, where the heroic nature of the act is held up in high regard even as it is presented as gruesome and in some basic sense disgusting. The nursing father outdoes the nursing mother, since he is ready to die for the sake of nourishing all the children and their mother. And the nursing father will not really die, since he can provide an endless supply of food without being in any way diminished or depleted.

Although not positing food made of male bodies, rabbinic texts equate manna and mother's milk and thus present both the deity and Moses as nursing figures. These nursing figures far outweigh all human mothers. Babylonian Talmud tractate *Yoma* 75a plays on the word "cake" used to describe manna in Numbers 11:8, changing the vowels to read instead "breast." Both the manna cakes and breast milk have a variety of tastes. The *Sifre* (commentary on Numbers) 89 compares the centrality of manna, which is so significant for those who eat it, with the breast, which "is everything" to the nursing infant. Yet another interpretation recounts that in the time of the persecution of the Israelites by the Egyptians, God provided the Israelites with two balls (breast-shaped rocks), one made of oil and one made of honey, citing "And he made him to suck honey out of the crag and oil out of the flinty rock" (Deuteronomy 32:13). God thus nurses the children of Israel with honey and oil instead of milk (Midrash *Exodus Rabba* 1.12 and Talmud tractate *Sota* 11b). In the rabbinic text *Pesikta d'Rab Kahane* 12, manna and nursing milk are both equated with the divine word, which is also customized to each individual person's needs, "the Divine Word spoke to each and every person according to his particular capacity."

The sacred food from the deity and Moses is copied in the rituals where rabbis are equated with nursing mothers when they set children on their laps and feed them "torah" cakes. These rites as in the rituals used when young boys begin their study of the Torah and are fed cakes by their rabbi teachers (Marcus, 1996, p. 77).

INITIATION RITUALS AND ENVY OF FEMALES

Initiation, J. Z. Smith (2004) points out, may be the equivalent in hunter-gatherer cultures of sacrifice in agrarian ones. His observation seems especially salient in regards to the topic of this essay since initiation rituals also appear to be based on envy of women. The female envy encoded in these rituals has been more widely noted in analytic literature, perhaps because it is mentioned so often in the anthropological data (Jaffe, 1968; Lidz & Lidz, 1977). Initiations are interpreted as a subcategory of fertility rites, since they assert that men too can bear children (Bettelheim, 1954, p. 45).

This was not Freud's view, nor that of many of his followers. Freud's particular stance on circumcision was that it was connected to castration anxiety and the Oedipal complex. He wrote, "Circumcision is the symbolic substitute for castration, a punishment which the primeval father dealt his sons long ago out of the fullness of his power" (Freud, 1933/1964, p. 122). Freud did not consider other theories, and most of his followers have stuck fairly closely to Freud's lines of interpretation. Hermann Nunberg (1947), for example, offers clinical evidence about circumcision fantasies that point to issues of bisexuality but repeats the strict Freudian interpretation. Freud's explanation is dependent on the universality of the Oedipus complex, a point that is highly controversial. The question is whether these rituals can also have another function, especially in societies where the jealous father is not a central figure in the cultural stories. These rituals are often undertaken by the man by choice and sometimes even repeated by choice. The rituals are seen as enhancing the men's status as more virile. Decades ago Bruno Bettelheim brought to the attention of the analytic community Margaret Mead's analysis of initiation rites as male attempts to take over female functions.[11] He argued at length in *Symbolic Wounds* (1954) that males are ambivalent toward their mothers, and that they envy the female sexual organs and their functions (p. 15). Since women also participate in initiation rituals, they may be able to temporarily make themselves into men via these rites.

The initiation rituals to which Mead, Bettelheim, and others draw our attention involve numerous ingenious means of genital mutilation by men. In some of these rites men make their genitals bleed in order to make themselves temporarily into menstruating women. In his 1970 study of New Guinea, Hogbin (1970) describes a complex set of rituals by which men "menstruate" and are thus able to cleanse themselves of contamination. This set of rituals is so important in Hogbin's analysis of the culture that it appears in the title of his book *The Island of Menstruating Men.* Menstruating men, like menstruating women, are considered "rekaraka," and must go into retirement, observe food taboos, and so forth. Variations in the treatment of the two genders are due to, as Hogbin explains, the fact that "men are socially more important" (p. 89). Also, the men do not menstruate every month; they may delay doing so until they suffer an illness where they may be suffering from some type of female pollution and in need of decontamination. Men are thus able to be female to the extent that it is useful to them, but to avoid the consequences of being too female, or female all the time.

Ruth and Theodore Lidz (1977) describe still other rituals in New Guinea in which men "menstruate" as a means of endowing themselves with female creativity, which they believe women possess naturally but which men must acquire via rituals. After they menstruate as part of initiation ceremonies, they then learn to play the sacred flutes.

A striking number of other initiation rituals in other religious traditions also involve drawing blood from male genitals. According to standard rabbinic practice, if a boy is born circumcised, or if a man who is circumcised converts to Judaism, then in order to convert to Judaism some blood must be drawn from his penis (Hoffman, 1996, p. 96). This blood is not defiling, in stark contrast to menstrual blood. It is no surprise circumcision is emphasized in the priestly source of the Hebrew scriptures, which denies to women as much as possible any role in genealogies.

Initiation also articulates with other, more explicit attempts by males to take on birthing roles, among the more famous "couvade," the practice by men of simulated pregnancy. In all of these instances one of the beauties of the rituals is that it is not a permanent change; men can experiment with being female temporarily. Men can symbolically undergo childbirth, lactation, and all the other roles, which are not open to them in normal life.

Endowing religious specialists with secrets is often presented as stealing the secret of fertility from women. Among the Yoruba, in the Itefa initiation ceremonies, male diviners take over the birthing role by "rebirthing" men into a new identity. The founding myth for the ritual claims that it was originally the wife of the deity of divination who told it to her husband. He then proceeded to produce 16 "children," that is, the 16 major divination signs. As a reminder of this origin a woman carries a closed gourd during the ritual (Drewal, 1992, p. 73).

Although women are completely excluded from sacrifice, they are able to participate in some circumstances in initiations. These rituals often exhibit aspects of penis envy, that is, during the rites women act like men and show off culturally male attributes such as courage and endurance. An intriguing question is why females are permitted to experiment with being males temporarily, while no equivalent experimentation is found in sacrificial cultures.

CONCLUSIONS

The fact that it is the mother who by nature bears children and offers food presents a problem: How is it possible that women have such an inherent advantage? It would appear to point to some kind of natural superiority of women. It is this dilemma that some rituals work hard to overcome by reversing, canceling, or denigrating the female advantage. Exactly how this is done varies from religion to religion and from culture to culture.

If we want to follow Andresen's advice and look for more sacrificial material in clinical work, we must consider that fantasies about sacrifice and initiation may relate to issues of bisexuality. People continue to have bisexual identifications throughout their lives. Religious rituals and myths can permit these identifications to be temporarily tried out in new ways or strongly reinforce standard societal norms.

We must also greatly expand on our notions of sacrificial fantasies. Bataille (1986) argued that sacrifice is the moment when the continuity of life and death is acted out, but our analysis points in a different direction. Sacrifice is the structural opposite of birth, the undoing of the natural birth experience via culturally enacted death. Ironically, the act of killing by choice, the "selective kill" described in J. Z. Smith's (2004) theory of sacrifice, seems to give the power of death and life to men. The sleight of hand, as it were, of sacrifice, giving birth by killing, redirects natural productivity to men.

It may not be surprising that myths and rituals, which are the creations of men, center on creative male deities from whom female principles are born. But Klein would have us take this issue very seriously, since the relationship with the breast is the basis of object relations, building the core of the ego.[12] Envy of the breast is part of the psychic development of every individual. She writes: "The whole is instinctual desire and his unconscious phantasies imbue the breast with qualities going far beyond the actual nourishment it affords" (1975, p. 180). In particular, "the fundamental envy of the women's breast lies at the root even of penis envy" (p. 199).[13]

The social implications of these unconscious structures of myth and ritual are enormous; envy of women is a basic problem that societies must struggle with. Sacrifice and initiation rites are both central opportunities to overcome male disadvantages temporarily, but the issue is in no way resolved.

NOTES

1. For a concise summary of several major theories of sacrifice see (Valeri, 1985, pp. 62–73). Jeffrey Carter's (2003) collection includes excerpts from many major theorists, although sometimes in rather abbreviated form. For biblical sacrifices in particular, see Anderson (1991).
2. Even in matriarchal societies sacrifices such as the Ashanti, or in bilateral descent traditions such as the Hawaiian, sacrifices are carried out by men exclusively and dominate the social world and create the most important social power relations.
3. This story raises numerous issues about sacrifice and sexuality, which are beyond the scope of this essay, and points to issues of sacrifice as a mode of resolving Oedipal conflicts. See Patricia Johnson's (1997) article, which argues that Antigone's decision to sacrifice herself for her brother instead of marrying her intended husband is also presented as an unresolved Oedipus conflict.
4. Looking for an unconscious meaning cross-culturally is a fraught enterprise; it is imperative to avoid reading one culture's notion of the feminine into another culture. Many analytic studies ignore this problem and simply equate, for example, femininity with passivity no matter the specifics of the cultural system.
5. Jay does occasionally mention myths about sacrifice, as for example the myth that Hercules became divine via a sacrificial fire that burnt away "all that his mother gave him," leaving him in the image of his father (Jay, 1992, p. 31).

6. Second Maccabees is a Greek text from the first century B.C.E. that is in Catholic and Eastern Orthodox Bibles to this day.
7. It is beyond the scope of this essay, but worth noting that the food women make for ritual purposes is often involved in debates about heresy. The tradition of denouncing women for making cakes for the Queen of Heaven, perhaps in the shape of female genitalia (Jeremiah 7:18, 44:19; cf. Hosea 3:1) reappears in heresiologist Epiphanius of Salamis's fourth-century denunciation (*Haeres* 78) of the "Collyridians" for making cakes for the Virgin Mother (Pope, 1977, p. 379). This tradition is perhaps continued all the way up to the making of hamantaschen.
8. These few comments on the incredibly complex meanings of the Eucharist are meant to be suggestive. See also Jay's discussion of these issues in the modern context (1992, pp. 112–127).
9. The Jataka tales are noncanonical Buddhist folk literature dating to approximately the third century.
10. In this story the ascetic pulls the hare out of the fire, but, as Ohnuma notes, the story demonstrates the Buddha's willingness to sacrifice himself.
11. In addition to Mead's book *Male and Female*, Bettelheim cites the work of Ashley Montagu, Gregory Bateson, and R. M. and C. H. Berndt.
12. See also Robert Paul's comments on the persecuting father of the biblical texts as "a derivative of the more primary persecuting breast of the Kleinian 'paranoid position,'" which he argues explain the "more uncanny and horrifying features of the male god" (1996, p. 103).
13. Similar to Karen Horney's (1967) statements that fear of the vulva is earlier than fear of the father's penis, and the dread of the penis is put forward to "hide the intense dread of the vulva" (pp. 458–459).

REFERENCES

Anderson, G. (1991). Sacrifice. In D. N. Friedman (Ed.), *Anchor dictionary of the Bible* (pp. 870–886). New York: Doubleday.

Andresen, J. (1984). The motif of sacrifice and the sacrifice complex. *Contemporary Psychoanalysis, 20*, 526–559.

Bataille, G. (1986). *Erotism: Death and sensuality*. San Francisco: City Lights.

Bettelheim, B. (1954). *Symbolic wounds: Puberty rites and the envious male*. Glencoe, IL: Free Press.

Carter, J. (2003). *Understanding religious sacrifice: A reader*. London: Continuum.

Drewal, M. (1992). *Yoruba ritual: Performance, play, ritual*. Bloomington: Indiana University Press.

Dundes, A. (1984). The Earth diver myth. In A. Dundes (Ed.), *Sacred narrative: readings in the theory of myth* (pp. 270–294). Berkeley: University of California Press.

Frazer, J. (1904). The origin of circumcision. *Independent Review, 4*, 4204–4218.

Freud, S. (1901/1960). The psychopathology of everyday life. In *Standard edition* (Vol. 6). London: Hogarth Press.

Freud, S. (1933/1964). New introductory lectures on psycho-analysis: Lecture XXXIII, Femininity. In *Standard edition* (Vol. 22, pp. 112–136). London: Hogarth Press.

Girard, R. (1977). *Violence and the sacred.* Baltimore: Johns Hopkins University Press.
Hoffman, L. (1996). *Covenant of blood: Circumcision and gender in rabbinic Judaism.* Chicago: University of Chicago Press.
Hogbin, I. (1970). *The island of menstruating men: Religion in Wogeo, New Guinea.* Scranton: Chandler.
Horney, K. (1967). *Feminine psychology.* New York: W. W. Norton.
Jaffe, D. (1968). The masculine envy of woman's procreative function. *Journal of the American Psychoanalytic Association, 16,* 521–548.
Janowitz, N. (2006). Lusting for death: Unconscious fantasies in an ancient Jewish martyrdom text. *Psychoanalytic Psychology 23(4)*:644–653..
Jay, N. (1992). *Throughout your generations forever: Sacrifice, religion and paternity.* Chicago: University of Chicago Press.
Johnson, P. (1997). Woman's third face: A psycho/social reconsideration of Sophocles' *Antigone. Arethusa, 30,* 369–398.
Klein, M. (1975). *Envy and gratitude and other works, 1946–1963.* New York: Free Press.
Lidz, R., & Lidz, T. (1977). Male menstruation: A ritual alternative to the oedipal transition. *International Journal of Psycho-Analysis, 58,* 17–31.
Lopez, D. J. (1995). *Buddhism in practice.* Princeton, NJ: Princeton University Press.
Marcus, I. (1996). *Rituals of childhood: Jewish acculturation in medieval Europe.* New Haven, CT: Yale University Press.
Nunberg, H. (1947). Circumcision and problems of bisexuality. *International Journal of Psycho-Analysis, 28,* 145–179.
Ohnuma, R. (1998). Gift of the body and gift of Dharma. *History of Religions, 37*(4):323–359.
Paul, R. A. (1996). *Moses and civilization: The meaning behind Freud's myth.* New Haven, CT: Yale University Press.
Pope, M. (1977). *The Song of Songs.* Garden City, NY: Doubleday.
Sered, S. S. (1994). *Priestess mother sacred sister: Religions dominated by women.* Oxford: Oxford University Press.
Sered, S. S. (2002). Towards a gendered typology of sacrifice: Women and feasting, men and death in an Okinawan village. In A. Baumgarten (Ed.), *Sacrifice in religious experience* (pp. 13–38). Leiden: Brill.
Smith, J. Z. (2004). *Relating religion: Essays in the study of religion.* Chicago: University of Chicago Press.
Smith, W. R. (1894). *Lectures on the religion of the Semites: The fundamental institutions.* London: A. & C. Black.
Valeri, V. (1985). *Kingship and sacrifice: Ritual and society in ancient Hawaii.* Chicago: University of Chicago Press.

7

The Evil Eye, Envy, and Shame

On Emotions and Explanation

BENJAMIN KILBORNE

Throughout the Mediterranean and the Middle East there persists today a powerful and fascinating belief system organized around the concept of the Evil Eye. Implicit in this belief system is the psychology of envy as the linchpin of human motivation, the keystone in the arch of human experience.

Why the belief systems organized around the Evil Eye are so powerful can be understood in the light of the distinction Gimbattista Vico made in 1744 between *il certo* (certainty) and *il vero* (truth). This, in turn, sheds light on Freud's 1919 paper on "The Uncanny" in which he speaks of the Evil Eye. However, there are distinctions to be made between the concept of envy in the psychoanalytic tradition and the concept of envy represented by Evil Eye belief systems. Both are equally important for clinicians, and both implicitly or explicitly conjoin the power of envy with the power of shame dynamics.

EVIL EYE RITUALS

The tradition of the Evil Eye and its functions in explanations for human misfortune and illness goes back thousands of years. One finds Mesopotamian (i.e., Assyrian and Babylonian) seals and amulets against the Evil Eye, as well as representations of the Evil Eye. In ancient and modern Egypt the symbolism of the Evil Eye is to be found not only in the iconography of Horus but also in numerous hieroglyphic writings. There is even an eye on the U.S. dollar bill, derived from beliefs of the freemasons and intended perhaps to ward off envy. In the United States conspicuous consumption has so far outstripped beliefs in the Evil Eye that most people do not even notice the eye on the dollar bill; still less do they give credence to the cautionary practices prevalent elsewhere. The avoidance of the subject of envy in the United States may also have something to do with the Horatio Alger myth that everyone can become wealthy. Therefore, in a land where the wealthy are to be emulated (and they can be), nobody need be envious, and the seeming absence of envy on the cultural radar screen can be a reinforcement for illusions of democratic equality. However, our ideals of equality, perpetuated by the Horatio Alger myth, actually get in the way of civic and social responses to and responsibilities for real inequalities. In this respect envy and greed can feed on illusions of equality while deepening the divide between rich and poor, which has grown exponentially over the past two decades. The most obvious form in which envy appears (disguised) is in "healthy competition" (read destructive rivalry) over conspicuous consumption (keeping up with the Jones): I am not envious, I am competitive, and my financial success reinforces my right to exist. By contrast, those who are poor or fraught with financial insecurity are, according to prevailing American values, brought to question their existence itself. In this way, the predominance of materialistic values (represented, for example, by the importance ascribed to the gross national product) provides those who succeed financially with culturally sanctioned ways of defending against shame and vulnerability. In the process, however, the American emphasis on competition and money undermines social responsibilities and human bonds.

Notions of looks that kill are to be found throughout the world.[1] There is a Polish story in which the hero, cursed by the Evil Eye, blinds himself in order to keep his children from being injured by his looks. Beliefs in the Evil Eye were prevalent in ancient Greece and Rome. Pliny notes that special laws were put into place so that those using the Evil Eye to injure crops could be held responsible. This power was termed *fascinatio* in Latin, and from it is derived our word "fascination." Most will no doubt be familiar with a variety of folk tales that deal with lethal looks, one of the most familiar being that of Lady Godiva, who forbade all the villagers to watch her as she rode naked through the village. One peeping Tom dared look and was punished by being blinded.

Children and young animals were thought to be particularly vulnerable to the nefarious effects of the Evil Eye, beliefs widely prevalent in the Middle East and Mediterranean today. For example, in Lebanon and Turkey eye amulets against the Evil Eye are placed on newborn babies and on their cribs. These are passed from generation to generation, so sons and daughters inherit the amulets they will place on their children, and these will be passed down to their children and their children's children. Readers will also be familiar with the magical hex signs on barns to ward off the Evil Eye. Although far less in evidence today, these used to be widely prevalent throughout the Western world (and elsewhere) until the Second World War.

But amulets were not the only means of warding off the Evil Eye. There are (and were) also gestures such as pointing one's forefingers in a fork at the one believed to have the Evil Eye, written charms often dissolved in water so that the afflicted might drink it, and spitting. For both the Greeks and the Romans spitting was a prevalent antidote to the poisons of the Evil Eye. According to Theocritus one must spit three times onto the chest of the person who is believed to be a potential victim of the Evil Eye.

Since the Evil Eye is thought to be rooted in envy, it is therefore believed to be imprudent to engage in any sort of conspicuous consumption or bragging. When praising anything the Italians would add *Si mal occhio non ci fosse* (may the Evil Eye not strike it), and the Romans *Praefiscini dixerim.* This expression was added after having praised oneself or complimented oneself and indicates that what was just spoken was meant neither as bragging nor as a challenge to the envious. Additionally, the word *Praefiscini* is derived from "fascinum, fascinare" from, which we get our words "fascinate" and "fascination."[2] What the Scots call "forespeaking" when praise is likely to bring on disease or misfortune can be illustrated by a number of rural sayings, such as the Somersetshire expression "I don't wish ee no harm, so I on't zay no more." Roger Bacon writes: "the times when the stroke … of an envious eye does most hurt are particularly when the party envied is beheld in glory and in triumph."[3]

THE EVIL EYE, ILLNESS, AND MISFORTUNE

Within the anthropological world, it is striking that to my knowledge there does not exist a major study of the Evil Eye as a belief system. Belief systems can be defined as those structures of thinking that circumscribe a familiar conceptual world and dictate assumptions. Generally speaking, psychoanalysts neither cite works on belief systems nor use the term at all. This is a shame, since the term provides us with ways of speaking within the same frame about religious beliefs and those beliefs characterized as "superstitions." In addressing the subject of the Evil Eye, Freud characterizes Evil Eye beliefs as "superstitions." In so doing he is drawing on a long history of thought categories in the West. The Judeo-Christian tradition is "religious," as are the other "religions" studied by comparative religion. Although Lowie (1924) and others have written on "primitive religion" in order to dignify what was regarded as "superstition," the distinction has clung to discourse in the social sciences and politics, and to this day has the ring of "us" (we have religion) versus "them" (they have superstition). We can see this, for example, in the speeches of President George W. Bush when he speaks of Islam. The pope, like President Bush, also calls up the specter of the crusades and their war against "the infidels."

In this chapter I will be focusing on the concept of belief systems in order to better provide a perspective on Freud's approach to the subject of the Evil Eye, and to speak about Evil Eye belief systems as social and cultural phenomena with a life and power that Freud did not allow himself the freedom to understand.

A variety of sources refer to practices that are collected in various works on magic, divination, and healing, but none of them describe the functions of beliefs in the Evil Eye as a part of an explanatory system designed to account for human suffering, uncertainty, and illness, and as a way of making human feelings recognizable.

Let me illustrate the functioning of beliefs in the Evil Eye with an example from my fieldwork in Morocco. As an anthropologist (and psychoanalyst to be), I was interested in dreams and dream interpretation as they relate to conceptions of illness and healing throughout the Mediterranean. I found that there are in Morocco two separate and distinct systems of dream interpretation, one by and for men based on the Koran and on principles of religious literacy and learning, and the other by and for women based on oral traditions (as distinct from Koranic authority) and including beliefs in the Evil Eye and the social functions of jealousy. I was in the position of being the foreign anthropologist in a society in which many activities segregated the sexes. As a man how was I to find a female field assistant who could take the dreams I wanted interpreted as a series to a woman specializing in the interpretation of dreams?

After considerable effort, I at last persuaded Aysha, an illiterate young woman in the Souss, a rural region in the High Atlas mountains roughly southwest of Marrakesh and east of Agadir, to be my field assistant. The inhabitants of the Souss are known to be profoundly attached to their land and place and also to have networks of grocery stores throughout Morocco and the French-speaking world. Those who do travel to Moroccan cities like Rabat inevitably build houses in which to retire in the Souss.

Aysha spoke both French and Berber and agreed to take the dreams I gave her in French and present these to a Berber female dream interpreter. The dreams in question were two dreams drawn from the Freudian corpus—the dream of the dead father (Freud's own dream) and the dream of the officer. The second, on which the interpretation focused, is one included in Freud's "Introductory Lectures."

> An officer in a red cap was running after her in the street. She fled from him, and ran up the stairs with him still after her. Breathless, she reached her flat, slammed the door behind her and locked it. He stayed outside, and when she looked through the peephole, he was sitting on a bench outside and weeping. (Freud, 1916/1974, p. 192)

The interpretation of the wise woman ran as follows: "The dream represents an obstacle (resistance) in the life of the dreamer, in her love-life particularly. Red is a lucky color in this dream. The dream was provoked by jealousy (i.e., the Evil Eye)" (cited in Kilborne, 1978a, p. 218).

When Aysha returned from the consultation she was thoroughly shaken. Not only had the woman interpreter/healer assumed the dreams to be Aysha's, but interpreted them in such a way as to overwhelm her through an interpretation of the effects of the Evil Eye on her relationships with men. The following is the narrative of the consultation.

The wise woman (who was illiterate) gave Aysha a talisman and instructed her to wash it in water until the letters and markings were dissolved. The "dreamer" was then to pour this water over a piece of red-hot iron heated in red-hot coals. These acts were to be performed in order to eliminate the "resistance" which the dream represented and about which the interpreter was to become increasingly specific.

It was a jealous and envious woman who put this "resistance" in the path of the dreamer, explained the interpreter. At this point in the consultation the "dreamer" admitted that there was, in fact, an envious person in her own family: her aunt. Once in possession of this bit of Souss family dynamics, the interpreter zeroed in with that sort of understanding of Souss family dynamics that only those brought up there could possess.

"Have you been to Casablanca?" asked the interpreter. "Yes," was the answer. From here, and because going to Casablanca meant going into dangerous territory, the interpreter grew more certain. "The day you intended to leave for Casa, your aunt touched you on your right shoulder with a gri-gri (a talisman), and she put another on the threshold of the doorway you were to pass through. When you got to Casablanca, you were suddenly dizzy; a sort of black veil seemed to appear before your eyes." Remember, the Souss is a seriously rural community, and Casablanca is the big city that is likely to produce dizziness in those who have known little but the wind in the hills, the rustle of trees, and the songs of birds.

Continuing, the interpreter pressed on. "Your aunt did this to hex your trip to Casablanca. The spell she cast also made you fickle. You passed from one boy to another, incapable of choosing among them. Even now you cannot make up your mind."

Disconcerted, Aysha ruefully admitted that the interpreter was right. In fact, she *had* felt dizzy in Casablanca, where she had planned to stay more than 4 days but had to cut her stay short, and she *did* have the impression that her relations with boys were jinxed.

In concluding the consultation, the interpreter/healer affirmed that 3 days previously Aysha had gotten into an argument with her boyfriend and that since neither had been able to speak. Again, Aysha said this was accurate. Whereupon the interpreter gave the girl a gri-gri to counter the effects of the Evil Eye and sent her on her way.

In this example the Evil Eye is used to explain misfortune, dizziness, fear of the big city, the girl's fickle nature, indecision, her problems with relationships, and the disappointments and hopes that she holds.[4] Seldom in a single consultation are we as analysts able to cast so wide a net, whatever our interpretations or theoretical orientation. The extraordinary effect of the consultation calls attention to the powerful and multidimensional functions of beliefs in the Evil Eye, and the importance of envy as a point of entry into the world of the emotions. It also calls attention to the power of envy, which it is the purpose of this essay to explore.

FREUD, "THE UNCANNY," AND THE EVIL EYE

It is a well-known fact that Freud's ideas about psychoanalysis grew out of his interest in hypnotism and occult phenomena in general, an interest widespread at the turn of the century. This widespread interest and fascination represented a real enthusiasm for and curiosity about the life and power of the mind, one which today is easy to underestimate. The very term psychoanalysis comes from the Greek *psuche,* meaning breath, the source of life. Psychoanalysis was, as Bettelheim and others have pointed out, a treatment for the soul.

When Freud wrote his paper on "The Uncanny," his aim was to explore what makes feelings powerful. Implicitly, he was exploring the bounds of psychoanalysis and its links to ideas about the soul, traditionally the province of religion. One of the reasons for the success of Freud's *Interpretation of Dreams* was precisely its reach: dreams traditionally were viewed as the means by which gods communicated with mortals, the means by which the Christian God and Jewish Yaweh made their wishes known. Freud sought to open the exploration of dreams so that he could describe them and explore their meanings with all of the passion of the naturalist, while at the same time appealing to those steeped in religious traditions. In this he was making use of the Judeo-Christian belief systems whose assumptions about the life of the soul (and the importance of tending to the soul) provide a backdrop to his magnum opus.

Freud's paper is of particular importance for the subject of the Evil Eye because of the associative materials Freud adduces in addressing and exploring the subject of the uncanny. Implicitly Freud links envy and shame through his discussion of the German word *heimlich* and through his interest in what makes feelings powerful. He identifies a dimension of the uncanny as "concealed, kept from sight, so that others do not get to know of or about it, withheld from others." This sounds like secret shame, and the shame of secrets. And then Freud continues:

> To do something *heimlich,* i.e., behind someone's back; to steal away *heimlich; heimlich* meetings and appointments; to look on with *heimlich* pleasure at someone's discomfiture; to sigh or weep *heimlich;* to behave *heimlich,* as though there was something to conceal; *heimlich* love-affair, love sin; *heimlich* places (which good manners oblige us to conceal) (1 Sam, v. 6). The *heimlich* chamber (privy) (2 Kings x. 27). Also "The *heimlich* chair" … "The *heimlich* art" (magic) … "A holy, *heimlich* effect." (1919, pp. 223–224)

Note here the biblical references, as well as the references to meanings relating to secrecy, toilets, concealment, love and sin, pleasure at someone else's discomfiture—all within the scope of shame dynamics. As though this were not sufficient, Freud amasses yet more biblical references. "'In the secret of his tabernacle he shall hide me *heimlich*' (Ps. Xxvii.5) … *Heimlich* parts of the human body, pudenda …' the men that died were smitten on their *heimlich* parts' (1 Sam. V. 12)."

Freud speaks of E. T. A. Hoffman's story of the Sand Man in which the theme of lethal looks and blindness (both motifs related to shame and destructiveness) appear clearly. The Sand Man is:

> a wicked man who comes when children won't go to bed, and throws handfuls of sand in their eyes so that they jump out of their heads all bleeding. Then he puts the eyes in a sack and carries them off to the half-moon to feed his children. They sit up there in their nest, and their beaks are hooked like owls' beaks, and they use them to peck up naughty boys' and girls' eyes with. (p. 228)

Elsewhere I have explored in detail the links between shame and looking, a link essential to an understanding of the Evil Eye (Kilborne, 2002).

After having discussed in detail stories of the double, another motif directly related to shame and superego conflict, Freud speaks of the Evil Eye in a manner evoking the Hoffman story and in the context of his remarks on superstition. "One of the most uncanny and wide-spread forms of superstition is the dread of the Evil Eye" (1919, p. 240). And Freud continues:

> Whoever possesses something that is at once valuable and fragile is afraid of other people's envy, insofar as he projects on to them the envy he would have felt in their place. A feeling like this betrays itself by a look even though it is not put into words; and when a man is prominent owing to noticeable, and particularly owing to unattractive, attributes, other people are ready to believe that his envy is rising to a more than usual degree of intensity, and that this intensity will convert it into effective action. What is feared is thus a secret intention of doing harm, and certain signs are taken to mean that intention has the necessary power at its command. (p. 240)

Although this passage, like so much of the work of Freud in English translation, is awkwardly rendered, several features stand out. First, Freud is trying to speak of very strong feelings as a part of the theory of the quality of feelings that he addressed at the outset of the paper. Second, he explains the intensity of feeling as a result of projected envy rather than, for example, the result of collective belief systems, shared cultural values, or legitimate mistrust. This is but one manifestation of Freud's disinclination to address the problem of belief systems. Third, the fear he associates with the intensity of feeling is "a secret intention of doing harm." This would appear to explain the power of envy through a theory of aggression and cruelty, and to explain away human destructiveness as the manifestation of the fear of inner destructiveness. This is important because Freud seems to be saying that the primary reason envy is powerful is because of internal drives rather than either the innate power of the feeling of envy or the power of envy in human relationships. Fourth, that the Evil Eye is associated with ways of reading human experience, a sort of divination through the reading of signs, which, one might infer, is distinctly different from the more rational scrutiny of the human experience embodied in psychoanalysis. And finally, Freud's material for this paper is drawn above all from literature and philology and from the Bible, as though these sources allowed him better to address his primary subject: a theory of the quality of feelings.

Stepping back for a moment from Freud's discussion of the Evil Eye and of the uncanny, consider his approach to the study of dreams, which also in important respects walks a thin line between reason and belief, science and religion, religion and superstition.

In the early Christian period, Christ became a healer in order to "absorb" the healing component in the cult of Asclepius. This, of course, Freud knew so well, since he explicitly set himself up as Asclepius, the God who heals through dreams, in his *Interpretation of Dreams*. But Freud also wanted to present his book as scientific. Hence, the seeming paradox: On the one hand he could present himself as a part of our ancient and classical (as well as Mesopotamian) tradition of healing, thereby drawing on enormous resources in our cultural imagination, while at the same time claiming a "scientific" status for his discipline.

Conflicts between science and magic, religion and superstition in the West have a very long history. Studies of incubation[5] or temple sleeping (the sleeping in sacred places in order to dream cures to ills, whether infertility, misfortune, deafness, or migraines) and studies of tarantism (the cult of dancing in southern Italy) demonstrate how linked with the history of Western civilization both are, and how many and how various are the overlaps. As De Martino (2002) observes apropos of tarantism in southern Italy, it struck root in Apulia where particular importance was attributed to musical catharsis and where the vigorous Christian polemic against pagan orgiastic cults resulted, paradoxically, in their absorption by Christianity. "Tarantism was grafted into two great polemics in the West: that of Christianity against the orgiastic cults and that of the new science against natural and ceremonial magic" (De Martino, 2002, p. 247). Despite the rise of science, these orgiastic and healing cults of antiquity have persisted in various forms to this day.[6]

Anthropological and historical sources are in accord concerning the syncretism of religion and science; one never fully replaces the next, as one religion invariably absorbs essential features of the one that preceded it. Why would psychoanalysis be any different?

Significantly, the first allusion to Freud's paper "The Uncanny" can be found in a letter to Sandor Ferenczi of May 12, 1919, in which Freud writes that "The Uncanny" has been completed. This is important for several reasons because it was Ferenczi above all the other members of Freud's circle who was focusing his efforts on what Freud refers to in the opening paragraph as "the theory of the qualities of feeling" (1919/1974, p. 219). The year 1919 was a turning point in the history of psychoanalysis, although it has almost disappeared from the view of contemporary writers. In the spring of that year Ferenczi married Gisella Palos, was given the first chair in psychoanalysis (at the University of Budapest), and was president of the International Psychoanalytic Association whose meetings in the fall would be devoted to the subject of war trauma. Freud's letter to Ferenczi, therefore, marks a high water mark of their friendship and collaboration; Freud's approach to the subject of the uncanny (with all the biblical and religious references) reflects a freedom to explore the unknown and the fringes of psychoanalytic understanding, which is virtually unequaled in his later writings.

In the summer of 1919 (after Freud writes his paper on "The Uncanny"), there was a revolution in Hungary, Ferenczi was stripped of his post, and in the Fall of 1919 at Freud's insistence, the presidency of the IPA was transferred to Ernst Jones, Farenczi's analysand. Subsequently the analytic community forgot that Ferenczi had ever been president of the International Psychoanalytic Association, and effectively erased him and the events of the year 1919 from its memory.[7]

The events of 1919, coupled with divergences between their clinical work and their theories, together with strains in their personal relationship, set Freud and Ferenczi on diverging paths. From this point on, Freud distanced himself from Ferenczi and never again would consider the question of what makes feelings powerful with the same reach into the nether regions of *heimlich* and shame.

ENVY AND SHAME

In the Kleinian tradition, it is commonly believed that envy is the linchpin of emotions, as it is in Evil Eye belief systems. But there are important differences between the two.

First, Klein and the Kleinians use envy as an offshoot of Freud's theory of drives. Children, their argument goes, are envious because they are sexual beings whose bodies are unable to satisfy their urges and needs. In these theories, envy is a function of the theory of drives rather than an emotion with power in its own right that deserves to be understood in its interpersonal context as well as from the vantage point of individual psychodynamics.

Therefore (and here I am extrapolating), because of the shame of children's dependency (and this is a theory of shame that makes shame an epiphenomenon of envy rather than a phenomenon in its own right), children come to envy those who have (or are imagined to have) the powers they themselves do not possess. Evil eye explanations, by contrast, inevitably designate a particular person in the patient's world as the source of the misfortune, evil, or sickness. Evil eye explanations are, as it were, two-person explanations and rely on shared belief systems.

Also, in the example we have cited of Aysha and her consultation with the wise woman, shame plays an important role. Aysha, a country girl who goes to the big city and is disoriented and frightened, feels she cannot have a satisfying love life and is deficient. The Evil Eye represents an explanation for her feelings of deficiency and shame over her limitations and functions to make them more tolerable. By ascribing to her difficulties a "cause" (her envious aunt), she can represent her feelings of shame to herself more easily and tolerate them because they can be recognized (i.e., by the wise woman).

Second, Klein's theory of envy implies the existence of primary narcissism, the weaning of which gives rise to envy. This developmental emphasis is nowhere to be found in Evil Eye explanations, which concentrate only on the here and now of the patient's situation. The thrust of explanation in Evil Eye belief systems focuses only on the present misfortune to be born; there is no room for references to the past except as direct illuminations of the present. And there is no concept whatsoever of infant and child development.

Third, Evil Eye explanations seek specifically to answer the question: Why am I sick, unhappy, or distressed? Here it is worth noting that asking the question in such a form implies feelings of sickness, unhappiness, and distress that are reinforced and validated by the availability of the question itself. For us, such questions are often thought to be the province of religion and not of science. In the light of our Souss example, Aysha's experience of having her unhappiness laid out before her can be attributed to the wise woman's assumption that the dreams she brought meant unhappiness to be explained and made sense of.

Although some psychoanalytic writers have dismissed Evil Eye beliefs as pathological, epistemologically, societies cannot be pathological in the same way that individuals are, so the very labeling of social practices and beliefs as "pathological" raises serious difficulties for students of the philosophy of the social and human sciences. When psychoanalysis strives for a *global* view and understanding of psychodynamics, conflating group and social phenomena with drive-oriented individual psychodynamics, it inevitably distorts its object. The concept of culturally constituted defenses was promulgated by Melford Spiro (Kilborne & Langness, 1987) several decades ago in theoretical papers of direct relevance for psychoanalysis. Such defenses can be shared; cultural values often serve not only to rationalize defenses and make them invisible to members of the society of which they are a part, but also to provide such defenses with powers of social (and individual) coherence and conviction.

Fourth, despite claims that Kleinian and indeed all psychoanalysis is essentially individualistic and that we are champions of individual freedom, the kind of social science explanatory system on which we rely would seem to be less specific and less personal than those of religious belief systems. The questions Why me? Why now? are the primary focus of what we may call Evil Eye explanatory systems. Although such non-European belief systems are known for their want of individualism and their reliance on group processes and collective symbols and representation, this emphasis (Why me? Why now?) seems to be more specifically individualistic than, for example, the explanation of envy as a manifestation of drives.

A discussion of the Evil Eye necessarily entails an exploration of the destructiveness of envy and shame, shame over both omnipotence and surfeit and over helplessness and deficit. The question what makes envy destructive is therefore close to the question what makes shame destructive.

In his recent book on shame and jealousy the British analyst Phil Mollon (2002) brings the work of Melanie Klein and Heinz Kohut together around the notion of shame, associating the destructiveness of shame and envy (Klein) with the healing properties of empathy. Although there is some merit to the position that shame can be caused by want of empathy and cured by empathy, such a position tends to distort or neglect internal and often unconscious superego conflicts and psychic disorientation. Those who hold to this position believe *the cure* lies in the other: for the patient suffering from toxic shame, the problem and *the pain* lies in the other.

As many writers have stressed (e.g., Wurmser, Lansky, Kilborne, Morrison), there is a direct link between feelings of shame and feelings of failure. Failure produces shame, as it stems from self-judgments (ego ideals). Shame experiences are by definition anxiety filled fears of being ashamed, and being ashamed is the very mark of failure. Just as chronic pain calls up fear of pain and anxiety over pain, so chronic shame experiences are filled with anxiety over the feelings of shame themselves, which, when toxic, are unbearable. What cannot be sufficiently emphasized is that feelings of failure and shame can become toxic when they form maelstroms, pulling the self down into itself. When this happens, Object Relations suffer and can become both impossible and threatening.

For those of us who struggle with all the ambiguities, conflicts, and uncertainties of shame dynamics, the precept that there is no single antidote to shame (such as empathy) may itself serve as a source of shame and humiliation for patients whose confusion results in shame-prone vulnerabilities. As I have explained elsewhere (Kilborne, 2002), clinicians are faced with the intractable dilemma of shame: the more ashamed one is, the more ipso facto one depends on fantasies and perceptions of how one is being seen. This, in turn, exacerbates shame vulnerabilities and contributes to narcissistic/paranoid defenses by attributing to the other powers he or she cannot and does not have as an attempted antidote to feelings of deficiency, limitation, and defect in oneself. The result often looks like envy.

As Wurmser (2000) has so pertinently noted, shame is directly related to the power of the inner judge. If the analyst, relying on notions that only empathy can cure shame, calls up or exacerbates the power of the inner judge in the patient, who condemns himself for not being sufficiently empathic or for thwarting the analyst's reliance on the power of his (the analyst's) powers of empathy, then the result will be damaging.

VICO, PSYCHOANALYSIS, AND EXPLANATION

Today many assume that because they do not believe in God, or because they accept the worldview of science, they do not need to acknowledge the explanatory powers of the divinity. Whereas it is the goal of natural science to dispel ignorance and explain rationally explicable phenomena like the movements of the heavens or the falling of an apple, the objectives of belief systems are fundamentally different and depend on asking fundamentally different questions. Broadly speaking, science tends to be based on what can be observed or experimentally replicated. Belief systems, on the other hand, depend on forces unseen and impossible to know except through the emotions. Only belief systems address the questions Why me? Why now?

Freud never addresses squarely the matter of how psychoanalysis might approach the subject of belief systems, although he does address the question of a *Weltanschauung* in his 1932 paper. However, he does so only by asking whether or not psychoanalysis is a *Weltanschauung*, not by wondering how psychoanalytic understanding might illuminate belief systems. He concludes his paper by observing: "Psycho-analysis, in my opinion, is incapable of creating a Weltanschauung of its own. It does not need one; it is a part of science and can adhere to the scientific *Weltanschauung*" (1932, p. 181).

As Giambatista Vico (1744) noted in the 18th century, there is a fundamental distinction to be made between, on the one hand, *coscienza* consciousness or conscience, and on the other hand, *scienza*, knowledge or science. The object of *coscienza* is *il certo*, or certainty; the object of *scienza* is *il vero* or the truth in the sense of universally applicable principles.[8]

A fundamental implication of this distinction involves the emotions. Emotions are pertinent for *il certo* because the concept and the epistemological domain it designates stem from *coscienza*, consciousness and conscience (both the same word in Italian and French). Our English distinction between the two words makes Vico's argument more difficult to understand. For Vico, emotional knowledge (what lies within the "modifications of the human mind") is an essential part of his argument. In fact, Vico makes emotions and consciousness the object of "certainty" (*il certo*), as opposed to the rational knowledge of the natural world (*il vero*). Setting himself against the rationalism of Descartes, Vico sees the origin of language, not in any rational need to formulate ideas, but rather in the emotions of awe and terror brought on by a violent thunderstorm. A primitive man and woman are sitting in a cave, unable to speak. There is a terrifying thunderstorm, with lightning and deafening cracks of thunder. Suddenly, and in response to overwhelming feelings, the man (a tenor?) bursts into song, the origin of language.

As Vico explains:

> Men at first feel without perceiving, then they perceive with a troubled and agitated spirit, finally they reflect with a clear mind. This axiom is the principle of poetic sentences, which are formed by feelings of passion and emotion, whereas philosophic sentences are formed by reflection and reasoning. The more the latter rise towards universals, the closer they approach the truth; the more the former descend to particulars, the more certain they become. (pp. 75–76 sections 218–219)

There are clearly many implications of Vico's distinction for psychoanalysis. One is that the world of men can be known, and that the natural world (the world God made) can never be understood with "certainty" (*il certo*), because it is awe-inspiring and beyond human grasp. Therefore, Vico is suggesting that too narrow a focus on the natural world to the exclusion of the human world is a sort of hubris, a manifestation of a sort of sclerosis of reason that does not allow for the passions or for the unknown and is quite implicitly anti-Cartesian. Whereas Descartes in his *Discourse on the Method* made monolithic doubt the centerpiece of his system and method, Vico made the distinction between two kinds of knowledge (*il vero* and *il certo*) the centerpiece of his. Also, for Descartes there is only one form of truth and certainty: that arrived at by doubting the testimony of the senses. This makes Descartes a closet sensualist in the cloak of a rationalist. Additionally, the method of Descartes does away with the distinction, so prevalent from the Renaissance to the 19th century, between the moral and the physical sciences. The result, if looked at globally, is to make reason scientific and science reasonable; it is to make knowledge only what can be proven and viewed as acceptable when seen in the light of prevalent theories of causality and logic.[9] Vico's anti-Cartesian stance sets him at odds with the entire sensualist-rationalist tradition; his approach can be seen to depart fundamentally from structuralist, poststructuralist, deconstructionist, and modernist assumptions, as well as from the assumptions of rational choice theorists, behaviorists, cognitivists, and neurobiologists. Much social science is predicated on observation that excludes the emotions of the observer as an essential part of what is observed. From Vico's perspective, such approaches therefore leave out *il certo*.

As he observes at the end of his book, "this Science [meaning the New Science of Man of which he writes] carries inseparably with it the study of piety, and that he who is not pious cannot be truly wise" (Vico, 1744, p. 426, section 1112). In other words, for Vico the human world is inscribed in the natural world, the domain of piety and awe. However, the human world can be known and understood, whereas its larger context can be grasped only insofar as it is given to humankind to understand universal principles and laws, and this understanding is subject to human limitation. To recognize that there is a basic distinction between the world of mankind and the natural world is, therefore, a basic act of piety; to conflate the two, as the empirical and sensualist tradition tends to do, is an expression of impiety and ignorance.

In what is perhaps the most memorable passage in the book, Vico writes:

> But in the night of thick darkness enveloping the earliest antiquity, so remote from ourselves, there shines the eternal and never failing light of a truth beyond all question: that the world of civil society has certainly been made by men, and that its principles are therefore to be found within the modifications of our own human mind. Whoever reflects on this cannot but marvel that the philosophers should have bent all their energies to the study of the world of nature, which, since God made it, He alone knows; and that they should have neglected the study of the world of nations, or civil world, which, since men had made it, men could come to know. (p. 96, section 331)[10]

Such an epistemological distinction is clearly present in the Moroccan material we have discussed, and fundamental to our notions of psychoanalytic interpretation and explanation. Psychoanalysis has historically positioned itself somewhere between these two. It admits the power of the emotions (drives being derived from theories of animal magnetism, mesmerism, hypnotism, paranormal phenomena, and fears of primitive promiscuity), while presenting explanations that seek to satisfy behaviorally scientific criteria (e.g., they can be observable and replicable). By contrast, behaviorism does away with the distinction and the tension between the two orders of explanation, making observation and universal principles the primary criterion for reliability and legitimacy, and thereby neglecting the internal world of thoughts and feelings, the world of human experience (Vico, 1984).

The recent attacks on psychoanalysis by Grunbaum (1985) and others have accused psychoanalysis and psychoanalysts of failure to present sufficient "evidence" to validate a presumed scientific "method." However, for clinicians (as opposed to those who do not have live patients in front of them), the psychoanalytic method, because it seeks to make emotions more bearable and therefore to use its explanatory system in the service of helping patients to recognize their own feelings and be less anxious about them, must do double duty: It must at once satisfy scientific criteria of validity and help equilibrate the world of the emotions. Therefore, its effectiveness in the first can be at odds with its effectiveness in the second, and vice versa.

Let me illustrate the conflict between explanatory worlds with an example from *Witchcraft, Oracles and Magic among the Azande* by the Oxford social anthropologist E. E. Evans-Pritchard (1940/1976). Evans-Pritchard notes that the Zande[11] (who occupied a portion of what used to be the Anglo-Egyptian Sudan) build their houses on posts, which sometimes give way. Evans-Pritchard tried to explain to the Zande that these posts were eaten by termites, and therefore the termites were the problem. However, the Zande were in no way satisfied by this explanation, since it was impersonal and depended on seeing termites as agents of destruction: termites were the cause and the collapse of a house was the effect. For the Zande, the real question was: Why was *that* particular person sitting under the house at *that* particular time when *that* particular house collapsed? Were a Westerner to explain to the Zande that the cause of the collapse was termites, the Zande would not understand why such an irrelevant fact could be put forward as useful, since it left the primary question unanswered.

It is therefore obvious in view of this example that explanations can be valued according to the kind of question asked. To the question Why do apples fall?, we have a ready answer: because of gravity. But that does not explain why *that* particular apple fell on *my* head (and not on the head of someone else) on *this* particular day and not another. This specificity of explanation is one of the resources of our psychoanalytic explanation and lends importance to the here and now of the transference and to analytic interactions. But we are unlikely ever to be able to defend our emphasis on transference against behaviorist critics who do not understand the questions we must ask as part of the exercise of our profession. However, this does not mean that we cannot muster more effective arguments against our detractors and defend out virtues with greater vigor than we have been able to do thus far. But it does imply epistemological considerations that help explain the difficulties that psychoanalysis faces in the contemporary world.

THE POWER OF ENVY AND SHAME: PARANOIA, EXPLANATION, AND INTERPRETATION

As I hope to have suggested thus far, much can be learned about the dynamics of envy and shame through a study of the Evil Eye. What makes the Evil Eye dangerous? What makes it powerful? How does its dangerousness and power shed light on envy? And how do belief systems such as the Evil Eye provide resources for human bonds and object relations?

As I have written elsewhere (Kilborne, 2002), much of what psychoanalysis has termed paranoia is directly related to shame and superego conflict. Therefore, the tendency to dismiss Evil Eye phenomena as paranoid leaves out the shame dimensions. Without an understanding of the Evil Eye as a belief system (including its shame dynamics), the phenomenon of the Evil Eye is reduced to "envy projected" and labeled paranoia. Once it has been so labeled, it is an easy step to dismissing it as "superstition," and therefore without any basis in reality. When Freud was writing there was great emphasis on reality. Reality (whatever it is construed to mean) becomes split between those who speak of psychic reality (Freud and those who follow him) on the one side and those who speak of social reality (Durkheim and his followers) on the other. Furthermore, "reality" is assumed to be higher on the scale of human development (progress) than "superstition." From the psychoanalytic perspective of Freud, the social dimension of Evil Eye experiences and their potential for communication are missed, and theories of psychic structure and drives can be relied on to fill in the missing pieces. This trend in psychoanalysis has persisted to the present day and can be seen in the writings of those who claim to be sensitive to cultural differences and traditions in psychoanalytic treatment yet omit the dimensions of shame dynamics, culturally constituted defenses, collective experience, and collective representations.

Such reductionism was, clearly, a hallmark of the social sciences at the end of the 19th and the beginning of the 20th centuries, when the "scientific" status of the various disciplines needed to be established. Durkheim, Halbwachs, Levy-Bruhl, and others focused on the collective dimension of human experience (social solidarity, collective representations, and so forth), but left out the internal conflictual dimensions.

Such reductionism further clouded the basic epistemological distinction made by Vico in his *The New Science*; it focused attention on *either* the individual *or* the social (but never the two in the same frame). The beauty of Vico's formulation is that it throws into relief the distinction, not between the individual and culture but rather between *il certo* and *il vero*.

The assumption that beliefs in the Evil Eye can be subsumed under our rubric of paranoia implies that they undermine object relations. As we have seen, the very opposite is the case. In societies where beliefs in the Evil Eye prevail, these can at once provide explanations for human misfortune and suffering and, because they entail shared values, actually reinforce human bonds. Inasmuch as this might be so, then the problem lies with those who would attach a label of projection, superstition, and paranoia to the complex phenomena and collective representations of the Evil Eye. It would be problematic because the very labeling suggests that the labelers do not recognize important dimensions of social experience and resources for human bonds, and also because they repeat the unfortunate distinction between us (who have religion) and them (who have only superstition).

For a variety of epistemological reasons, the psychoanalytic concept of projection is problematic. Literally, projection means getting something from here to there, getting a projectile from point A to point B. To do so one needs a source of power or force. In the example "I hit you" it is obvious that "I" is the actor and you are being acted upon. However, in the Freudian and psychoanalytic concept of projection, the power resides in the aggressive wishes of the one being acted upon. As a result the "actor" is implicitly turned into a fantasy of the "acted upon," whose aggressive drives are what is most powerful and most to be feared. The inside has triumphed over the outside; internal phenomena are real, whereas outside phenomena are epiphenomena.

Paradoxically, then, it is the danger and power (aggressive drives?) of the one injured that takes center stage, not the danger of the one doing the injuring. Victim becomes victimizer. The concept is further muddied by the Kleinian emphasis on projective identification.

By contrast, the Italian concept of *Jettatore* is far more parsimonious as an explanation since it incorporates the notion of throwing or hurling and is unambiguous about who is doing what to whom. The angry powerful one is doing the hurling, and the receiver of what is hurled is at risk of injury. Also, the concept is clear about the role of envy as the motivating force of the *Jettatore*. What gives the *Jettatore* power is the power of envy, which is both implicitly and explicitly assumed in Evil Eye belief systems.

To say that what gives envy power is projection and paranoia, which is what Freud and others have implied, is to miss the power of envy itself as an extremely powerful emotion related to internal judgments and superego condemnations and, therefore, to the basic sense of identity. It is also to miss the power of shame, the shame, among other dynamics, of feeling envious (and the anxiety of feeling without). Shame dynamics constitute an essential part of the cultural values and defenses so prominent in Evil Eye phenomena.

Shame is powerful for a variety of reasons. In toxic forms it can threaten the right to existence, and undermine the feeling that object relations can be possible and worthwhile. Envy can be a badge of unrecognized shame; one wants from others what one feels one lacks oneself and must have. Rather than feel the lack, one feels envious, as though the other has wrongly deprived oneself of exactly what was needed. When we associate the feeling of envy with the dangerousness and superstitiousness of others, are we not using the concept of envy as our Western way of avoiding feelings of loss and limitation? And are these associations and this avoidance not then further defended against by turning the envy that we associate with the Evil Eye into paranoia, and then suggesting that societies privileging envy as an explanatory system are paranoid and not individualistic? The implication being that we are not to be thought of as envious (since we have so much others want), and that others are somehow lesser because their envy is dangerous and ours is not, they are paranoid and we are not.

Envy as a response to intolerable feelings of limitation, loss, and deficit thus comes bundled with shame and resentment. And, as beliefs in the Evil Eye demonstrate so abundantly, envy and shame can both be directly related to looking and being seen, to the theme of lethal looks.

But if looking can be associated with lethal looks, and looks can be dangerous, so too can not looking. In fact, not looking can have devastating consequences for child development. Relating envy and looking to unlovability and the shame it causes, it would appear that the unresponsiveness of parents or caregivers to an infant or child leads to fantasies of omnipotence in the child (who believes that he or she can make the parent adequate and undo the injury), which then makes looking that much more shameful. If the child feels that others who look will detect his or her omnipotence, the response will be to hide and feel envious of those who can be proudly visible (i.e., those who do not need to hide).

Unresponsiveness leads to shame, which causes omnipotent fantasies to grow, and omnipotent fantasies breed yet more shame. Under these circumstances, when omnipotent defenses are challenged, human frailty, blindness, and fallibility become that much more threatening and shameful. In this way envy can be relied on to avoid feelings of limitation and loss, since the focus is on not allowing others to see one's omnipotence (itself a defense against unbearable shame over feelings of limitation and loss).[12]

How then are unresponsiveness, envy, and looking, particularly lethal looking, related?[13] If it is the response of loved ones to one's shameful feelings that allow them to be tolerated, then nonresponse on the part of parents or caregivers reflects an intolerance of their shameful feelings, which comes out as an intolerance of the responses of children to feeling unseen and unrecognized, and, consequently, unlovable.[14]

Nonresponse, often organized around eyes that do not see, leads to an experience of soul blindness on the part of those on whom one depends for faith in human connections. This experience, in turn, makes one dependent on those who cannot see, and therefore who cannot see the one looking to them for response (linking blindness and nonresponse to shame). Such disorientation leads at once to hiding and rage at not being able to find the person looking, which then makes the looks of the disoriented that much more threatening to them. Enter envy. Envy then steps in to provide an orientation and defense against feelings of disorientation and disconnection, both sources of shame.

NOTES

1. See Kilborne (2002) for a discussion of the dynamics of lethal looks and their relation to narcissism.
2. I am indebted to Leon Wurmser for invaluable assistance with the translation of this passage, and for the links to our words "fascinate" and "fascination."
3. See "Evil Eye" in *The Encyclopaedia Britannica* 10th edition. The references cited in this section can mostly be found in this entry. For additional references to the Evil Eye and practices associated with it see, for example, Doutte (1909), Fahd (1966), Peristiany (1965), and Westermarck (1926/1968).
4. Although the girl had to memorize the dreams because she could not read, and then translate them into Berber, and allowing for slippage, her strong emotions over the consultation were beyond the slightest doubt. For her the experience was extremely powerful.

5. For a discussion of contemporary incubation practices see Kilborne (1978b, 1990). For a discussion of Greek incubation, see Edelstein and Edelstein (1945).
6. The contemporary cults of physical fitness and the cult of the body represent thinly disguised efforts at staving off the effects of aging and defending against anxieties over death, just as are the Evil Eye belief systems, the cult of tarantism, or the cults of incubation practiced to this day throughout the Mediterranean.
7. Roughly 10 years ago I learned that Horatio Etchegoyen, then the president of the International Psychoanalytic Association, realized that Ferenczi's picture was not among those in London of the presidents of the International Psychoanalytic Association. A number of analysts wondered if Ferenczi had ever been the president of the IPA. These events of 1919 were, I have come to understand, essential for an understanding of the history of psychoanalysis; their importance cannot be denied and neither can their repression.
8. For Vico, knowledge of the natural world, perceived through the five senses, is associated with the passions and with what men can know from the inside, as it were. In the 18th-century tradition of the sensualists (e.g., Hume, Locke, Helvetius, La Mettrie (*L'Homme Machine*), however, the two kinds of knowledge are conflated, and empirical observation is held up as the standard by which the reliability of knowledge can be judged.
9. There is some irony is Heisenberg's choice of terms when he describes "the Uncertainty Principle." In the light of Vico, what Heisenberg is studying is necessarily uncertain, since it can only be "true."
10. Vico elaborates on the origin of gods in the following passage: "Thus it was fear which created gods in the world; not fear awakened in men by other men, but fear awakened in men by themselves" (1984, p. 120, section 382).
11. Evans-Pritchard refers to the tribe as the Azande, and groups of individuals as the Zande.
12. Soul-blindness of a person on whom one depends leads them to suffering in isolation, and experiences of being altogether cut off, like Philoctetes of Sophocles, alone on the island with oozing wounds, caught up in the agony of his pain.
13. Use of pain to defend against deeper pain of shame and vulnerability; physical symptoms to hide omnipotence. If only I felt better, everything would be fine. But nothing is fine, and the reality of the horror and tragedy cannot be avoided without consequence.
14. In addition, such shameful feelings call up anxiety over loss and limitation.

REFERENCES

De Martino, E. (2002). *The land of remorse: A study of southern Italian tarantism* (D. L. Zinn, Trans.) London: Free Association Books.

Doute, E. (1909). *Magie et religion dans l'Afrique du nord.*

Edelstein, E., & Edelstein, L. (1945). *Esclepius* (2 vols.). Baltimore: Johns Hopkins University Press.

Evans-Pritchard, E. E. (1940/1976). *Witchcraft, oracles and magic among the Azande.* Oxford: Oxford University Press.

Fahd, T. (1959/1966). La divination Arabe; etudes religieuses sociciologiques et folkloriques sur le milieu natif de l'Islam. *Sources Orientales,* 2–3.
Freud, S. (1900–1901/1974). The interpretation of dreams. In *Standard edition* (Vols. 4–5, pp.). London: Hogarth Press.
Freud, S. (1916/1974). Introductory lectures. In *Standard edition* (Vol. 16, pp.). London: Hogarth Press.
Freud, S. (1919/1974). The uncanny. In *Standard edition* (Vol. 17, pp. 218–256). London: Hogarth Press.
Freud, S. (1932/1974). The question of a Weltanschauung, new introductory lectures. In *Standard edition* (Vol. 22, pp.). London: Hogarth Press.
Grunbaum, A. (1985). *The foundations of psychoanalysis: A philosophical critique.* Berkeley: University of California Press.
Kilborne, B. (1978a). The cultural setting of dream interpretation. *Psychopathologie Africaine, 12,* 77–89.
Kilborne, B. (1978b). *Interpretations du reve au Marc.* Claix: La Pensee Sauvage.
Kilborne, B. (1990). Field notes.
Kilborne, B. (2002). *Disappearing persons: Shame and appearance.* Albany: SUNY Press.
Kilborne, B., & Langness, L. L. (1987). *Culture and human nature: Theoretical papers of Melford E. Spiro.*
Lowie, R. (1924). *Primitive religion.* New York: Liverwright.
Mollon, P. (2002). *Shame and jealousy: The hidden turmoils.* London: Karnac.
Peristiany, J. B. (1965). *Honour and shame in the Mediterranean.* London: Weidenfeld and Nicolson.
Vico, G. (1774/1984). *The new science* (T. Bergin & M. Fisch, Eds.). Ithaca, NY: Cornell University Press.
Westermarck, E. (1926/1968). *Ritual and belief in Morocco* (2 vols.). London: Macmillan.
Wurmser, L. (2000). *The Power of the inner judge: Psychodynamic treatment of severe neurosis.* Northdale, NJ: Jason Aronson.

8

"Evil Eye" and "Searing Look"

Jealousy, Envy, and Shame in the Magic Gaze

HEIDRUN JARASS AND LÉON WURMSER

In this essay we will expand on Benjamin Kilborne's anthropological and philosophical study of the Evil Eye by adding additional evidence for the widespread belief in the magically powerful eye and for the psychodynamics involved in it. Clinical and literary experience allows a broader interpretation of the underlying dynamics of the Evil Eye and related phenomena than just by projected envy. Jealousy appears to be an equally important factor, as is more generally the projection of various aspects of superego condemnation, not only in the direction of guilt, but cardinally in that of shame: I.e., not only is the eye, and by extension, the entire face the powerfully effective carrier of dangerous emotions like envy and resentment, but it is also the organ par excellence of shaming, and with that also a paramount herald of superego sanctions, seemingly from the outside, yet very poignantly by externalization of inner accusation and self-blame. In its turn, this superego condemnation is rooted in traumatic early experiences of shaming and blaming—the devastating look of annihilating dehumanization and instrumentalization. Yet, if we think of the negative force of eye and face we also must consider its opposite: the charismatically effective, love and enthusiasm inspiring look and facial expression.

Both versions are clearly rooted in some deeply magic experiences of the omnipotence of thought, perception, and gesture—a form of cognitive and perceptual regression ("topographic regression" [Freud, 1900/1953/1968]). Thinking, perceiving, and being perceived are processes that have become again or have remained vehicles of power and destruction on the one side, of loving union, ecstatic merger, and enthusiasm on the other side.

After some further material from religious and literary tradition and some clinical vignettes illustrating the role of warded-off jealousy, we will study a case in detail where the penetrating gaze played a considerable role.

"EVIL EYE" AND "SHINING COUNTENANCE" IN JEWISH TRADITION (LW)

In a passage in the Talmud tractate Bava Metzia, the "Middle Gate," that deals with the themes of vanity, shame, and mortal humiliation in the life of the great and imposingly large scholar Yochanan bar Nappacha, the leading "Amora" (Talmudic teacher) of the second generation (3rd century C.E., in Palestine):

> Rabbi Yochanan would go and sit at the gates of the ritual bath. He said: "When the daughters of Israel come up from [their] obligatory immersion, let them meet me, so that they may have remarkable (*shapiré*) sons like me, students of the Torah like me." The Rabbis said to him: "Are you not afraid, sir, of the Evil Eye?" (*la mistefé, mar, me'ená bishá?*) He said to them: "I come from the descendants of Joseph, over whom the Evil Eye has no power (*delá shaltá be ená bishá*), as it is written: 'Joseph is a fruitful bough, a fruitful bough by a well (*ayin*)'" (Gen. 49.22). And Rabbi Abbahu said: "Do not read: 'by a well', but [rather he stands] above [the power of the eye]'." "*Ayin*" means both well and eye. Since the wellspring is, as it were, an eye in the desert, Joseph was standing above the force of the eye.[1]

This vignette is followed by the longer tale where Rabbi Yochanan mortally offends his brother-in-law, disciple, and debate partner, Resh Laqish, by comparing him with robbers, an allusion to his early past as a gladiator. Resh Laqish falls into a deep depression about the humiliation and dies from shame; Rabbi Yochanan in turn succumbs to the crushing grief and guilt about this death.

The same tractate describes how deeply offended and humiliated another scholar, Rabbi Eliezer ben Hyrkanos, was who, because of his stubbornness with which he insisted upon his interpretation, was banished. Rabbi Aqiva was sent to let him know of his excommunication:

> "Rabbi, it seems to me that [your] friends are staying away from you." He [Eliezer] too rent his garments and took off his shoes, and he slipped down and sat on the ground. His eyes streamed with tears. The world was smitten: one third of the olives, and one third of the wheat, and one third of the barley. And some say: even the dough in a woman's hands swelled. It was taught: "There was a great calamity on that day, for every place upon which Rabbi Eliezer laid his eyes was burnt." So it is said: "Anyone who shames his fellow in public is as if he sheds blood." (B.M., 59B, 58B; Steinsaltz, 1989–1999, pp. 238, 226)

The story continues with Eliezer's prayer to Heaven for redress, which leads to the death of his adversary and brother-in-law, Rabban Gamaliel; because the gates of Heaven open up when the prayers of offended dignity (*ona'áh)* knock on them.

In these passages we have on the one side the *magical power of looking*, and on the other side the *lethal effect of shaming and ensuing resentment and revenge*. Both narratives deal with the magical power of looking and appearing, positively as well as destructively: In the first story, gazing at a beautiful and scholarly man would have the effect of the birth of beautiful and scholarly sons, but the Evil Eye could destroy this power of appearance. In the second tale, the eye of resentment (i.e., of the feeling of suffered injustice in form of severe humiliation and rejection) is seen as possessing a metaphysically annihilating power that burns the world of nature and kills the shaming authority.

The word for envy in Hebrew is *roa ayin*, evilness of the eye, and *en-hará*, the Evil Eye, in Jiddish, *enhóro*, is even nowadays often referred to, as is the protective formula, *"bli en-hará"* "without the Evil Eye," in the sense of "Heaven forbid!"

Yet, there is a counterforce: At the beginning of the Sabbath, the parents bless their children with the words: "May God bless you and guard you. May God let his countenance shine upon you and show you grace." Here the theme of the shining countenance, as antithesis to, and yet in secret connection with, the lethal looks appears.

When Moses came for the second time down from Mount Sinai, bearing the two Tablets of Reminder (literally of Witnessing: *edút*), he was not aware that the skin of his face was radiant (*qarán*, from the same stem as *qéren*, "horn," whence the image of Moses with horns, for example, in the sculpture of Michelangelo) since he had spoken with God (Exodus 34:29). In response to this splendor, his brother Aaron and the other Israelites shrank from him. Moses hid his shining face behind a veil (*masswéh*) (v. 33), a passage suggestive of another one in which it is written that God's face itself cannot and ought not be seen (Exodus 33:20): "You cannot see My face, for man may not see Me and live." In the theme of the sanctified face we see represented at once awe-inspiring power from which the ordinary shrink in fear and the blessing of human happiness and peace.

JETTATORE

If we now narrow the focus, let us contrast this showing of face as an expression of divine power and blessing to the concealment of face in Selma Lagerlöf's novel *The Miracles of the Antichrist* ([*hon*] *"blygs så, at hon inte törs visa sitt ansikte"*, p. 60: "she is so ashamed of herself that she does not allow herself to show her face"). In that novel set in Sicily, Lagerlöf tells the story:

> In Catania there was once a man with the "Evil Eye" (*det onda ögat*), a *jettatore* (someone who "throws" the evil look). He was almost the most dreaded Jettatore on Sicily. As soon as he appeared on the street people rushed to point bent fingers at him as a protective gesture. But this did not help at all. Whoever encountered him had to be prepared for an unhappy day. He would find his food burnt and the old fine jelly bowl shattered. He would get informed that his banker had stopped his payments and that the little note he had written to the wife of his friend had fallen into the wrong hands. Mostly a jettatore is a long, lanky guy with a pale, shy face and a long nose lying over his upper lip and hacking down on it. God has set the parrot's nose as a sign upon the jettatore. Yet everything changes, nothing remains constant. (p. 209, trans. LW)

Here the Evil Eye has frozen into a human stereotype, a stranger and an ugly person, who looks different from the average people and should be ashamed for his unusual appearance. Again it is the appearance that should stand for the essence, and, by looking and showing, this essence disturbs the everyday life of the others and thus causes calamity and bad luck. But what stands behind this phantom of the evil, harm-causing eye? It needs to be deepened psychoanalytically.

SHAME, ENVY, AND RETRIBUTION (LW)

Throughout the world it is commonly believed that the eye is the window of the soul. It is what we could call with Goethe, an "*Urphänomen*," a primary or basic experience. It is a window through which the inner life, the soul, radiates outward and communicates––shining or punishing, oppressed or wrathful, envious or vengeful––but also loving, admiring, and forgiving. Yet, it equally is a window through which others look and thus penetrate into the soul, where what is hidden could presumably be uncovered and the secrets revealed, a deep experience where our shame anxiety whispers to us: "Those who look me in the eye will be able to read my thoughts. Everything that is covered up will come out, every fault unveiled, every guilt will be pulled to the light of day, every evil intent will be unmasked."

"An unknown [unconscious] envy lies in the squint-eyed look of your contempt" ("*Ein ungewußter Neid ist im scheelen Blick eurer Verachtung*"), says Nietzsche's Zarathustra (1883–1885/1988, p. 38). It is the anxiety about having to be ashamed for a defect, an unworthiness felt in the self.

Already from the language we guess that the Evil Eye deals with projected shame, projected envy and perhaps jealousy, and with projected revenge, but now turned against one's own self.

In his paper "The Uncanny" (1919/1955/1968), Freud explains:

> One of the most uncanny and wide-spread forms of superstition is the dread of the Evil Eye (*dem bösen Blick*, lit: the evil look). … There never seems

> to have been any doubt about the source of this dread. Whoever possesses something that is at once valuable and fragile is afraid of other people's envy, because he projects on to them the envy he would have felt in their place. A feeling like this betrays itself by a look even though it is not put into words; and when somebody is conspicuous by noticeable, and particularly by unattractive, attributes, people are ready to believe that his envy is rising to a more than usual degree of intensity and that this intensity will convert it into effective action. What is feared is thus a secret intention of doing harm, and certain signs are taken to mean that that intention has the necessary power at its command. (p. 240, modified by LW)

Freud sees in this phenomenon, just as in "The Uncanny" altogether, "something which is familiar and old-established in the mind and which has become alienated from it only through the process of repression" (p. 241). Thus it is a negative, aggressive feeling state that manifests itself in projected form.

However, there is more to the Evil Eye than projected envy; there are other essential dimensions of the power of these beliefs. The eye is most of all a window of the conscience: looking into the conscience and looking out from the conscience; this look may indeed be the lightning bolt of the conscience's power. Johanna Vennemann (2001) adds, therefore: "A judging, condemning message goes out from the Evil Eye which draws redoubled power because it is unspoken" (p. 168). The superego component in it is evident: the Evil Eye is a punishing, condemning eye; by "omnipotence of thought" (Freud, 1919/1955/1968) it spreads everywhere disaster and curse. We think that the Evil Eye derives much of its power from its function as a symbol for the superego, and in particular, as a penetrating and unmasking eye, it represents the shame part of the superego.

Single eyes that characterize horrifying beings abound in literature, for example, the Greek Cyclops (literally "Circle Eye") and Tolkien's "Fellowship of the Ring" and its movie version, where Sauron's omnipresent eye spreads horror.

EXORCISING THE EVIL EYE: A CHILD OBSERVATION (COMMUNICATION, MRS. KRONBERG-SÖDDE)

Fanny, a 5-year-old girl, was adopted at the age of 18 months from an orphanage in Romania. She had been born prematurely; not even a birth certificate existed for her: she had not been "picked up" at the hospital by her 15-year-old mother. After entering the orphanage, she never left its rooms until the day of her adoption. She was malnourished with corresponding signs of deficit and with motor restrictions (she could not yet walk). It was more by accident that friends from Austria adopted her: After Ceaucescu's downfall, the adoptive parents were bringing aid to the institution. Fanny was clinging to the adoptive mother and for hours did not let her go. Thus she had chosen her parents. Thanks to physiotherapy and exercise, she turned into a robust child who enjoyed sports. The adoptive parents moved with her to a Spanish island. At age 5, Fanny spoke both German and Spanish fluently.

My contact with her parents was brought about by Fanny; she was able to spellbind her environment by her great social competency. What was striking were her unconditional demands for twosomeness; her attacks of jealousy were vehement.

One day when she was 5, I picked her up after judo training. She was irate and flashed with indignation about her friend David who had taunted her by saying that she was going to marry Sebastian. My suggestion that David might be jealous because in the past few days she had not paid any attention to him anymore infuriated her even more: "I do not want him to be jealous! David is not my friend anymore!"

I tried to mitigate this severe attack by explaining that after all, she knew this feeling from herself, that she was often angry when her mama was talking with her papa or when I spoke with her father and wanted to step in between. But this enraged her even more. She screamed: "I am not jealous!" and in order to emphasize her protest, she stretched out her index and middle finger in a V-form and three times jabbed with them against my eyes, with the words: "Forget, forget, forget!!!"

There is a kind of epicrisis to this vignette: "Fanny is now 16 years old and keeps us all very busy with her temper tantrums and refusals. She is speaking now four languages, but refuses to be 'schooled' and has just been thrown out of boarding school. Unfortunately, a few months ago her parents have separated and her mother has rejected her: 'You are not my child. You do not have my genes!' This has of course led to a retraumatization, and she is completely derailed."

We (LW&H) have a few thoughts about this story: This is a child and youngster who has been severely, early, and cumulatively traumatized. After her rescue from total dilapidation, she developed a considerable amount of social competence with the help of which she tries to keep control over her surroundings, but most of all about her emotions, thus trying to prevent herself from tumbling down into overwhelming affect storms and the void of total isolation. She experiences the feelings of jealousy her friend David is having and showing as extremely threatening. They are for her, because of the fear of loss of control, particularly over her own jealous and retaliatory impulses, so frightening that she has to break off contact and relationship. One could also say that the author's remark worked as a kind of direct drive interpretation, eliciting the regressive defense by magic action.

Something comparable is happening now, 11 years later: Not only is it the time of puberty where things anyway are violently shaken up, but the only family she has ever known has broken apart and she has been ruthlessly expelled by her adoptive mother. The earlier conflicts are massively reactivated and she feels ever more menacingly that she does not have a grip on her life anymore.

It is not only a fear of her own jealousy that is at play in this brief interaction, but we might also surmise that she is envious of the boy who has so much more direct access to his feelings, both of love and of jealousy, without being overwhelmed by them, than she can have. For her, it threatens to be the fall into emptiness.

GHOSTS, VAMPIRES, AND THE "EVIL EYE": THE FEAR OF THE JEALOUS OTHER (LW)

In a second vignette we would like to bring excerpts from the case of a 27-year-old lawyer, Alexa, from the U.S. Midwest, seen long ago by a male colleague and her case communicated to us.

She enters treatment because of great social anxiety and often deep depression, a pervasive fear of being shamed, persecutory dreams and fantasies, and a generalized feeling of uncanniness. She flees from her panic and deep despair into sleep. Since childhood she is afraid of darkness, very specifically sensing the uncanny presence of ghosts, especially of vampires, that would jump on her and kill her. In grade school, after seeing some vampire masks during the Carnival, she became so terrified by them that for several days she could not go to school. She is deeply fearful of the Evil Eye and has formed a number of talismans that should protect her from these murderous threats. She is able to fall asleep only if she wears a cross on her chest. Partly as a protection against her anxieties she also uses various drugs. She clearly lives in a magic-animistic universe. The image *is* reality, it is concrete, the real thing; it is a presentation, not a representation. In a dream at the beginning of analysis she saw corpses and dismembered body parts draped around the treatment room. She does not tolerate separation and separateness; her universe is controlled by secret connections and relations. Thus the boundaries between agents of influence must be dissolved.

Alexa's ability to symbolize appears to be defensively blocked, rather than simply stunted. At the same time she is deeply afraid of being considered crazy and sent to the hospital. Clearly, there is more generally a blurring of the boundaries between imagination and perception, between dream and reality, between concrete and symbolic, between animate and inanimate.

She sought treatment after her boyfriend had "betrayed" her with other women. In the interviews the therapist feels "excluded" by her monologic speech. The marriage of the parents seemed good, but when the patient returned at age 13 from a vacation, she found them suddenly separated, after the mother had fallen in love with another man. She went with the mother, her 4 years' older brother with the father. She had not known how disturbed the marriage of the parents had been; their separation was a "huge break" for her and she felt "excluded." More recently, her stepfather was felled by a severe chronic illness and is now being cared for by the mother. An interesting detail: After the acute onset of his illness, Alexa was entrusted to give directions to their house to the ambulance driver, but was as if paralyzed and failed to do so, thus delaying the urgently needed help: there was conscious competition with the stepfather for mother's love; he himself had been a very jealous man.

Then her brother, who always had been a problem child, hyperactive and provocative, with attention deficit disorder, is now also severely handicapped and being cared for by her mother. The patient asks herself what catastrophe she has to produce in order to attract her mother's attention, and there is clear survivor's guilt. "Mother has everything under control," is a refrain, but she also was at times agoraphobic and claims to be clairvoyant: "You cannot keep anything secret from her." Her mother's eyes are therefore seen as penetrating into the soul, as unveiling what is hidden. The mother's view is: "You can never give enough to men." Her father is described as weak, distant, intellectual, soft––and devalued by her mother and her as "schizoid-compulsive."

A scene from her childhood is that she is sitting in her father's lap. Her mother intervenes, says she should not do this, and pushes the father away. The premise is that sexual excitement could not be contained.

She remembers having admired her rule-breaking brother and having been in love with him, being able to appease him, but being punished together with him. Yet, he was also very jealous and envious of her and of the praise and attention she got as the "good child" and for her scholastic success. There was permanent arguing between brother and mother. At the behest of her mother, she had to hide her school work and her grades to avoid his furious envy and temper tantrums. Once she touched his penis, and he told this to their mother. He kept tormenting her with her anxieties and tried to decapitate her doll. She also remembers that up to his near death, there had continuously been much rivalry between them, in the form of both envy and jealousy. The mother had told him: "You have your mama, you do not need a girlfriend." In fact, he did not have one and was living at home.

At an early age in kindergarten, Alexa engaged with a boy in sexual plays; they were surprised by her mother who quietly again closed the door. She felt embarrassed about it but was not punished for it. Some shame may have a root there, both felt by herself and recognized in her mother's eye.

From adolescence on, she involved herself in friendships with mostly dysfunctional men who exploited her in various ways. With her current boyfriend, there is also much competition; she envies his success but devalues his "running after recognition." We may assume a brother transference to her lovers. One of her lovers "would most have liked to marry my mother," and there was much competition with all of them.

At the same time as she is terrified of a possible psychosis she is highly functioning, successful, and recognized in her work. She still firmly believes in the real existence of ghosts, of a hidden, utterly uncanny reality behind the phenomena. There is both a yearning for death and a fear of death.

In the analysis, the conflict between the great closeness to her mother and the feeling of hatred against her is an important topic. She felt she had been dropped and her unbroken (*heil*) world had been shattered by her mother's seemingly sudden adulterous affair. The ghosts represent not only the fear of her own affects and impulses, especially her conscious incestuous wishes toward her brother, but also the early denied surmises of what was hidden by the family façade. She wants also to be taken care of by her mother, and at the same time there is an "uncanny anxiety and foreboding" that she would be the next case for chronic care and that her mother would drive her into her death. In fact she is still being financially supported by her mother (until the later phase of treatment). Being afraid of the secret power of others, she protects her own will by distancing herself from them, which is in turn mirrored in the split countertransference––keeping emotional distance, yet sudden impulses to embrace and kiss the patient. Very often she cancels the appointments, asks for substitute hours, remains unexpectedly away––clearly a drama of the "excluding first in order not to be the excluded third," the fantasy scenario of jealousy. There is a strong but disavowed transference love; but the fragmented quality of transference, dreams, and speech reflects the discontinuity in the early relationships, presumably mostly with her mother (and then continued with her brother).

Much of her experience appears in sexualized form, especially as projected sexual curiosity (e.g., "hidden men in bushes"), or when she was sitting as a child with her brother under the table, listening like spies to the talk of the adults and suddenly grabbing them. In this enacted fantasy she again intruded into a world from which she felt excluded, transgressing a boundary and participating in the secrets of the adults––references to the primal scene. We may assume that part of what went on in that world of secrecy was very overstimulating, causing massive overexcitement. The vampire teeth represent terrifying and also titillating penetration, perhaps derivatives of the sadomasochistically interpreted primal scene and the denied aggressions between the parents. The jealous implications of the primal scene were much later repeated when she placed herself (as an adolescent!) in the bed between her mother and stepfather.

Correspondingly, she fears being sexually abused and overstimulated by her analyst, or to the contrary, neglected and abandoned, in sync with what we know about the family scenes. She feels deep humiliation by the Evil Eye, the looks of strangers; it is a matter of annihilation and extinction, and the therapist's looks are felt to be evil as well. After all, the analyst is in a sense also clairvoyant and penetrates into her inmost soul. Alexa experiences him as controlling, vampirelike devouring, and sucking her out, and avoids looking in his eye; as a countermeasure she is the one who sets the times of appointment. Her face is often masklike. At the end of the session she appears more open and looks at the analyst. In a dream about her father and boyfriend and reminiscent of an abortion she had years ago, she chases a ghost away by yelling at it: "You are the sad child!" Here the ghost appears to represent her guilt feelings for the killing of the embryo and the survivor's guilt. Yet, there is also clear evidence for her mother's jealousy and her own fear of it. She has the fantasy that she and her brother were "wolf children," exposed in the wild and growing up without parents, reflecting the sense of discontinuity in the early relationship and the insecurity of attachment.

In turn she calls her analyst "the jealous structure" that holds her back and does not allow her independence. In reality, the therapist has to reduce the treatment because the insurance has run out, but is willing to continue seeing her if she pays herself at a reduced fee. In the meantime, she has become financially independent. She projects her own jealousy of the luckier siblings onto the "jealous setting" and the analyst, and declares her autonomy by traveling to Europe, both in dreams and reality. But there she feels (in a dream) haunted by hidden murderers, rapists of children, and robbers––projections of her own murderous jealousy. Still, she has been able to transform much of her aggression into productive forms: as self-assertion and professional success––instead of the paranoid projections, the blurring of the boundaries between animate and inanimate, between life and death, and the attempts at dehumanization. She dreams of an island where no being is said to be born nor to die, a realm between life and death, just like the ghosts, that are named the "undead." There the truth would be revealed to her: to find her roots.

THE "VULTURE EYE" AND "THE HELLISH TATTOO OF THE HEART" (HJ)

In Edgar Allan Poe's (1983) story "The Telltale Heart," the protagonist is fascinated and horrified by an old man's eye, and as a result of that terror and fascination, kills him: "He had the eye of a vulture––a pale blue eye, with a film over it. Whenever it fell upon me, my blood ran cold; and so by degrees––very gradually––I made up my mind to take the life of the old man, and thus rid myself of the eye forever" (p. 799).

He keeps asserting and appealing to an invisible dialogue partner that he is only "nervous" and that his senses are very keen but that he certainly was not mad. Even in that there is a break in the basic senses of trust and an anxiety about losing control, we may presume a fear of judgment, but couched in a fear of death (the eye specifically of the vulture). We think––as we will witness in the case presented below––of a soul blind mother and the lack of the "eye dance" (*Augentanz*), the back and forth of loving response between baby and mother. The threat of the eye is the fear of the archaic, condemning, and especially shaming superego, death being a correlate of the archaic pitiless superego. He tries to appease his own dread, his own sense of the abyss of not having been seen and heard, and to control his archaic superego and the rage about his helplessness:

"[I] spoke courageously to him, calling him by name in a hearty tone" (p. 800).

He could do his deed, however, only when the eye was open: "it was not the old man who vexed me, but his Evil Eye" (p. 800). Planning his murderous deed, the narrator speaks of barely containable feelings of triumph. The dangers seemingly are outside: "the shutters close fastened, through fear of robbers" (p. 800), but the hinges of the door creaked. The robber and murderer comes from within, the projections totter and become ever more brittle.

"The groan of mortal terror" of the victim is matched by his own horror. The "dreadful echo" and the "death-watches in the wall" function like a row of mirrors that multiply his own anxiety to infinity. Yet, now he not only attributes it to his victim, but he brings it about in a massive role reversal (Sandler, 1976a, 1976b, 1989, 1993; Sandler & Sandler, 1994), and this successful externalization is accompanied by the same sense of triumph already felt beforehand during the planning. He is split between empathy: "I knew what the old man felt, and pitied him," and that immense relief: "although I chuckled at heart" (p. 801), an ambivalence of human sympathy and cold dehumanization. The old man tries to console himself, the murderer empathically infers, but, again triumphantly: *"All in vain;* because Death, in approaching the old man, had stalked with his black shadow before him, and the shadow had now reached and enveloped the victim. And it was the mournful influence of the unperceived shadow that caused him to feel––although he neither saw nor heard me––to *feel* the presence of my head within the room" (p. 801, emphasis in the original).

As he directed the thin ray of his lantern upon the victim's head, it "fell full upon the vulture eye. It was open—wide, wide open—and I grew furious as I gazed upon it. I saw it with perfect distinctness—all a dull blue, with a hideous veil over it that chilled the very marrow in my bones" (p. 801). Added to the terrifying eye was the ever increasing sound of the old man's beating heart, *"a low, dull, quick sound—much such a sound as a watch makes when enveloped in cotton"* (p. 801, emphasis in the original). With a yell he threw himself upon the old man and suffocated him with his heavy bed (p. 802): "His eye would trouble *me* no more." He dismembered and hid the corpse and as the police knocked, alerted by the shriek of the old man, he opened them "with a light heart." He offers them chairs, "while I myself, in the wild audacity of my perfect triumph, placed my own seat upon the very spot beneath which reposed the corpse of the victim" (pp. 802–803). The officers felt convinced by his manners that everything was in order, but the ease and comfort of the murderer suddenly waned as he started hearing first a ringing and then the muffled beating sound. While he became more and more agitated the three policemen continued chatting amiably. He takes this as scorn:

> Was it possible they heard not? Almighty God!—no, no! They heard!—they suspected!—they *knew!*—they were making a mockery of my horror!—this

> I thought, and this I think. But anything better than this agony! Anything was more tolerable than this derision! I could bear those hypocritical smiles no longer! I felt that I must scream or die!—and now—again! hark! louder! louder! louder! *louder!*—"Villains!" I shrieked, "dissemble no more! I admit the deed!—tear up the planks!—here, here!—it is the beating of his hideous heart!" (p. 803, emphasis in the original)

The controls have collapsed; all the externalizations and projections were of no avail; the abysmal terrors of shame and guilt have returned.

We turn now to a shift in perspective on this story, to that of the reader's own "eye." In his "countertransference," the reader is immediately pulled into the shame and superego conflicts and the diverse defensive maneuvers against these, and he turns into a possible projection screen of the intolerable feelings of the I-narrator. Thus he begins his story by referring the reader to the overinvestment ("hypercathexis") of his sensory modalities: "The disease had sharpened my senses" (p. 799). At once he assumes with the observing part of his ego that, because of these defensive maneuvers undertaken out of fear of punishment, the reader could take him for crazy. Already at this point, the I-narrator establishes with the reader a familiar relationship, in the sense of what J. Sandler (1976b) describes: that the narrator has a certain presumption how the reader is listening to his utterances, namely that he condemns him, that he does not enter into his inner experience and inner world, and that he does not try to understand them in their emotional significance.

The assumption that this extent of sharpening of the senses might be looked at as abnormal is derived from the reality testing of the narrator himself, he is unable to experience and keep this conflict as such within himself, but he rather at once entangles the reader in an interaction by fascinating him (i.e., by casting a spell). Instead of the narrator, it is now the reader who suspects that the nature of the "disease" may lie in severe inner conflicts. Vicariously, he feels that what it is all about is the control of an abysmal anxiety, of a dread of being condemned, which the narrator projects onto the reader and then compels him into taking over that role (Sandler, 1976b, 1993).

The I-narrator claims that in truth he would not have any problem with the old man were it not for his vulture eye (similar to the patient who at times is sure he would not have any problem were it not for the symptom). But why is it just this eye that exerts such an utterly upsetting effect upon the narrator? This could have to do with the fact that the eye is the seam between the subject pole of shame and other superego affects (the agency of self-observation) and its object pole (the way how the outside world views the subject, or, in this case far more importantly, how the subject fantasizes how it would be viewed from the outside). In other words, in this doubleness of subject pole and object pole, which meet in looking and being looked at, the affect of shame becomes integrally tied in with the superego (which it originally is not). The narrator may be so deeply terrified and agitated because on the one side he still believes that he could get rid of all his conflicts by projecting them upon the vulture eye and by externalizing them while at the same time having a muted foreboding that the horror (the "awe") is really residing within himself. Yet, he tries now, by turning passive into active, to control on the outside what oppresses and frightens him so very much in his inmost self. In an actualization of his relationship fantasies, he secretly, during the night, positions his own eye in the bedroom of the old man who is deeply sleeping and therefore absolutely helpless and impotent. He carries a closed lantern, as if mirroring the closed vulture eye and "responding" to it. Now he has the absolute control over the "opening of the lantern"; this is like the casting of a gaze full of fantasized destructive powers, in accordance with the contents of his shame fantasies. In this way he has the control over looking at, peering into, showing, and being seen. In the opening of the lantern slit, light ray and vulture eye meet, and it seems as if the narrator believed he could, by this action, banish and master the shame fantasies inherent in this encounter. By naming the old man he tries to strengthen his power and control over him and over whom he represents, and in his chuckling he triumphs over the other's helpless exposure.

At the peak of his fantasized power over the contents of his conflicts and shame fantasies his defensive efforts seem to increase yet more: "the shutters were close fastened, through fear of robbers" (p. 800). "Robbers" could perhaps be understood as a metaphor for the contents of conflicts shuttered behind the defenses.

In the further course of the story, these defenses start crumbling: "a groan of mortal terror":

> [I]t was the low stifled sound that arises from the bottom of the soul overcharged with *awe*.[2] I knew the sound well. Many a night, just at midnight, when all the world slept, it has welled up from my own bosom, deepening with its dreadful echo, the terrors that distracted me. I knew what the old man felt, and pitied him, although I chuckled at heart (p. 801, emphasis in the original).

Through the "empathy" with the old man he begins to recognize as his own the mortal horror that hitherto has been, for defensive reasons, completely projected; in rudiments, he senses it now as something that is emerging from his own depths, and the reader might, again vicariously for him, ask himself: What are the contents of this terror?

The topic of shame, and more generally of condemnation, is introduced at the point when he is afraid that the neighbors could hear the loud beating of the heart. Here he seems again to displace by projective identification his own inner conflict onto the object pole, onto the fear of being viewed by the other with condemnation. At issue is his self-condemnation and his shame about his wish and yearning for another human being, for somebody loving. (We give here more weight to shame than to guilt because it gives greater coherence to the interpretation.)

When he dismembers the body of his victim it could be interpreted as a metaphor for his defensively motivated attack against the part of his own self that is being beset by these shame-evoking longings and against the object interaction represented within that elicits this yearning.

"When all the world slept" might represent the profound loneliness and abandonment, and in the "dreadful echo" it is the resonance of the terrible dread of condemnation by an archaic, implacable superego.

We mentioned before that this terror is, as in endless mirrors, reflected into limitless space. Also, he turns his own hopelessness in front of such a pitiless inner object from passive into active by triumphing over the helpless attempts of the old man to gain control over his fear of death; in his own stead he lets him suffer the powerlessness imposed by such a cruel and fatal force. Now he is master over life and death and over all the dreadful feelings.

This implacable superego corresponds to a precipitate of a soul-blind interaction with the early objects. Not being seen and not being recognized lead to a deep sense of shame, which manifests itself in the representations of self and objects and in those of the interactions with them.

THE PENETRATING GAZE AND PERVASIVE SHAME: "DUEL INSTEAD OF DUET" (HJ)

We would like now to illustrate these multiple meanings of the magical, especially the penetrating, look in another clinical example. It comes from the psychoanalytic psychotherapy of an elderly scholar conducted by one of us (HJ). He had sought help after a severe public humiliation (a review in some newspapers that ridiculed a scholarly work of his and accused him of Nazi sympathies).

What is really at issue here is a very common form of scientific and literary discussion of his thoughts; but within himself it was experienced as intensely traumatic. He described how he had felt: "I was pilloried; it is like a huge bell on which one hangs." He assumed: "I have done great damage to my work that could have become a work of the century." He was afraid this could never be repaired and added: "I notice how I identify more and more with the reproach of anti-Semitism." He had completely lost his immense scientific creativity; and his lectures, which he usually could give with much ease, now extracted from him the greatest of energy. All this threw him into deep depression. Only with extreme efforts was he able to resist the continually intruding impulses to throw himself in front of the onrushing train, which would, in his fantasy, separate his head from his members and scatter his body parts over a large area.

The fact that he has experienced the public discussion of his work to such an extent as a traumatization makes me suspect that earlier experiences of not being seen or of being wrongly perceived—experiences rooted in the soul-blind attitudes of the primary objects—may have led to various unconscious fantasies and representations, or in the concept of Winnicott to the formation of a "false self," and how the strivings of the "true self" have to be hidden behind shame fantasies. The "true self" is taken as the reason for being unlovable and "unworthy to live" ("*lebensunwertes Leben*," a core term in Nazi ideology)—and that the feelings triggered in him had to be hidden behind shame fantasies: that he has lost his right to live because the world has discovered his inner shortcomings. These themes break through in the here and now of his current life situation. However, I do not at this point have an idea what he is exactly feeling when he is being seen. What seems clear is that he equates his being seen with his inner life's being aggressively penetrated by the gaze of others, and that something frightful within him could be uncovered.

This theme of aggressive penetration is reenacted between us in our first encounter. When I opened the door and greeted him, he looked deeply into my eyes in an arrogant and sexual way, which immediately made me feel helplessly exposed to an unpleasant and outrageous sexual intrusion. I was aware of a sense of intense dislike, a fear of being subjugated, a violent wish to reject him and to cut contact with him. As soon as we were in the consulting room and had sat down, he launched into a series of sexual remarks, in particular about the pattern of my curtain, in a way that made me feel anxious, bullied, ashamed, and incompetent. He seemed unable to talk about the concerns that had brought him to analysis. He could only show how superior, powerful, and in control he really was. I had great difficulties in maintaining my analytic attitude, as I felt overwhelmed with a sense of humiliation and powerlessness. The understanding of his provocative behavior as a defensive posture helped me to make sense of my feelings, which I understood mirrored his own helplessness and shame.

Therefore, I dealt extremely cautiously with him. I controlled my words more than usual, and at the same time I felt how a part of me rebelled against thus being controlled. In the course of the session when he was talking about his symptoms, it was impossible for me to experience the depressed feelings he described. Rather, I felt humiliated and repelled instead by his crass sexual allusions; yet I also sensed a very great pressure from him to admire him. I believe that in this first session I could not say much more as an analyst than that it must have been certainly very hard for him to have been forced by his depression to seek help with me.

In retrospect I think it was good that I did not say more because with certainty he would have experienced the interpretation of our interaction as an attack. He wanted on the one hand to be seen, but on the other he wanted to control precisely what was seen of him.

After this turbulent entrance, he quickly reverted on the couch to his professional role of lecturing. Although I am at first mentally stimulated by his interesting and clever "lectures," I am soon struck by the devaluing undertone. He wants to be seen by me as the "splendid professor," while

I should be the "little, dumb (and female) therapist." He finds my interpretations––"it is not easy for you not to view the setting of lying on the couch as an attempt by me to make you feel small and to put you into the inferior position"—"interesting," but quickly disappears into higher spiritual spaces. I feel attacked, irritated, incompetent, small, ashamed, and keep asking myself if I am really capable of helping him. The intensity of the feelings triggered in me gives me a sense of how much the show of competence is for him equated with being loved and worth living. In turn, the "true self" is taken as the reason for being unlovable and "unworthy to live."

Already here it is evident how his superego and shame conflicts manifest themselves in his fantasies about seeing and being seen and about their destructive effects: the annihilating force of humiliation. In an "actualization" of what he had experienced in his primary relationships, he now ascribes these horrific effects to the critic's Evil Eye.

Following Joseph Sandler (1976b), we understand as "actualization" the enactment of an important unconscious or preconscious fantasy by the patient in the relationship with the therapist. Role pressure is exerted on the other person toward behaving in ways that would conform to the fantasy. We consider it important that the therapist is as comprehensively as possible capable to engage in this so that it can be put into words and understood by the patient within the relationship, as will be immediately shown. In the actualization in the here and now it is important to perceive affectively and strongly together this role pressure and the intended role reversal, not merely to recognize them and talk about them as projections and externalizations. The danger of intellectualization is always prominent with patients like Mr. A.

A few words about his history. He describes his parents in this way: His father was a physician, about whom he states already in the first sessions that he had low self-esteem and that he, Mr. A, had from early on, to assist in stabilizing. His mother helped him in the office. He saw her as a "strong personality," extremely controlling toward her husband and the other members of the family. Feelings were something one should be ashamed of and almost appear to have a life-threatening dimension: When the father was upset the mother ran to measure his blood pressure, telling him he should control himself. She was an "austere, cool, and strong personality." At home, as he said, she had everything under control. Harmony had to prevail, and all conflicts were denied. There were never any arguments. The mother bragged that already at age 1 he had been toilet trained—a story that fills him even now with resentment.

At this point I would like to make a few remarks about a time in his analysis where I felt deeply moved about how much he must have felt controlled: "One root of my problems certainly lies here." It became gradually more possible for us to thematize his feeling controlled and his compulsion to be controlling in the here and now of our therapeutic relationship. He can address this as it becomes clearer to him how he is treating the analytic hour as if he were sitting on the potty with me: he arrives and delivers "his things" like an automaton. There is no space for pleasure, no room for playing, no variation of the sequence. Then he leaves as if it had not had anything to do with him or what I could interpret to him. During this session, the parallel to his impotence in the marriage impresses me; there he also cannot bring drive wishes into the relationship and thus remains "clean" in this very early sense.

But back to his biography: He thoroughly adapted to the wishes of his parents. There was a 3 years' younger sister who, in contrast to him, rebelled more. She was jealous of his being the favorite good child, and he envied her for being more able to be herself. Although younger, she played teacher toward him and bossed him around.

The father was said to be against the Nazis, but the father's brother joined the SS as a volunteer and remained an "incorrigible Nazi"; he took the adolescent A. to movies that glorified German soldiers. Against the background of his experiencing his mother as castrating and his father as weak, the homosexual and misogynous undertone in these propaganda films certainly proved quite attractive for the patient as adolescent.

A secret that he reports with extreme shame is that during a carnival event when he was about 20 he dressed up as Hitler, under the motto "historical terror cabinet." He still suffers much under this reminiscence. Following the public insinuation about anti-Semitism that had plunged him into the severe crisis, which had brought him into treatment, we may assume that he felt seen-through in his secret fantasies. The identification with Hitler served as a powerful defense against his own absolute powerlessness and smallness. It also would appear as if he created by his masquerade a counterpart in destructiveness to his mother seen as so castrating. This permitted him to fight against his mother's power. Thus he fought for his emotional survival in the oedipal triangle a labile balance between the father whom he experienced as disappointing and weak and his overwhelming mother. The book review struck this labile situation like a lightning bolt and turned everything upon its head. Now he felt overpowered by all his hate, his sadism, and his destructive fantasies.

His whole education is described as very antisexual: It was all about duty, orderliness, and reason. Everything that had to do with play, fantasy, pleasure, and wishes was utterly dangerous. When he once was caught *in flagranti* with a young girl helping in the house there was a "tremendous catastrophe"—expulsion (*Rausschmiß*) of the pretty, young servant and shattering of the mother's image of the good son. Later, he married a woman who, in his words, was spontaneous, impulsive, vivacious, and erotically attractive—but detested by his mother. Her wished for daughter-in-law was according to Mr. A "an erotic neuter." His sexuality with her was from the beginning not very gratifying for both. He had premature ejaculations and asked her to masturbate him, which she more and more refused. He increasingly rejected her and engaged in a number of affairs, and it appears that she also sought compensation in liaisons of her own. He barely ever mentions his two now adult children. His extramarital love relationships were and are more satisfactory, but seem to be split off: He denies any emotional participation and is detached while the partner keeps pleading for his love.

In the further course of treatment, he was able to profit from the sessions so that he could find his way back to his scientific brilliance while I became aware that there was something grandiose and rejecting in his habitude. He attributed this improvement exclusively to the medication: "It has absolutely nothing to do with you!" He also did not make the connection between our relationship and the recurrence of his suicidal tendencies after separations from me, caused by his frequent leaves for lecture tours or excursions. When I suggested an increase in the frequency of our sessions after one such interruption that had triggered massive suicidal impulses, he seemed to be full of regret, but declined: "After going through my full calendar I unfortunately cannot fulfill your wish." It was apparent that he had projected his longing into me and treated the issue now so as if I were the one who could not tolerate the long intervals between the sessions.

In fact, in the following session he is quite desperate. His suicidal impulses are hard to control: "For Heaven's sake, help me! I cannot pull myself out of the swamp by my own collar! I cannot bear any longer your cold, detached, and distant attitude. I urgently beg you to do something!" I answer that he is pleadingly stretching his arms out for help from me and experiencing me as unreachable and sadistically turning away from him, and I ask him if this seems familiar to him. He is shaken by the power of projection and says that all this makes him think of his mother. I make a connection to the last session: "Perhaps you are afraid to be abandoned by me because you could not comply with my suggestion of an increase in sessions, just as you recently told me that your mother was retreating emotionally when her little granddaughter expressed her own wishes." What I do not address at this point is his deep sense of shame when he gets in touch with the needy little boy within, whom the adult part hates so strongly. In his life up to then he has learned to show himself as sovereign and to expect as little as possible from his cold mother.

That Mr. A gained now more access to his anxiety of "mother's cold, judgmental gaze" represented a milestone in his treatment. It became ever clearer how the critic's look hid the gaze of his mother. Now we also uncovered a crucial biographical detail: During the Nazi time, his mother had taught at so-called "mother schools" about infant care according to the ideas of Dr. J. Haarer ("The German Mother and Her First Child," 1934, quoted in Chamberlain, 2000). What in these recollections was now emerging and in what I could sense in my countertransference feelings, offered us much illustrative material about the child rearing during the Nazi time: the drill to regularity that left little leeway for the inner life, for the child's own state of feeling, and no opportunity for what Haarer very negatively called "*Tändeln*" (playful dawdling and spontaneity).

Especially striking was "the refusal of mother's face" and its impassivity during nursing, bathing, diapering, and feeding the infant. Eye contact was to be avoided and thus the early "eye dance" between mother and baby blocked—the playful, even dreamy togetherness of mother and baby during feeding and taking care of the infant, mother's joy about her playing with the child. In this way one of the cardinal foundations for "a relationship to the emotional center of the mother" (Chamberlain, 2000, p. 38) was made impossible. Also the inductions to obedience are revealing, quoted now directly from Haarer (cited by Chamberlain, p. 40):

> "At the age of playing, obedience must be obtained; that means, unconditional obedience without distraction, without reward or promise and without threat of punishment." In the ideal case, the child of 2 ½ years should be steered solely by the eyes of the mother. "The properly trained child soon does not require anymore even a first hint of punishment. He knows very well of his own what would follow this or that misbehavior, or he receives enough warning by one look at the mother's face."

It might be seen that there is a contradiction between the avoidance of eye contact and the steering of the child by the mother's eye. But it is, after all, a matter of how the child feels he or she is being perceived—either as an object to be controlled and steered or as a living part of a relationship that he or she joins in shaping.

Those eyes that control, threaten, and also penetrate ("I can see it in your face if you are lying or have done something"), as Chamberlain continues, are reminiscent of the most important national socialistic newspaper, the "Völkische Beobachter" (i.e., "the ethnic observer"; "*völkisch*" is a very nationalistic and racist adjective coined by the Nazis).

Chamberlain asks:

> May it be that the person who early on had been refused access to the center of the Other, to her soul, later on can be brought much more easily to annihilate that human being whose existence had been declared useless, like a "dead" thing, a "soulless" insect? Sometimes this was not possible anymore when by chance glances were exchanged and contact occurred, if but for a brief moment, during which presumably there was a recognition and memory of the fear of death. There are several reports of such remembering that some people were not able to kill anymore at that moment; others felt for the rest of their lives haunted by those eyes, and yet at times, such a memory of an earlier fear of death would make some even more furious and cruel. (p. 41)

In his analysis, Mr. A increasingly found better access to his loneliness and his inner distress about the unreachability of his mother, a distress repeated and worked through in the transference to me. He also could now recognize more clearly his severe guilt feelings for his own impulses and assumed he had sent the other person into flight. He realized that his impulses differed from those of the people around him and could trace them to their genetic context with his mother. He had to realize that he was not as sovereign as he had liked to view himself and was very ashamed about this presumed weakness. Yet it appears that these guilt feelings served by and large as defense against the preponderance of shame conflicts.

Here again Haarer's thoughts about the "loving manipulation of the child" are quite revealing. The child should be left unsure of the love and acceptance by the mother. "It is dangerous to show the child that her love is unshakeable, regardless and without restriction." She should withdraw her friendliness from the child when she is annoyed. The child must learn that it can regain her love only by obedience. Haarer calls this "loving manipulation" (*"liebevolle Beeinflussung"*) (cited in Chamberlain, 2000, p. 136). The child should never feel secure in his trust. Especially when he shows his anxiety and tries to cling to her, he has to be intentionally shown rejection: "The more clearly he shows his anxiety the more strongly the mother is misusing it by causing more insecurity, called loving manipulation, in order to reinforce obedience. Particularly useful is the child's anxiety when he is defiant" (p. 136). Thus the child's fear of the loss of love is used to suppress all his attempts at autonomy and independence. His wish to function on his own has to be broken by the threat of such punishment.

M. Mahler (1975) describes the phase of separation and individuation as a time in infantile development where the mother does not represent anymore the only center in the child's life but where the variegated outside world becomes increasingly more fascinating and attractive. This is not a simple time for child or mother because, in spite of the child's autonomy strivings, it remains very important for him to be able to find a way back to the safe harbor of his relationship with the mother. However, if these autonomy needs are punished with loss of love there arises for the child an almost unsolvable conflict. He has to decide between his own self and the relatedness to his mother. In all likelihood he will then decide for himself to return to the symbiosis, a symbiotic attachment, however, which is also, because of the traumatic quality of the experience of dependency, felt to be very dangerous—duel instead of duet. Thus, both dependency and independence are interpreted as threatening (what we also know as the vicious circle between separation guilt and dependency shame) (Wurmser, 1981, 2004, 2007).

With these insights, Mr. A was gradually able to distance himself somewhat from the enmeshment with his mother. He recalled how the holidays always had to be celebrated at his mother's, although his wife did not like it: "The only possibility not to appear [at mother's] would be for me to be dead." With the help of a cat, Mr. A and his wife found a way to excuse themselves from some of these forced visits.

Shortly before the expiration of the insurance coverage for the analysis, he gave vent to some very strong transference feelings: He accused me of "being like a sphinx, a person of respect with the aura of unapproachability, avoiding eye contact," and that I am asking him to lie down just because it belongs to the rules. "Why would she do this?" he asked himself. He answers his own question: that she is doing this so that he would not penetrate her with his eyes. He believes that *I am afraid of his penetrating eye*. What underlies this fantasy is of course that he has no other relationship fantasy about reciprocal seeing than this form of mutual destruction, not of being able to be creative and fruitful with each other—"duel instead of duet," the sadomasochistic "fearful symmetry" (Novick & Novick, 1996)—and that she tries to protect herself in this way.

He also claims I protect myself against him by the therapeutic setup and am humiliating him that way, and he is afraid I would hypnotize him: that with my eyes I would exert power over him—*eo ipso* a source of shame for him. I say: "With Haarer it is so that the good mother steers her children with the eyes." Being shamed is being equated with the fear of death. He had experienced his public humiliation as something so terrible that he had been thinking of throwing himself under the train; he had no right to live anymore.

In the transference, I become such a cold mother who looks at him without any interest. He does not know where I would turn my gaze to. In one of these sessions, he fantasizes that he is lying in a baby carriage that I am pushing. I fantasize the eye contact with the baby and say: "It is for you as when, being in the baby carriage, you could not imagine that your mother would look joyfully at you." He: "It was only *her cold look, icy*." This means his total worthlessness. He cannot imagine that I could warmly look at him. He says: "You just want to establish the relationship in order to destroy it again by your 'analyzing' me." This is actually his projection: He himself attacks and devalues everything by his undermining (*zersetzend*) way of "analyzing." It has to be assumed that he has not experienced warm, loving, and empathic eye contact with a female, maternal vis-à-vis so that he knows to interpret the women's gaze only in one dimension, namely that of sexualization. Until now, women have been sexual objects whom he could dominate. The analyst is for him now a novel phenomenon that he cannot understand at first: She is not interested in sex with him, but offers him her constant, regular, and safe presence, a space to think together with him about his issues. Right now, she has to be for him a peculiar little animal. He bites prophylactically because he has no idea that in the relationship one could do something together.

Intellectualizing has helped him all his life so that he does it also in the analysis. It is the *transference of his defense by intellectualizing, a projection of this defense onto the analyst*: "You attribute to me what has helped you all your life." He tries to analyze me: that I am a very vulnerable person and have a hard shell in order to protect myself. Maybe he has recognized something real but he does use it as a hook to fasten his projection on.

I answer: "The professional shell is something that creates the space where we can reflect together. By my distancing and refusal I protect the dialogue, not only you and myself," and I continue that the eye contact means for him injury and shame, instead of understanding and empathy, and that he experiences the analytic situation as stimulating and frustrating and at the same time as an opportunity for intellectualization.

In his monology, he can explain everything to himself, he does not need anybody and thus does not have to feel helplessly surrendered (*ausgeliefert*) and does not get in touch with his great yearning for an empathic eye. Was he a bit angry because he could not in this setting have any eye contact? Perhaps so, because he wants to find in my eyes what gradually has become more permissible.

In fact, it is more and more noticeable that Mr. A is now able to experience a kind of warm and loving feeling toward me and other people in his outside life. In his sessions he now speaks with more understanding about his female students, and he also allows himself to be more touched by the worries of his own children. Again and again, however, he needs to be reassured by me that his being touched is not a sign of weakness and unmanliness.

At this point, the number of sessions paid by the insurance was about to run out. The patient experienced this as a severe threat of separation. He discussed a dream in which an unknown woman wearing gray clothes was coming for him. He woke up crying with terror. In his associations, the woman reminded him of his analyst and of death.

For him separation was being experienced as death, and death itself as a huge narcissistic slight. He is not immortal. In his own written work he has succeeded in reawakening the life of great artists, to resurrect them from the *shame of mortality*.

I inquire what might have triggered the shame on the day before. The content of the previous session had dealt with sexual transgressions on his side and renewed temptations of this kind. Above all, I had tried to address a number of incidents some considerable time ago when he had actually harassed me sexually and nearly assaulted me. Certainly he had at least tried to sexually seduce me.

Thus behind the two prominent and conscious themes of separation and death was hidden a third one—shame; it was also playing a vital role in the patient's mental economy: *the wish to be seen was countered by the fear of being penetrated by the eyes*. In the meantime Mr. A had succeeded during his sessions to enter into a fruitful dialogue with me and being more seen as himself. Yet, this stood in crass contrast to his need to ward off his feelings of impotence by "sexual harassment." Increasingly his destructive fantasies of symbiosis entered into the therapeutic relationship.

The awareness of separation and death would indeed shatter his grandiose attempts at invincibility and force him to face his limitations and anxieties that he might feel ashamed of. Talking now about separation means a kind of security against having to cope with the topic of shame—and his acted out self-object relationship fantasies.

Death is, however, in its own right a huge narcissistic slight: having to realize that the self is not immortal—but more: a failure and end of all his endeavors to still transform the cold and merciless eye of his mother into an empathic, receptive one that would allow him to partake of her inner treasures. The eye stands here for the entrance gate to the inner self of the mother from which he feels barred and through which he now tries to forcibly enter into her, and more generally women's inner space, when they refuse him ready access. The same had occurred in the first interactions between us.

However, death also reflects his anxiety that the defenses against the immense impulses for revenge resulting from his being excluded might fail. In one of the sessions he had been able to formulate this understanding with the words: "The little Mozart in me probably serves the protection against the little Hitler in me." With that he refers to his great creativity; he has published a great number of articles in professional journals and several books, including some standard works. He is also well known as a painter.

As already mentioned, in his own work he succeeds in reawakening the great artists to life—to resurrect them from the shame of mortality. In an act of revenge he is thus able to break his mother's prerogative in her Janus-faced potency: of both giving life and bringing death, and to deny his dependency on her by grandiosely giving rebirth to the great figures of history. In this way he can triumph over her in her procreative functions—showing the great importance of *womb envy*.

In the last hour before the end of insurance coverage he talked about his having "shot all my powder," that he did not have anything more to say. I countered that these times—when he had been feeling that way—had often been our most fruitful sessions because then we could develop something together, something that we had in common. He replied: "Yes, then I left the sessions surprisingly content. But this happened only because you then picked up the ball and made something out of it. When that did not succeed the ball went in the wrong direction." I asked myself in the ensuing silence whether what came across now was envy of my "inner potency" and that I could be myself and resist his attacks. Could he be ashamed about his own emptiness and sense of defeat? In my countertransference thoughts I am preoccupied at this moment with "dead inner spaces."

He speaks of his gratitude that I had done such an excellent work with him, but then also that I had a Janus head: He does not know what it means for me that he comes to sessions. He has understood in the meantime what analysis means: that he says something; that I then take that within myself and digest it, and that I then give something back to him that he can take and in turn do something with. I say: "Yes, we do that so together."

He then says something that I do not remember verbatim anymore but the image intrudes in my mind of a small child that busies himself to explore the inner life of his toy: to cut open his doll in order to find out how what is within functions. He wants to know it perhaps so that he could also better control its functions. Or does he do it to fight off his envy of the inner aliveness of the other, or does he struggle with his feeling excluded from the inner world of the other? I tell him that he is perhaps uncertain what is happening with his image in my inner world and that he asks himself if he really is also reaching me in my inner world. He simply responds that I practice a technique. I say: "In that case I could be a machine and take everything that you tell me and spit it out again."

He replies: "Let's switch the roles for once. If I put myself in your place—excuse me that I say this so, I would not know if I could do this: always to listen to what someone else is telling, to have to be with my entire interest with someone else. I would often digress and be somewhere else with my thoughts."

I tell him: "You are uncertain how I am with you, how I am silent with you, whether then I am also with you or completely absent and distant," and I think of the "refused face" of the mother.

Then he says: "You need the analytic attitude in order to protect yourself against me. You have never come to my lectures where we then would have had an opportunity to go and drink a glass of wine together."

I reply: "You take my giving you the opportunity to bring everything to your hours that afflicts or moves you not so much as an offer but as an attempt on my side to belittle you and to shame you, and you would like for once also to let me feel this shame 'on the outside.' You still have trouble imagining that I would do something because I think about you within myself. And I think: 'In his world, he can only think of a relationship as serving one's own gratification of pleasure, that means that for him relationships are still much duel and little duet.'"

At the end of this session he asks me as he is leaving: "When is it allowed to have again a relapse?"

He would have had the possibility to understand yet more, but his anxiety and shame are too great, and he does not want to continue the analysis. He feels narcissistically too vulnerable. When we think of the "Haarer mothers" and we remind ourselves that his mother was one of them, we can understand his fear better. This had been an education toward strict obedience to authority and a suppression of feelings, especially those of tenderness or weakness. The children were left crying for hours. The eye demanded submission and turned away with cold disapproval from the needy infant.

He experiences his dependence on the analysis as a deep slight and he tries to avoid this by letting the therapy taper off. Alternatively, he tries to transform the analytic relationship into a reality enactment so that he would not have to deal with these feelings. In that case, he could be lord and master; there would not be any separation and weakness. He would penetrate me genitally rather than my eyes be experienced as penetrating him.

The dream of death, where an unknown lady was coming for him before the break-off of the therapy, proved to be prophetic. A short while after he had left the therapy, at a birthday celebration for his mother, he suddenly succumbed to a heart attack—in a macabre irony of what he had said before about the obligatory celebrations with his mother.

He had described it as a "large bell of not being perceived" under which he was living: the uncomprehending and objectifying look of his mother. He needed his "false self" of triumphal success and public acclaim, and when this crumbled under the onslaught of criticism, he felt his life's work was destroyed and his life was not justifiable anymore. It was also a mortifying "vulture eye" that penetrated him, and no triumph could last in front of it. And this was the transference before his sudden death.

CONCLUDING REMARKS: "SEE HOW GREAT THE POWER OF SHAME IS!"

In the *Mask of Shame*, one of us (LW), described a clinical observation that is not rare:

> His own magic eye was needed to find the lost face of his mother and to undo, once and for all, by magic expression, the wound of basic unlovability. The face that he sought also had just such a magic eye. It was beckoning, admiring, and promising healing love. These two sets of unconscious wishes: to find love through searching and through expressing, were defended against by shame. ... Love resides in the face—in its beauty, in the music of the voice and the warmth of the eye. Love is proved by the eye, and so is unlovability—proved by seeing and hearing, by being seen and heard. (1981, pp. 94, 96–97)

Unlovability is proved by the disdainful look, by the punishing and envious or jealous eye, by the accusing voice, and in particular by not being seen and heard as the one who one is. "A child can be loved without being given the nipple; but love cannot exist without face and music. ... To be unlovable means not to see a responsive eye and not to hear a responding voice, no matter how much they are sought" (p. 97).

In regressive states and fantasy, the duality of action, both of showing oneself and of perceiving, turns into a means of merger and destruction; thus the eye becomes a source of magic power of sexuality and aggression. Curiosity and fascination, self-presentation and self-exhibition may have a hugely seductive and vindictive effect. We hear it hinted at in Clemens Brentano's poem "Zu Bacharach am Rheine (Lore Lay)" about the sorceress Lore Lay (Loreley) drawing all men who see her into perdition and later on, in Heine's poem, becomes the nymph singing in the middle of the Rhine, drawing the boatmen by her songs to their death: *"Die Augen sind zwei Flammen, mein Arm ein Zauberstab"* (The eyes are two flames, my arm is a magic wand).[3]

The eye becomes a means of unbidden penetration. "It is as if vision is then used as a proximity sense" (like taste, smell, touch and proprioception) "enabling a part object relationship to be re-established" (Steiner, 2006, p. 947). The sequence of *shame→envy and jealousy→revenge→feared retribution by even more archaic forms of humiliation* turns into a characteristic vicious cycle, a cycle of repeated traumatization, internalization of such traumatizing relationships, and of inviting its repetition by "actualization." Most importantly, the superego takes over the work begun by the early object relationships. The "inner judge," the "inner dwarf" (Wurmser, 2007), owns that inner eye that implacably humiliates; it becomes the carrier of envy and resentment: "You do not deserve anything good! How dare you! How can you have any pleasure when others have suffered so much—because of you?" It punishes the self mercilessly, onto death, and it brings about in the interaction with others the very thing it fears most and wants to avoid most assiduously. The *core of the Evil Eye is the pernicious power of conscience,* above all of its unconscious parts. Admiration and idealization or humiliation of others may hide the sequence outlined, but this inner Evil Eye keeps breaking through with its own kind of penetrating gaze, its own kind of magical and searing force.

Such regression of the cognitive and perceptual processes is due to trauma with its many forms of overstimulation and overexcitement, or of self-annihilation by fragmentation and devastating shame. A few concluding words about traumatogenic shame are therefore in order here.

The feeling of shame in its multilayeredness and depth is prominent among the frightening affects induced by trauma. In many cases, like with Alexa and Mr. A, much of psychoanalytic work may consist in listening to the sense of current slights that seem to confirm the feeling of one's own unworth and the burning resentment about the suffered injustices. In fact, the analysis itself can become traumatizing, as a repetition of this original link between trauma and shame within the transference, or rather, within the real relationship with the therapist. What is this original link, however?

1. One root may indeed be *massive shaming* as part of the trauma, and that seems to be a self-evident connection. But there is far more that we uncover in our analytic work.
2. Very commonly it is *the shame about the intensity of feelings* in general, the great anxiety to express them and the anxiety of inner and outer loss of control. It is so often the premise in the family, supported by cultural prejudice, that it is a sign of disgraceful weakness and thus of vulnerability, to show, or even just to have, strong feelings (the Haarer mothers!). This causes a very strong tendency to be deeply ashamed. The body, especially sexuality, may be far less strongly shame inducing than this alleged weakness of having strong feelings: feelings of neediness, of longing, of tenderness, of being moved, of being hurt. Many look then for a partner who is an antishame hero: someone emotionally untouchable, impenetrable, invulnerable, a disdainful ruler. One aspect of transference may indeed consist in trying to evoke in the analyst a countertransference reaction of distancing and angry rebuff, visible in both patients

studied. Looking for the acceptance by such a figure and merger with him or her would remove the shame of feeling and wishing too strongly, but it means an almost incorrigible masochistic bondage and a renewed and deepened sense of disgrace.

3. Then shame is caused by the experience that one has not been perceived as a person with the right for one's own feelings and will. The other person's *soul blindness* evokes the feeling of great worthlessness; the other's contempt expressed by disregard for one's own inner life is matched by self-loathing. I mentioned how analysis itself may be shaming and thus inadvertently repeat the traumatogenic shame. There are many ways of doing this: Sometimes it may be silence to a question, sometimes a sarcastic comment, often direct drive interpretations, and, what I see particularly in my supervisions in Europe, the unempathic, forced relating of every aspect to transference. All this can be felt to represent being soul blind. Incomprehension and tactlessness are experienced as a renewed deep insult and shaming.
4. Typically in severe traumatization in childhood, *sexualization* is then deployed as an attempt to regulate affects, again very noticeable in both cases. Both the flooding with affects and the very archaic defense by sexualization lead to an overwhelming feeling of shame. On an additional front line of defense, aggressive wishes, impulses, and fantasies are thrown in as means to reestablish control; they should stop the further tumble in that regressive spiral. This archaic equation of traumatic affect storms, sexualization and aggression leads, on the one hand, to global forms of defense, above all of turning passive into active, denial, externalization, and projection, and as a result to the observable dissociative phenomena and, on the other hand, to massive countermeasures by the superego in the form of the same absoluteness and pervasiveness of shame and guilt. Much of this hypertrophy of the superego consists in the dominating fantasy of omnipotent responsibility set up as protection against traumatic helplessness: "It is in my power to prevent abuse, or the fighting between the parents, or the dissolution of their marriage. If I do not prevent this the calamity is all my fault."
5. Every kind of excitement turns, as affect regression, into *overexcitement* and *overstimulation*, and this has to lead inevitably to a crash, to a very painful disappointment and the overwhelming sense of shame for "having been made the fool again." This traumatic, passively experienced process is again and again turned around into something actively reenacted. How so? It happens in that way that every joy, every gratification, every expectation, everything good has to be broken off and changed into something negative and bad. It may seem as if it were unconscious guilt that would make it appear as if one did not deserve to be successful. This may certainly contribute. But that dangerous, mortifying, shame-laden excitement appears to be more important: "It is too dangerous to sense pleasure

and joy; it will be abruptly taken away or it will become unbearably intense and totally unfulfillable." Thus the inner judge, the archaic superego, has to prevent all pleasure. It stands to reason that the *negative therapeutic reaction* has a crucially important source in this preemptive thwarting of joy and pride in success.

6. Closely connected with this is a sixth reason: that of the *intrapsychic passivity*. David Rapaport (1953) wrote about the passivity of the ego. Often, what appears to be ordained from the outside is in truth an inner passivity in regard to affects and drives, but also and no less so a passivity vis-à-vis the threatening and hammering superego. There is not only profound anxiety about being helplessly delivered to these inner powers, but also shame for such *inner ego passivity*. Outer victimhood is very often its externalization: a repetition on the outside in the vain attempt to resolve it within.

Such multiform traumatogenic shame predisposes to archaic and massive forms of jealousy and envy, which then in turn are reflected in the cruelty and destructiveness of the conscience. All this is projected in the form of the Evil Eye, of magic look, of Medusa's horrifying face. In a "trauma compensatory scheme" (Fischer & Riedesser, 2003), it may find its antithesis in the radiant face of divine inspiration and blessing.

In the Talmud (Gittin 57a) a story is told how a man was wrongly, on the basis of a mixing up of his name, invited to a banquet given by a foe of his. When the host discovered him, he threw him out, although the guest tried to pay for the entire banquet in order to avert the public humiliation. Deeply shamed he went to the Roman emperor and accused the Jews of sacrilege, whereupon the Roman army laid siege to Jerusalem and eventually destroyed it. The story ends: "It has been taught that Rabbi El'azar said: 'Come and see how great the power of shame is (*bo ure'eh kama gedolah kocha shel busha*), for the Holy one espoused the cause of Bar Qamtza and destroyed His House and burnt His Temple.'"

ACKNOWLEDGMENTS

We thank Dr. Benjamin Kilborne, Mrs. Anne-Marie Sandler, and Mrs. Kronberg-Gödde, for their very helpful suggestions and corrections in this essay.

NOTES

1. Rabbi Yose bar Chanina interpreted from another source: "'And let them multiply like fish in the womb of the earth'. Just as fish in the sea are covered by water and the [Evil] Eye has no power over them, so too the [Evil] Eye has no power over the descendants of Joseph" (B.M. 84A, pp. 121–122, Steinsaltz [1989–1999] translation, but somewhat modified).

2. Here in the sense of great fear, although today usually a fear mixed with admiration.
3. We are grateful to Professor A. Bacher for this reference. The immediate context of these verses is: *"Herr Bischof lasst mich sterben, / Ich bin des Lebens müd, / Weil jeder muss verderben, / Der meine Augen sieht. / Die Augen sind zwei Flammen, / Mein Arm ein Zauberstab— / O legt mich in die Flammen! / O brechet mir den Stab!"* (Translation: "Lord bishop let me die, I am tired of my life because everyone has to perish who sees my eyes. The eyes are two flames, my arm a magic wand—O put me in the flames! O break the staff over me!")

REFERENCES

Chamberlain, S. (2000). *Adolf Hitler, die deutsche Mutter und ihr erstes Kind. Über zwei NS-Erziehungsbücher.* Giessen: Psycho-Sozial Verlag.

Fischer, G., & Riedesser, P. (2003). *Lehrbuch der Psychotraumatologie* (3rd ed.). München: Reinhardt.

Freud, S. (1900/1953/1968). The interpretation of dreams. In *Standard edition* (Vols. 4 & 5). London: Hogarth Press.

Freud, S. (1919/1955/1968): The uncanny. In *Standard edition* (Vol. 17, pp. 217–252). London: Hogarth Press.

Haarer, J (1934). *Die deutsche Mutter und ihr erstes Kind* (J. J. Lehmanns). München: Verlag.

Lagerlöf, S. (1897/1989). *Antikrists mirakler.* Norbok AS, Norway (originally Bonniers, Stockholm, Sweden).

Mahler, M. S., Pine, F., & Bergman, A. (1975) *The psychological birth of the human infant: Symbiosis and individuation.* Basic Books, New York.

Novick, J., & Novick, K. K. (1996). *Fearful symmetry. The development and treatment of sadomasochism.* Northvale, NJ: Jason Aronson.

Nietzsche, F. (1883–1885/1988). *Also sprach Zarathustra.* München: Musarionausgabe.

Poe, E. A. (1983). The Telltale Heart. In *The unabridged Edgar Allan Poe.* Philadelphia: Running Press.

Rapaport, D. (1953/1967). Some metapsychologial considerations concerning activity and passivity. In M. M. Gill (Ed.), *Collected papers of D. Rapaport* (pp. 530–568). New York: Basic Books.

Sandler, J. (1976a). Dreams, unconscious fantasies and "identity of perception." *International Review of Psycho-Analysis, 3,* 33–42.

Sandler, J. (1976b). Countertransference and role-responsiveness. *International Review of Psycho-Analysis, 3,* 43–48.

Sandler, J. (Ed.). (1989). *Projection, identification, projective identification.* London: Karnac Classics.

Sandler, J. (1993). On communication from patient to analyst: not everything is projective identification. *International Journal of Psycho-Analysis, 74,* 1097–1108.

Sandler, J., & Sandler, A.-M. (1994). Phantasy and its transformations: A contemporary Freudian view. *International Journal of Psycho-Analysis, 75,* 387–394.

Steiner, J. (2006). Seeing and being seen. *International Journal of Psychoanalysis, 87,* 939–952.

Steinsaltz, A. (1989–1999). *The Talmud* (I. Berman, D. Strauss, et al., Transl.). New York: Random House.

Talmud: *Hebrew/Aramaic edition of the Babylonian Talmud,* 1962. ed. Rabbi M. Zioni, Jersusalem, Bne Braq. Engl. translation, 1936, ed. Isidore Epstein, Soncino Press, London.

Vennemann, J. (2001). Der böse Blick. *Jahrbuch für klinische Psychoanalyse, 3,* 166–172.

Wurmser, L. (1981). *The Mask of Shame.* Baltimore: Johns Hopkins University Press (Republished Northvale, NJ: Jason Aronson, 1994).

Wurmser, L. (Ed.). (2004). Superego revisited—relevant or irrelevant? In: The superego—A vital or supplanted concept? *Psychoanalytical Inquiry, 24*(2), 183–205.

Wurmser, L (2007). *Torment me, but don't abandon me. Psychoanalysis of the severe neuroses in a new key.* New York: Rowman & Littlefield.

9

Shame and Envy

ANDREW P. MORRISON AND MELVIN R. LANSKY

It is to Melanie Klein that psychoanalysis is indebted for the most nuanced, original, and powerful conceptualization of envy that we possess. Klein clearly distinguished envy from covetousness and made clear not only that penis envy was not itself simply a matter of desire for a penis, but also that envy of the penis was not the bedrock and irreducible origin of envy. Her clarifications have definitively advanced psychoanalytic understanding. Post-Freudian psychoanalytic consideration of envy begins with the contributions of Klein. We pay tribute to this major contribution to psychoanalytic understanding, but we disagree with Klein's privileging of the primacy of innate aggressivity, that which she calls the death instinct (Thanatos), in the phenomenology of envy.

For Klein, envy is innate, the death instinct turned outward in the form of aggressive attack on the presumed goodness and self-sufficient completeness of the other. It is here that we believe that Klein excessively attributed the derivation of both Thanatos and the phenomenology of envy to the drives. We see those attributes that are attacked by the workings of envy as functioning through self-conscious comparison to make the subject feel incomplete, needy, and ashamed before one who is complete, giving, and intact. Klein considered envy in terms of the paranoid-schizoid position, which she elaborated masterfully but, in our opinion, incompletely. That "position" vis-à-vis internal objects is dominated by paranoid anxieties and is handled by schizoid mechanisms. We agree with this characterization, but suggest, in the following way, that Klein did not fully understand the type of paranoid anxiety that is present in the paranoid-schizoid position. We believe the "paranoia" in the paranoid-schizoid position, at least with regard to envy, to be paranoid anxiety specifically about what is felt by the subject to be deliberate humiliation and relegation to rejected or insignificant status on the part of a dominant other on whom the subject depends intensely. It is paranoid shame that characterizes the paranoid-schizoid position with regard to envy. The paranoid-schizoid position thus becomes a state of exquisite persecutory shame anxiety in which the source of shame is projected and felt to be the deliberate intent of the other to humiliate and stigmatize. This paranoid anxiety is handled by schizoid mechanisms (hence the name paranoid-schizoid position, which originated with Fairbairn).

It is the schizoid handling of these shame-infused paranoid states—the withdrawal from the social and moral order—that we see as the operation of the destructive instinct, Thanatos. Freud (1940) writes:

> we have decided to assume the existence of only two basic instincts, *Eros* and *the destructive instinct.* ... The aim of the first of these basic instincts is to establish ever greater unities and to preserve them thus—in short to bind together; the aim of the second is, on the contrary, to undo connections and so to destroy things. (p. 148)

Following Freud, we suggest that the essence of Thanatos is the (unconsciously motivated and executed) withdrawal and disconnected state of moral obliviousness that we see resulting from fulminant shame, connected only secondarily to aggression. In our view, then, envy is instigated by shame, and is, thus, a variant of narcissistic rage, not evidence of a primary aggressive drive. Although Kleinian theory and clinical practice have evolved broadly since Klein's original formulations, we still see traces of a privileging of innate aggressivity and a neglect of shame dynamics persisting in the work of contemporary Kleinians (Spillius, 1993).

Envy reflects the destructive idealization of another considered in relation to oneself, representing comparison of self to other, with the self assuming the lesser position (Morrison, 1989, 1996). The Kleinian perspective on envy, then, emphasizes its destructive attributes—the self's refusal to tolerate that the other might possess qualities or bounty that one needs, desires, or cherishes. From Klein's viewpoint, this destructive rage originates in infancy, is directed toward negating the needed/desired breast, and represents the early manifestation of the destructive instinct (Freud's Thanatos). Although jealousy is essentially triangular and involves a whole object, envy is often, though not always, experienced toward part-objects, and is usually aimed at spoiling the object's "goodness" (Segal, 1977). Since an ideal object can neither be found nor tolerated, all hope is lost and one sinks into the mire of despair. As Adam Phillips (1994) notes in his Foreword to Harold Boris's (1994) reflections on envy, "poverty is exactly what's at stake in envy: a state of mind in which one is nevertheless poor" (p. x).

Boris contrasts desire with hope, concluding that "hope arises from preconceptions of how things and experiences should be" (1994, p.19). Envy results from recognition of what it is that one should have in order independently to meet one's own needs (for the infant, a breast). The possessor of that "something" is, inevitably, someone else (or, potentially, something else). Alternating with idealization of that "something" is the tendency to trivialize or disparage its value (Boris, 1994, p. 36), or to seek revenge against the possessor for the immutable value of that which is possessed. We see this situation as implying the workings of self-conscious comparison with the other—in a dyad or in a multiple party relationship—in which the attributes of the other in comparison to those of the self generate shame about the inequity and basic self-inferiority over needs requiring the (presumably self-sufficient) other for fulfillment. This shame, in turn, triggers envy, which serves in fantasy to repair the sense of inferiority and shame by tearing down the other.

In her essay on envy, Spillius (1993) presents a contemporary Kleinian, richly phenomenological view. She demonstrates that Klein included environmental with constitutional factors in determining the strength of envy, but, in our view, she still fails to appreciate the role of shame. With Boris, Spillius notes that "Any difference may be attacked by envy, but goodness is its special target" (p. 1202); this viewpoint, while an accurate representation of the analyst's observations, may not, Spillius points out, coincide with the understanding or self-view of the patient. The patient is, in all likelihood, more sensitive than the analyst to the basic asymmetry of the analytic situation with its resultant sense of inferior status. This shame dynamic is noted, but its consequences tend not to be appreciated by Spillius or by others in the Kleinian school. As generally conceived by Kleinians, the sources of envy tend to be unconscious and destructive; as patients approach the depressive position, the sources of envy become more conscious, generates guilt, and can be worked with analytically.

Envy tends to be experienced "when the individual compares himself with someone superior in happiness, reputation, or in the possession of anything desirable" (Spillius, 1993, p. 1203). Those who feel justified envy and a persistent sense of grievance tend toward deep narcissistic vulnerability, with feelings of inferiority and unlovability. Their rage may be expressed directly toward the "superior other," justified with a thirst for vindication; as examples, Spillius quotes Satin in Milton's *Paradise Lost*,[1] and Lansky (1997) reminds us of the opening declaration of envy in Shakespeare's *Richard III*.2

It is our contention that one central piece is missing from the Kleinian vision of envy, even as represented contemporaneously by Spillius. If envy reflects comparison with someone superior, this comparison must be against a self felt to be inferior, lacking, or in some way defective. Envy is built on comparison, and therefore must reflect self-consciousness. To the degree, then, that the self is found wanting or needy—inferior, unworthy, bad—there is likely to be an accompanying, self-derogatory affect emanating from the ego ideal, the seat of standards and ideals for the self. This affect is shame, experienced directly, or, more often, as signal affect—signaling the danger of being flooded with shame. Although guilt occurs often in clinical situations, it arises in response to the aggressive wishes or actions that have been instigated by shame experiences (such as self-critical feelings over being so constituted as to feel hatefully toward so fine an other). Guilt often screens underlying shame, and this may conceal the basic shame dynamic that is central in the investigation of processes involving envy. We emphasize the importance both theoretically and clinically of often hidden instigatory shame that arises when personal deficiencies are called into bold relief by the shining luminosity of the admired/envied other.

Spillius differentiates between impenitent (or conscious, "legitimate") envy and ego dystonic (unconscious, destructive toward a "good" other) envy. As shame so often is hidden from awareness, so too is envy (similarly odious and self-conscious) frequently unconscious (Lansky, 1997). Both experiences are responses to narcissistic vulnerability, built as they are on convictions of defect and unlovability with accompanying fantasies of "injustice ... having been cheated or damaged" (p. 329). These "injustice" fantasies are similar to Spillius's "impenitent" envy.

Envy may result from the activation of a predisposing sense of shame," not infrequently originating in identification with the same-gendered parent who is felt to be contemptible (Greenson, 1954). Predisposition toward shame, associated fantasies of unlovability, and a triggering experience of shame (usually unconscious and experienced as unbearable) present a sequence that often leads to, and is screened by, destructive envy and its consequent guilt-related dynamics. This can occur in the psychoanalytic setting, where the analyst may be seen as "whole" and superior, with the patient feeling intolerably needy and defective by comparison (as at times of vacation, with the patient's assumption that the analyst will be serenely happy, with no thoughts about him or her while the patient is left disconnected and desolate; or with bitter convictions of the analyst's "perfect" family life). The analytic setting itself, with its inherent power differential, contributes to patients' feelings of envy and shame.

In the case of envy, we find, as in so many other clinical situations, that shame experiences (narcissistic wounds) trigger more visible symptomatic conflicts, which give rise to aggression and guilt. These conflicts over aggression, in turn, screen the antecedent shame dynamics. In our experience, a theoretical and attitudinal overemphasis by the analyst on aggressivity and destruction at the expense of antecedent shame conflicts puts the patient in a basically contemptible light and so compounds the shaming aspect of the analytic situation. This attitudinal bias, then, if it remains unacknowledged, generates even more envy in the patient, which in turn, confirms the patient's escalating view of him- or herself as basically nasty and contemptible.

We underscore the fact that interpretation of envy in the analytic setting frequently itself leads to more shame, in that exposure as envious highlights a childlike and primitive attempt to aggrandize one's lovability by tearing down another who may appear to be more lovable. The shame resulting from exposed envy offers one significant explanation for the fact that envy itself tends to remain hidden. Shame that cannot be tolerated and remains unconscious may lead to unacknowledged envy, although it might as likely serve as a trigger to justify the projected, "impenitent" envy described by Spillius. Narcissistic rage unleashed by shame experiences or fantasies may find expression as envious outpourings toward an admired other. Envy can be seen as one type of defense against unbearable shame. As shame is recognized and becomes more bearable (i.e., the self is experienced as more secure in its lovability and acceptability and becomes able to be examined in analysis) related envy tends to become more ego-dystonic, a reflection of Klein's "depressive position."

We will turn to a clinical example of Spillius (1993) to try to indicate this relation of shame to envy. Two sessions are described in the analysis of Mrs. B, immediately following a series of "good" sessions in which she had felt helped and understood by Dr. Spillius. Mrs. B was disgruntled and ornery and reluctantly told her analyst a dream in which Mrs. B was dancing with her grandmother, who was lively. The patient was "half enjoying it but half afraid she [grandmother] would have a heart attack and die." Dr. Spillius interpreted mixed feelings of the patient toward the analyst, suggesting that Mrs. B feared for the strain that the analytic dance was putting on her, as she enjoyed the energy of the dance but seemed unaware of her own constitutional weakness. Mrs. B then allowed that there was something ridiculous about her grandmother, as about Dr. Spillius, who had in fact developed and grown a garden in her yard despite the fact that her house was "overlooked" by other houses.

Spillius interpreted the garden as Mrs. B's analysis, suggesting that she was showing her analyst up as silly for being unaware of how superior Mrs. B now felt herself to be. The patient responded triumphantly that Dr. Spillius was "overlooking" that she (patient) would spoil everything because of her "bad constitution." In the next session, she continued to denigrate the analyst for being the "incompetent granny," while simultaneously idealizing and exalting her for her status and her Ph.D., with which she identified and seemed to merge. Dr. Spillius suggests, too, that the patient had needed to denigrate the empathy and understanding that she had shown in the "good" sessions, because empathy/goodness is a sign of weakness, inferiority, unsafety, and even persecution. Mrs. B felt ashamed of family members whom she thought to be weak and ineffectual; Dr. Spillius adds: "I believe that she despised weakness in others because she believed unconsciously that she herself was weak, inferior, and unlovable … [she mourned] the loss of the ideal self that she would like to have been" (p. 163).

Spillius refers to Mrs. B as an example of someone with impenitent envy (justified grievance) experienced from the paranoid-schizoid mode. In the comment just quoted, she offers an explanation for the patient's contempt of weakness, reflecting the very attributes of shame that we have been considering, including even the wide gap experienced between the perceived and ideal self. However, it seems to us that Dr. Spillius doesn't accord shame the central position it deserves in the generation of Mrs. B's contempt and underlying envy of her analyst (i.e., the extent to which the patient is, herself, "granny" in the dream in comparison with her analyst). As is typical of many Kleinians, Spillius seems to overlook the fact that the paranoid-schizoid position is a shame state in which shame is experienced as deliberately inflicted by the other as a form of contempt, stigmatization, or exploitation.

Mrs. B attributed something "silly" to Dr. Spillius as to her grandmother, which she apparently related to gaucheness in siting the garden, the weakness inherent in empathy and understanding, and in being able to "pull the wool over her analyst's eyes" with regard to her constitutional need to spoil the analysis. Her envy reflects the power she attributed to her analyst to soothe and understand, the deep hope that she still maintained of being helped, and, of course, envy of her analyst's accomplishments and stature.

As Spillius suggests, these attributions represent Mrs. B's own negative comparisons of herself to her analyst, and her shame about her own incompetencies. About Dr. Spillius's garden, for instance, Mrs. B had felt that as long as the yard was a mess, "it didn't matter, there was nothing to see." Spillius interpreted this as representing the analysis, but it seems to us that the "messy yard" serves more closely as a representation of Mrs. B herself—"a mess; nothing to see." Inchoate, insignificant—images so evocative of shame. So too is Dr. Spillius's "silliness" a projection of Mrs. B's own feelings about herself—for yearning to be soothed and understood, for not having the power and status of a PhD. Mrs. B felt justified in her anger and envy—her grievance is legitimate—because somehow she had been shortchanged, "overlooked" (like Shakespeare's Richard, Milton's Satan). We can infer that her shame is unbearable and, therefore, unacknowledged and projected as contempt and envy onto her silly/weak–strong/competent analyst.

DISCUSSION

Envy is a complex emotion that emanates from self-consciousness and from comparison of self with other. The other is exalted and hated for his or her presumed superiority or completeness. In the case of contempt, the other is despised, "lowered" in comparison with an elevated sense of self. We are suggesting that central conflicts in negative self-evaluation involve shame, and as such shame and defenses against it instigate envy and contempt. Pride has been suggested as an opposite sense of self from shame (Nathanson, 1992); the individual with pride has no need to envy the other, nor is he or she likely to resort to contempt for some "less fortunate" soul.

In the case of Mrs. B, we have tried to indicate how shame (about failure, inferiority, need) underlies and instigates her envy of her analyst. Spillius emphasizes the "impenitent" (or "justified") nature of Mrs. B's envy. The example also nicely indicates how readily envy can be converted into contempt, a projection of shame into the other, serving to ward off the pain from recognizing envy and the shame that both underlies and accompanies it. Mrs. B seemed to envy her analyst's stature, her achievements (e.g., PhD), probably her home, and, particularly, her capacity to understand and empathize with her pain. It seemed that she was unable to bear her envy of Dr. Spillius or her own deep shame and self-loathing that generates it. In order to keep her shame and envy hidden, then, she transformed these feelings into contempt, believing the shame to belong to Dr. Spillius.

We agree with Spillius that the patient's envy was probably greatest in relation to the sequence of "good" sessions and her analyst's ability and power to provide them. We think this was so because Mrs. B felt weak, pathetic, and ridiculous for needing her analyst (all words central to the language of shame [Morrison, 1996]), but also because it exposed her to the danger that her needed analyst might ultimately abandon or disappoint her, potentially leading to further trauma. In this instance, envy and shame remain unconscious (with shame here also resulting from exposure as being envious) because they remain unbearable.

Shame and shame anxiety (a form of signal anxiety [Lansky & Morrison, 1997, Chap. 1]) serve as warnings of imminent threats to connection with the other (the attachment-bond). Such a signal may well be unconscious, but nonetheless it represents an attempt to repair or restore the bond (as in pathological accommodation to a noxious demand from a needed other [Brandschaft, 1993]), or to remove oneself from the other who threatens rejection or loss. Envy and contempt exemplify the latter, attempts through withdrawal to deal with the dangers from a sense of relative unworthiness and shame. From this perspective, envy and contempt are reflections of a shame-derived vision of Thanatos, as protective withdrawal from connection with needed objects. This contrasts with Klein's view of envy as a primary, aggressive drive emanating from a Thanatos that is instinctual.

As a response to shame representing anger and disdain, envy exemplifies narcissistic rage that attempts to deal with experiences or threats of injury. While seeking distance, however, it achieves the paradox of maintaining connection with the feared but needed other. This connection is, we believe, what Bion (1977) had in mind by the H or Hate bond. One may be obsessed with the object of envy or contempt, especially when this preoccupation serves to defend against unconscious, unbearable shame. When this obsession is played out in the transference (as was the case with Mrs. B), it exemplifies what Morrison (1994) has called the one-and-a-half person psychology—the patient, the analyst-as-other, and the analyst-as-created to meet the patient's needs (for containment, responsiveness, or for an adversary).

The central thesis of this communication is that envy is a comparative and self-conscious emotion lying "downstream," as it were, from shame. The analytic treatment of envy is well served by attunement and sensitivity to hidden shame, and by tactful efforts to bring underlying or unacknowledged shame to light. These efforts have the highest likelihood of yielding greater understanding and acceptance by the patient of the defensive needs for envy, and a broader capacity to face, accept, and modify shame that previously has been kept underground and unacknowledged. Such "bypassed" shame serves as a trigger to destructive pathology that leaves the patient and others bewildered and uncomprehending. Interpreting clinical situations involving envy through the shame that triggers it is clinically more effective than attempts at interpretation of more manifest and visible aggressive dynamics that are responses to that shame. Indeed, in our view, interpretive strategies short circuiting the shame that underlies envy risk acceptance by both patient and analyst as a type of "inexact interpretation" (Glover, 1931), or acceptance of the abrupt exposure of patients' attempts at regulating narcissistic equilibrium in a way that evokes even more shame.

NOTES

1. So farewell hope, and with hope farewell fear,

> Farewell remorse: all good to me is lost;
> Evil be thou my good;

Paradise Lost, Bk. IV, 1, lines 109–110.

2. But I, that am not shaped for sportive tricks,

> Nor made to court an amorous looking-glass;
> ...
> Deformed, unfinished, sent before my time
> Into this breathing world, scarce half made up,
> ...
> And therefore, since I cannot prove a lover,
> To entertain these fair well-spoken days,
> I am determined to prove a villain
> And hate the idle pleasures of these days.

Richard III, I,

REFERENCES

Bion, W. (1977). *Seven servants*. Northvale, NJ: Jason Aronson.
Boris, H. (1994). *Envy*. Northvale, NJ: Jason Aronson.

Brandschaft, B. (1993). To free the spirit from its cell. Chapter 16. *Progress in Self Psychology, 9,* 209–230.

Freud, S. (1940). An outline of psychoanalysis. *International Journal of Psycho-Analysis, 21,* 27–84.

Glover, E. (1931). The therapeutic effect of inexact interpretation. A contribution to the theory of superstition. *International Journal of Psycho-Analysis, 12,* 397-411.

Greenson, R. (1954). The struggle against identification. *Journal of the American Psychoanalytic Association, 2,* 200–217.

Lansky, M. (1997). Envy as process. In M. Lansky & A. Morrison (Eds.), *The widening scope of shame* (pp. 327–338). Hillsdale, NJ: Analytic Press.

Lansky, M., & Morrison, A. (1997). The legacy of Freud's writings on shame. In M. Lansky & A. Morrison (Eds.), *The widening scope of shame* (pp. 3–40). Hillsdale, NJ: Analytic Press.

Morrison, A. (1989). *Shame: The underside of narcissism.* Hillsdale, NJ: Analytic Press.

Morrison, A. (1994). The breadth and boundaries of a self-psychological immersion in shame. A one-and-a-half person perspective. *Psychoanalytic Dialogues, 4,* 19–35.

Morrison, A. (1996). *The culture of shame.* New York: Ballantine.

Nathanson, D. (1992). *Shame and pride: Affect, sex and the birth of the self.* New York: Norton.

Phillips, A. (1994). Foreword. In H. Boris, *Envy* (pp vii–xi). Northvale, NJ: Jason Aronson.

Segal, H. (1977). Psychoanalytic dialogue: Kleinian theory today. *Journal of theAmerican Psychoanalytic Association, 25,* 363–370.

Spillius, E. (1993). Varieties of envious experience. *International Journal of Psycho-Analysis, 74,* 1199–1212.

10

Envy and Admiration Among Women

ROSEMARY H. BALSAM

> You may take it as an instance of male injustice if I assert that envy and jealousy play an even greater part in the mental life of women than of men. It is not that I think these characteristics are absent in men or that I think they have no other roots in women than envy for the penis; but I am inclined to attribute their greater amount in women to this latter influence. ... The discovery that she is castrated is a turning point in a girl's growth.
>
> *S. Freud (1933, p. 126)*

Freud, as we know, famously specialized in unraveling the envy of girls and women about boys and men. His story of female envy is observable over a century after he first described the idea. But in considering that "penis envy" was "bedrock" (1937, p. 252) Freud merely articulated his now dated gender theory. Since then (especially in the 1970s and 1980s) well-known advances in feminist cultural psychoanalytic scholarship plus the postmodern turn in critical theory have shown the limitations of his view on all aspects of the sexed body's relation to gender, including his opinions about female envy, because of its phallocentric bias.

I have been curious about the great variability in the quality and the intensity of envy that I have clinically encountered in the inner world of women on the couch. By no means, therefore, is this affect a troublesome universal phenomenon in all adults. I suspect, that as Karen Horney noted about penis envy in 1924, there are universal envies of early childhood such as her sense of a primary penis envy, but that as a person grows up such envies undergo transformations (Dahl, 1996). The penis envy that will manifest itself virulently in adult life will be an overdetermined secondary and pathological envy. Here, I will be working from the surface of consciously stated envy "downward," in a classical model of a structured and layered psychic apparatus. My ideas need not challenge, for example, the metapsychological suggestions of say Klein or Bion on the intense role of envy in development, especially in its early form. I am influenced mostly by a contemporary ego-oriented and cultural approach, because for me, this approach lends itself most to questions about individuality, character dynamic composition, and the internalization of individualized parental objects. This essay therefore will address aspects of what psychodynamics help create painful envy and how it may become sustained and manifested as a feature of ongoing intrapsychic conflict in some women.

TOWARD SPECIFICALLY FEMALE ENVY

Brenner (1982) has wondered, sensibly I think, whether or not it is actually even possible for a female to fear losing a penis (thus causing a true "castration" anxiety), since she has no experience of ever having possessed the organ. Freud had similar occasional although dismissed doubts. This kind of thinking is a first step to distinguishing females from males in Freud's and his followers' psychoanalytic concept of the developing body. If penis envy is considered normative in girls' development, this requires a normal female to hold a basic delusional body image of possessing a penis that she lost. This is mental gymnastics designed to create a neat "one-sex" theory. As an ego body *basis* for female psychology, it is misdirected (Balsam, 2003; Horney, 1924). Brenner ends up concurring with Freud's normative (but inadequate) view that a girl's *fantasy* of being able to have a penis is a good enough basis for experiences of her feared body loss or deprivation, and hence her inevitable envy of men. This reasoning about men is only a variant in female development. Many have referred to Freud's as a female theory of "lack." Brenner acknowledges, as does Freud, other deep anxieties in women such as the fear of loss of love, but neither mentions any other female body anxiety as fundamental, beyond this already distorted "woman-without-a-penis" version.

Anxieties that accompany the *ownership* of a *female* body may be equivalent in their insistence to a male's castration anxiety.[1] The shifting theoretical role of general female body anxieties toward the contemporary focus on the female-qua-female opens up new and exciting territory to survey, such as thinking about specifically female-to-female envy, a topic still seldom studied.

When male hegemony was most challenged during the 1970s in the United States—a turning point also in gender theory—a socially newly nurtured camaraderie among women was occurring. The advertising flier for a 2006 issue of *Women's Studies Quarterly* on "Envy" edited by Jane Gallop, reminds us that "New Wave feminists discarded women's envy in favor of the concept of Sisterhood." The sisterhood, though healing in many ways, was supposed to be ideally and mercifully free of negativities that were perceived in males such as competition, hurtful aggression, and envy. Nowadays we can evolve beyond moral condemnation of these affects and aims and ask more about what they mean in their specifically female versions.

ADMIRATION AND ENVY

Intense concerns over what the body or person may lose or has lost, or alternatively has never possessed, can well be accompanied by abiding envy of what others are perceived to have. Envy goes hand in glove with the have-nots troubled relationship with the perceived haves. A stage in this emotional sequence that has drawn little commentary and is less noticed is a state of admiration that blends into idealization (Sandell, 1993). Sandell, following Klein, in this only titled paper in the literature dealing with the relationship of admiration to envy, viewed admiration as secondary and compensating for a primordial instinctual envy that is natural in a Kleinian object relational scheme of the mind. I would like to postulate the reverse—that admiration may actually *preexist* envy, perhaps especially in women—but I do agree with Sandell that the two emotions seem to bear a special relationship to one another.

Admiration literally means "to wonder at" (Latin: *ad*, to or at, and *mirari*, to wonder). In various dictionaries words such as "amaze," "awe," "astonish, "miracle, "marvel," and "pleasure" are placed in conjunction as explanatory. This suggests a focus on a quality of the other, and for my purposes in working on a body ego, I ask, what quality of the body is amazing or miraculous and to whom? Most immediately one thinks of a child in a child's body looking at her (or his) parents or older siblings. Let us, for the sake of overbrevity and space, postulate that obvious gender specific "amazements" are (a) pregnancy and childbirth and (b) penile erection. In many individuals then, this attitude of wonderment involves a mental representation of a quality of a desired person and, if conscious, the individual will "look up to" "wonder at" the amazing quality of this desirable object. The act of "looking up to" per se can be surrounded by emotional thorns. It involves a physical sense of being smaller, casting the eyes upward, a visually distorted view from below the field of vision of the other that even enhances the size of the other. Looking up often encodes the anxieties of dependency of the small child on its big parent or sibling. It can encode the small one being at the mercy of the strength of the bigger one; a potential for the big one having control over the little one because of physical superiority. Admiration probably can be more easily mitigated if the physical capability of the small one is thought in the future to be able to accomplish the amazing quality for her- or himself, for example, achievable body enlargement by the small admirer, or the possibility of equalization through growth and emulation. This kind of ability to imagine the future of a body one inhabits is subject to one's ego maturation. So if growth potential avenues appear blocked for whatever reason for the small admirer, then admiration itself can become dangerous and feared to be toxic.

I believe that marked envy occurs when this initial state of admiration, for whatever unconscious reason, is perceived as dangerous. Rapid repression occurs and in its place the intense admiration can secondarily turn into a bitter, hopeless envy, the emotion that is often described by patients as very painful—"searing," "burning," "all-consuming," "fierce," "intense"—many metaphors involving self-immolation, fire, and destructive conflagration. Neither is envy easy to digest: "it makes you green" or is "bitter" (as in nausea): nor is it easy to tolerate or ameliorate in treatment. To eliminate the pain of unrequitable admiration or the envy itself, leads to consequences: such as attempts to diminish the other in order to assert moral superiority to right the balance of loss of self-esteem and feelings of inferiority; or expressions of rageful destruction toward or even imaginative annihilation of the other's envied difference. (I am focusing only on individuals in analysis and not on groups.) All of these reactions toward the object of envy are radical internal efforts by the individual to rid herself (or himself because the mechanism of handling the emotion itself is not gender specific at all) of this profound pain. A gleeful but falsely reassuring triumph can be experienced briefly by a formerly envying subject, freed for the moment of the discomforts of admiration or envy of the now denigrated object. The gleeful person in a short-cut to freed "postenvy" mode has become magically in fantasy big instead of small, powerful instead of weak, strong instead of puny, on top instead of on bottom, amazing instead of ordinary—the actively envied one in fantasy instead of the one passively at the mercy of all this internal pain.

Envy seems to be one of the more painful emotions in the human repertoire, perhaps because it often seems to the individual that there is no "cure" for it. Of unpleasurable affects, anger will come and go, anxiety will be soothed, sadness will fade away. Envy tends to stay put once installed. No matter how powerful the subject wishes to be, he or she can never become or take over completely the identical part of the other that is so unconsciously unbearably admired and desired. If much of the imbalance is cemented in a version of a child's mentation, then time cannot be stopped for the now adult to right the bitterness of imbalance.

Once one begins to deal in fantasy, then symbolization opens the way to the value of, say, female penis envy as symbolic of social power (Grossman & Stewart, 1976). The sexed body matters, however, for the gist of interpretation. It matters if the analyst hears a woman's envy of men's sex as an envy of men per se, or as a flight from her own undervalued femaleness (Horney, 1926); or a woman's envy of another woman as a commentary on her own femininity.

FEMALE BODY ANXIETIES AND CONSEQUENT ENVIES

As I stated in a lecture on female exhibitionism (2004):

> There are many different kinds of genital and female body anxieties that we have learned about over the years since Freud, e.g., those concerning loss of virginity, penile penetration anxiety, or rape anxiety which Bernstein (1990) and Richards (1996) believe to be the female counterpart of castration anxiety; or those arising from loss of control of flow in menstruation, to which Ritvo (1976) alerted analysis in his studies of adolescent females; or of pubertal and pregnancy expansion in the breasts (Balsam, 1996); or anxiety in the tasks of anticipating and grasping in fantasy the elasticity of the abdominal cavity, the uterus and the vaginal canal during natural childbirth to which implicit attention has been drawn to by Deutsch (1945), Raphael-Leff (1995) and Pines (1993), and to which I would like to add. These are all specifically female body anxieties, which widen the scope well beyond the specific anxieties associated with a fantasized loss of a personal penis. (Balsam, 2004)

Any of these anxieties could be addressed in relation to the concepts of admiration and envy I suggest above.

Here I will use a case to show two unconscious routes to one patient's experiences of vituperative envy: maternal fertility and maternal pregnancy and childbirth.

CASE MATERIAL

The patient was in analysis supervised by myself by telephone and personal contact from a far away city. The analyst was a woman. The case is disguised except for the shape of the conflicts over admiration, envy, and some of the unconscious female body connections that became revealed in the analytic process.

Judy was a tall, stately, married, childless businesswoman in her 30s, who to the analyst and outsiders looked strikingly attractive with manicured hands, well-coiffed premature snow white hair, high cheek bones, and skillfully and carefully applied makeup. In consultation she appeared very competent, a good self-observer, and was deeply interested in other people. The first 6 months of her treatment were taken up with intensely angry reactions and bitter tears about having been passed over for promotion at work. She had thought she was everyone's darling. She spent hours telling of all the individuals who had assured her she was a shoe-in for senior vice president. Some even told her she would be the chief executive officer (CEO) in a few years. How could this be false? It wasn't. She was right in her estimate of herself, she averred.

The analyst, knowing that there were many steps Judy would have had to realize to become a CEO, began to notice the number of times she quoted her friends' "sureness" that she would be a CEO, and realized that this statement was not offered just as a bitter aside, but that Judy actually seemed to take it very literally. She was convinced that the promoters had it "in" for her because they were too envious of her accomplishments, or they were too dumb to notice her brilliance. She felt better when she thought this, but no reflection was possible. Meanwhile, Louise, a woman with whom Judy had been friendly, also competed for the vice president job and got it.

This increased Judy's fury and she spent hours convincing her analyst that this other woman was useless, inferior, shallow, inconsequential—in short, the very opposite of anyone who could be admired. Louise was despised. Judy felt moments of gleeful triumph, such as I have described above, in putting her down, once "accidentally" pushing the "send" button to the entire company on an email supposedly meant for a few cronies that sneered at Louise's new high-heeled shoes because they were ill fitting, or making catty comments in sotto voce earshot in meetings. (This reminds me of our issue editor Leon Wurmser's comment when I told him I was writing about female envy, and he quoted Dostoyevsky as noting that females' envy toward each other was like the "biting of mares"!)

Here are the kind of statements Judy made about Louise: "She's like a bug—so small they won't even see her behind a lectern. And she has this little high squeaky voice. Her legs are short and thick. She has no boobs and a big fat belly. Plus she's as dumb as a plank. She comes from Nowheresville, was educated at East Cupcake Junction and she has two ugly kids, and her mother is crazy."

"Wow!" said her analyst. "You certainly dislike her!"

"Of course [between the lines … you dummy!] I hate her. I wish she were dead. She's dumb and fat and I can't stand her." After this outburst a few days after the acute disappointment, Judy was increasingly sad and sorry for herself. She began to tell about their past.

"Louise actually was once one of my best friends. You wouldn't even know, given the things I say about her now. I hardly even recognize where this is all coming from. Yes, I feel just terrible about the job and I do still feel that I deserved it. But I have to admit, Louise deserves it too. She wasn't that bad a choice. Maybe they chose her because she's not going to be having more kids, whereas I was honest with them and said I couldn't be sure if I might soon get pregnant. No matter how much progress we make in the workplace, that's always an issue [sigh]. … I should take them to court."

The analyst and Judy slowly pieced together the following story that for the analyst and me made emotional sense of Judy's tumultuous wrathful envy at Louise.

Envy was an emotion by no means foreign to Judy. Nor was it confined to Louise. It was just that Louise was the latest target. Judy often had had bosom female friends at school and in college who at some point would surpass her in a shared ambition and thus cause a similar major disruption in their friendship. Former friends would become sworn enemies. She had encountered some of these ex-school pals at reunions and she was shocked to find that many were delighted to see her again, and in fact had not harbored the same hateful envy toward her that she had toward them. Being also a person capable of reflection and analysis, Judy was able to tackle the apparent differential and ask herself what this meant. She came from a family of four sisters where she was the oldest. Her father was a businessman who kept himself unavailable to the girls. The relation with her father was therefore one source of envy, because he took up her mother's attention and Judy had a longing and envious sense of the exclusivity of the parents' relation. Judy connected this emotional constellation with her envied imagined sense of her friend Louise's inclusion at the board meetings with senior vice presidents.

Meanwhile, her analyst became pregnant. Judy's transferential reactions revealed her inner life and the female-to-female envy that loomed far larger in her pantheon than her envy of her father, which had been more resolved and better integrated through developing her capabilities in his shared business world.

First of all, Judy failed to notice the obvious pregnancy until the sixth month. (This is a sign of trauma in this area.) When her analyst finally needed to draw attention to it, Judy fell into a fretful rage and started to miss appointments. Much began to emerge about her fury at her mother's enlarging body—the little girl's awe and vast admiration of the increasing girth, and yet her own inchoate burgeoning vast anxiety of the intuited future that waited her own little body. She remembered stroking her mother's belly and being told that someday she too would become like that. She felt the baby kick. She was at once terrified, awestruck, and amazed—by definition, filled with admiration that was simultaneously unbearable because of the acute fear about her own tiny body in comparison to her mother's, and a terror that she knew somehow she was supposed to contain a baby someday. She had night terrors then about becoming small "like a bug" that now could be analyzed. For Judy, this event occurred three times during her growing up, each time at crucial moments of her own body development—at age 5, 11, and 14. Much more could be said about the details of her intense envy of women with children, but it should be easy to see how this girl's intense admiration of her mother's body capability was too frightening to sustain, due to the strain of an attempted female identification thwarted by her own problems of conceptualizing a trajectory for her own little body's functioning. This mother also was so preoccupied with the babies themselves that Judy, being the oldest, lost out to much of her body contact and companionship. Related themes evolved in the transference. Judy was very anxious about the separations, about her own body, and about fantasies of becoming pregnant (which she actually did in the following year). She felt highly competitive with the analyst, cried about her having only an interest in her own "damned procreation" while she, Judy, was suffering about work and Louise. Judy's dreams helped to point to many female genital anxieties about the loss of her hymen (Holtzman & Kulish, 1996); her fears and excitement about carrying a baby (animal dreams of camels, kangaroos, elephants, fat ladies of Victorian side shows); and her thrill and terror of childbirth and delivery (reaching the peak of "Mt. Venus," diving for pearls, falling short in a marathon, losing the trophy at the Open).

This stage of the analysis was conducted in the presence of intense envy directed at the analyst, her pregnancy and her baby, and her husband. Judy was sarcastic, full of put-downs, denigration and trying to make her "feel small" the "way I do," and defeating the analyst's competence.

The analyst had a hard time not retaliating. But the occasional breakthrough of intense genuine admiration for this analyst was where she and I fully appreciated the relation for Judy between overwhelming preconscious admiration for her as a creative female, and her pained and painful conscious envy. Future fantasies of Judy's own pregnancy were a way to acknowledge to herself that she too could become the object of embodied female admiration as she gradually mitigated her envy and integrated a more mature body image.

CONCLUSION

Admiration, envy, and competition toward other women are prominent features in the emotional lives of many women. The fate of such emotions will depend very much on the way the family has helped the little girl metabolize her inevitable childhood awe and admiration of the strange mysterious and massive belly that one day, the family says, will be also her inheritance, but which she simultaneously, because of her immaturity, has a very difficult time comprehending. This particular aspect of not only being like her mother, but in a sense "becoming [a] mother" is the source of major elements of suppressed female admiration for the adult female body and hence also her capability of vituperative envy.

NOTE

1. These days many of us hope to educate contemporary psychoanalysis into using the simple, accurate, and encompassing term "female genital anxiety" (Dorsey, 1996; Long, 2005) and dropping the misleading old terms "phallic stage" or "narcissistic phallic stage" in favor of "first genital phase" (Parens, 1990). We can now provide a solid rationale for a language representing the female body qua female.

REFERENCES

Balsam, R. (1996). The pregnant mother and the body image of the daughter. *Journal of the American Psychoanalytical Association, 44* (Suppl.), 401–427.

Balsam, R. (2003). The vanished pregnant body in psychoanalytic developmental theory. *Journal of the American Psychoanalytical Association, 51*(4), 1153–1179.

Balsam, R. (2004, December 10). *Women showing off: Notes on female exhibitionism.* Paper presented at the Psychoanalytic Center. Cleveland, OH.

Bernstein, D. (1990). Female genital anxieties, conflicts and typical mastery modes. *International Journal of Psycho-Analysis, 71*: 151–165.

Brenner, C. (1982). *The mind in conflict.* New York: International University Press.

Dahl, E. K. (1996). The concept of penis envy revisited: A child analyst listens to adult women. *Psychoanalytic Study of the Child, 51,* 303–325.

Deutsch, H. (1945). *Psychology of Women, Vol. II.* New York: Grune and Stratton.

Dorsey, D. (1996). Castration anxiety or feminine genital anxiety? *Journal of the American Psychoanalytic Association, 44* (Suppl.), 283–302.

Freud, S. (1933). New introductory lectures: Lecture XXXIII Femininity. In *Standard edition* (Vol. 22, pp. 112–135). London: Hogarth Press.

Freud, S. (1937). Analysis terminable and interminable. In *Standard edition* (Vol. 23, pp. 209–255). London: Hogarth Press.

Gallop, J. (Ed.). (2006, Fall/Winter). Envy. *Women's Studies Quarterly,* 34(3 and 4).

Grossman, W., & Stewart, W. (1976). Penis envy: From childhood wish to developmental metaphor. *Journal of the American Psychoanalytic Association, 24*(Suppl.), 193–212.

Holtzman, D., & Kulish, N. (1996). Nevermore: The hymen and the loss of virginity. *Journal of the American Psychoanalytic Association, 44* (Suppl.), 303–332.

Horney, K. (1924). On the genesis of the castration complex in women. *International Journal of Psycho-Analysis, 5,* 50–65.

Horney, K. (1926). The flight from womanhood. *International Journal of Psycho-Analysis, 12,* 360–374.

Long, K. (2005). The changing language of female development. Panel report. *Journal of the American Psychoanalysis Association, 53*(4), 1161–1174.

Parens, H. (1990). On the girl's psychosexual development: Reconsiderations suggested from direct observation. *Journal of the American Psychoanalysis Association, 39,* 743–772.

Pines, F. (1993). *A Woman's Unconscious Use of Her Body.* New Haven, CT: Yale University Press.

Raphael-Leff, J. (1995). *Pregnancy: The Inside Story.* New York: Aronson.

Richards, A. (1996). Primary femininity and female genital anxiety. *Journal of the American Psychoanalytic Association: 44* (suppl): 261–281.

Ritvo, A. (1976). Adolescent to woman. *Journal of the American Psychoanalytic Association: 24*(suppl): 127–137.

Sandell, R. (1993). Envy and admiration. *International Journal of Psychoanalysis, 74,* 1213–1221.

Index

R

S

T